# The typical forms of English literature; an introduction to the historical and critical study of English literature for college classes

Alfred H. Upham

Copyright © BiblioLife, LLC

This book represents a historical reproduction of a work originally published before 1923 that is part of a unique project which provides opportunities for readers, educators and researchers by bringing hard-to-find original publications back into print at reasonable prices. Because this and other works are culturally important, we have made them available as part of our commitment to protecting, preserving and promoting the world's literature. These books are in the "public domain" and were digitized and made available in cooperation with libraries, archives, and open source initiatives around the world dedicated to this important mission.

We believe that when we undertake the difficult task of re-creating these works as attractive, readable and affordable books, we further the goal of sharing these works with a global audience, and preserving a vanishing wealth of human knowledge.

Many historical books were originally published in small fonts, which can make them very difficult to read. Accordingly, in order to improve the reading experience of these books, we have created "enlarged print" versions of our books. Because of font size variation in the original books, some of these may not technically qualify as "large print" books, as that term is generally defined; however, we believe these versions provide an overall improved reading experience for many.

# THE TYPICAL FORMS
## OF
# ENGLISH LITERATURE

AN INTRODUCTION TO THE HISTORICAL AND CRITICAL STUDY OF ENGLISH LITERATURE FOR COLLEGE CLASSES

BY

ALFRED H. UPHAM

Professor of English in Miami University

NEW YORK
OXFORD UNIVERSITY PRESS
AMERICAN BRANCH, 35 WEST 32ND STREET
LONDON, TORONTO, MELBOURNE, AND BOMBAY
HUMPHREY MILFORD
1917

*ALL RIGHTS RESERVED*

*Copyright, 1917*
BY OXFORD UNIVERSITY PRESS
AMERICAN BRANCH

# PREFACE

THIS book, derived from several years of experience with college classes, is intended primarily to be used with the now popular introductory courses in literature that approach their subject by way of representative types or literary forms. It undertakes to provide for a number of these typical forms a somewhat extended account of their development as phases of art, a briefer statement of their accepted standards of technique, a suggestive list of topics for study, and a bibliography of collections and critical discussions. It is not intended to supplant the reading and interpretation of literary documents, but rather to supply a basis of understanding and conviction, upon which such interpretations can be made more intelligently. Hitherto such material has been brought to the attention of students by means of lectures, or through assigned readings in various books of reference. But freshmen and sophomores in college are not skilled in note-taking, and the reference reading they do is often poorly digested. It should be an immense advantage to have in their hands a readable syllabus of this fundamental information.

Just how the book may be employed most effectively must be determined by individual instructors. Some will omit certain types and chapters, as the time allotted to the course may require. The author himself presents the drama in a separate course. The various divisions of the book are planned to suggest class-room discussion, where that is preferred, or may be assigned as private reading and tested largely by the student's ability to apply theory to the specimens of literature under consideration in class. In any event the first-hand acquaintance with the literature is all-important. Collections or anthologies of the various types have been described at some length in the bibliographies. The examples they contain should be analyzed and compared according to schemes easily derived from the sections on technique in this book. For the shorter forms actual attempts at developing the student's own imaginative impulses into finished products will clarify his mind surprisingly. The subjects for reports should serve the several purposes of enlarging the student's knowledge, of giving him practice in organizing and expressing information, and of further illustrating the substance of the course by more extended comparisons.

It will be a matter for regret if the usefulness of this book is limited to classes and class rooms. The entire treatment rests upon the assumption that the students who use it are already readers of reasonably good literature and will continue to be so throughout their lives. Its aim is to enable them to approach all their reading with more intelligent judgment, and keener, richer appreciation. Literature is presented as a vital thing, inspired by very real and immediate impulses, and responding readily to the increased demands made upon it by the complex experiences of today, or the still more complicated ones of tomorrow. The book is submitted even to the reading public outside college halls, many of whom find it difficult at times to give a reason for such literary taste and discrimination as they practice.

Obviously a book of this sort is full of obligations. Certain larger features of indebtedness are indicated in the text or in footnotes. Numerous others are implied in the lists of critical discussions appended to each chapter. Two special instances, of a more personal sort, are gratefully acknowledged here. One is the genuine patience and apparent interest of three successive college classes, who permitted this material to be tested upon them until it took final shape. The other is the constructive advice and friendly coöperation of the General Editor of this American series of Oxford publications, whose experience and judgment have contributed largely to make the book what it is.

# CONTENTS

| CHAPTER | | PAGE |
|---|---|---|
| I. | Formation of Types | 1 |
| II. | The Popular Ballad | 13 |
| III. | The Lyric | 38 |
| IV. | The Epic | 84 |
| V. | The Personal Essay | 117 |
| VI. | The Novel | 148 |
| VII. | The Short Story | 191 |
| VIII. | The Drama | 211 |
| | Index | 267 |

# I

## FORMATION OF TYPES

**Literature an Art**

LITERATURE finds its place in the studies of youth and the affections of men and women by virtue of the fact that it is one of the fine arts. It ministers to none of men's material needs, does not increase their physical comfort, and is not valued primarily for the lessons it teaches or the information it conveys. Furthermore, its enjoyment is limited to no individual or group of the elect, but is open to all who can understand and appreciate. Such qualities as these distinguish the fine arts in general from the practical arts, the crafts whose product has material utility.

**Art and Imitation**

The expression "fine arts" is comparatively modern. Aristotle thought of them as "arts of imitation"; the French still call them *beaux arts*—that is, the "beautiful arts." Both these terms are more significant than our own somewhat negative one. For these arts find justification in the pleasure they impart by means of beauty, and this beauty depends upon the perfect portrayal or imitation of the artist's imaginative impression of some phase of life. It is not enough that art in any form should merely reflect people and things as they pass. The waxen policeman we almost speak to in a museum is no more a work of art than the clever imitation of a bumblebee performed on a violin. The personality, the impression, the mood of the artist,—this human element must intervene between life and its imitation in order that we may have art.

The enumeration of the fine arts involves some difficulty. To the Greeks they were music, poetry, dancing, painting, and sculpture. Architecture was classed with the practical arts, being regarded as in no sense imitative except for its ornamentation, which belonged in the province of sculpture. Even today we feel that there is more of practical utility about architecture than belongs to any of these others. Dancing was for a long time omitted from the list, and has but recently been restored, largely under European influence. Various other arts are still more debatable. Acting, for example, is certainly imitation intended to give pleasure, but it is too often slavish copying. Tapestry-work properly done may involve equal skill and charm with painting. Pottery, one of the most primitive of arts, has once more come into favor. The arts of the goldsmith and of the landscape-gardener have been in high regard ever since the Italian Renaissance.

**The Fine Arts**

The position of poetry among the fine arts has never been questioned. The sonnet, the tragedy, or the lover's serenade obviously presents not life but the poet's impression of some large or small cross-section of experience, unified and revitalized by his creative imagination into a thing of beauty. Time cannot affect this condition of things, but it has brought certain important modifications. For one thing we must now understand the word "poetry" to include all imaginative literature, for the boundary line between prose and verse has always been defined but vaguely, and various forms of literary prose have developed in modern

**Literature— The Intellectual Side**

times. This very development has emphasized the fact that literature, unlike the other arts, usually carries with it a burden of thought, a message for the intellect as well as an appeal to emotion and fancy. Men feel the need of this intellectual content to give weight and dignity to literature, but they no longer accept the doctrine that poetry is made pleasurable in order to sweeten some bitter moral pill.

Literature or poetry, under present conditions, has peculiar difficulties in reaching us. Painting, sculpture, architecture, the dance, are there before us in their complete beauty, and we have only to open our eyes to see and enjoy. Music we do not regard as music until it is performed, and then our pleasure is immediate. All of these are for all people, without distinction of race or language. Once men depended for their poetry on the minstrel's song or the rhythmic chant of the story-teller, and literature and music were closest of kin. Now we sit in silence over a book of printed characters, and imagine the sound of ringing words and well-turned phrases into which these characters may be translated. It is as if we were all musicians so trained that we could hear the harmonies by reading printed notes,—and each nation had its particular system of notation. There is, however, one compensation. There has been only one Mona Lisa, only one Cathedral of Rheims. Before the development of the phonograph many people had little or no opportunity to hear good music. But good books are plentiful and cheap, and he must be poor and ignorant indeed who cannot re-create for himself the fancies of Shakespeare or the fiery message of the Hebrew prophets.

**The Medium of Letters**

As already intimated, poetry was no sooner devised as a form of artistic expression, than it began developing,—making various adaptations to meet various conditions of performance. Some of these adaptations were so wide in their appeal that they promptly became more or less permanent and conventionalized; some disappeared with certain temporary conditions that had given them birth; still others were developed farther until eventually they made a place for themselves. Thus there have arisen certain types or typical forms of literature, *genres* as the French call them, by a process not unlike that of evolution in plants and animals.[1] Often in the course of this evolution critics have undertaken to classify these types or divisions of poetry, with results that could not hope to be final. Aristotle, and the Italian critics after him, based his division on the method of presentation—in action, narrative, or song—and the class of people whose life was portrayed. Thus tragedy was the drama of gods and heroes, comedy that of the common people; while the narrative forms were divided into epic poems and satirical lampoons. Francis Bacon and Thomas Hobbes left lyric or song poetry entirely out of consideration; it appeared to them remote from life and concerned chiefly with rhetorical display. Bacon adds instead "allegorical poetry," while Hobbes subdivides his dramatic and narrative types into three classes, thus: poetry of the court, tragedy or epic; poetry of the city, comedy or satire; poetry of the country, pastoral comedy or eclogue.

*Differentiation in Forms of Poetry*

Since the literature of any particular people has been so distinctly an evolution of types, it will be clearer and probably more accurate to approach the divisions of English literature from this historical point of view. Our

[1] Cf. Chapter I of Ferdinand Brunetière's *L'Évolution des Genres*, Paris, 1890.

earliest popular literature may be supposed to have taken the form of ballads, crude songs based on local experiences, composed impromptu, and chanted to the accompaniment of dance-movements. Thus there were present from the beginning the three essential elements of narrative, song, and action— the last no doubt often imitative in character. Indeed the ballad, though it has survived to our own day, promptly separated into lyric ballad and narrative ballad, both retaining considerable dramatic force.

**Primitive Ballad Poetry**

For a long time this dramatic instinct for imitation through action could express itself only in ballads, or in pantomime and equally rude farce. Then it was appropriated to the uses of the church, and employed in performing sections of bible story (the miracle plays) or versions of the world-old conflict of vice and virtue (the moralities). The facility learned in dramatizing episodes from the bible was soon applied to secular history. Then the connected experiences of heroes, in history or legend, were organized with a greater sense of form, with classical drama as a model, and English tragedy appeared. Comedy developed in a similar way by putting motive and character into the old farces and by acquiring mastery of technique from Latin models.

**Development of Drama**

Among the early ballads, which were largely narrative, occasional ones appeared that were concerned with emotion, supposedly the personal feeling of the author. Soon these developed into a class by themselves, and the expression of human emotion in song became so popular by the days of Queen Elizabeth that England was "a nest of singing birds." With the growth of national

**Lyric Forms**

feeling in this period came the patriotic, or national song, which a little later found its highest expression in the ode. The personal lyric in the meantime was becoming constantly more subjective and introspective, and so involved in thought and phrasing that it did not lend itself to the music of a song. It remained true to its original limit of a single unit of emotion, and appeared in any one of several verse forms already in common use. Closely akin to the lyric poem, indeed in its most attractive form a kind of prose lyric, is the personal essay, which grew up in England coincident with the decline of Elizabethan lyric and the rise of prose to a position of literary importance. It remained for the next lyric period in English literature, the romantic activity of the early nineteenth century, to reveal the higher possibilities of the essay to express private feeling and imagination.

From the narrative element in the primitive ballads a somewhat more complicated family-line has descended. From the beginning, no doubt, such experiences or adventures were selected for telling as had "point" to them,— some central fact that established them as units of narrative and set them apart from other happenings. Often this was a matter of intrigue and deception, with satisfaction to be had from seeing an easy victim fleeced or a scheming rascal checkmated. Thus developed the broad, popular verse-narrative called the "*fabliau*," a favorite with the late Middle Ages, and best known to us in certain tales of Chaucer. Gradually this passed from verse to prose, and took the name of "*novella*" in Italy and Spain and "novel" in England, though it was really just a short story, as such things were understood in and about the year 1700. The modern short story had its birth less than a hundred years ago

*Narrative Types*

from a union of some of these old-fashioned well-told tales with the new imaginative and emotional spirit found in romantic literature.

The narrative ballads, throughout their history, displayed a certain interesting tendency. They were much inclined to unite with others dealing with the same or a similar personage into larger units or cycles. In case this personage was sufficiently heroic, the ultimate result was a form of popular or folk epic. This is seen at its best in the Old English poem, *Beowulf,* and is approximated in the *Little Gest of Robin Hood.* In classical literature the logical progress was from this amalgamated popular epic—as seen in the Homeric poems—to a unified, self-conscious imitative product like Virgil's *Æneid.* Later still the elements of love and adventure in the epics were developed independently into long romances, first in prose, later in verse, and finally in prose again. England, however, took little or no part in these developments. England produced no imitations of *Beowulf,* and the cycle of Arthurian romance, for which she furnished the material, was developed chiefly on foreign soil.

Epic and Romance

Both literary epic and prose romance came into England as a part of her Renaissance awakening. Only two great specimens of the former stand to her credit, Milton's *Paradise Lost,* representing the tradition of Virgil, and Spenser's *Faerie Queene,* of the type of the romantic epics invented by Italy. Prose romances were not widely cultivated, translations from the French being more popular, and soon gave way to the growing power of realism that trimmed the romances of their extravagances and brought them down to earth as

Emergence of the Novel

eighteenth-century novels. The novel has maintained its popularity for two centuries, varying between the two extremes of photographic realism and romantic fancy.

The literary forms enumerated are by no means the only ones produced and cultivated in the long evolution of literature in English. One might add a considerable list of types very much in the fashion at one time or another, or still enjoying an unbroken, if somewhat modest, popularity. Fable and epigram, memoir and familiar letter, literary biography and didactic poem, all have their place in the history of literature. In the limited space of a book like this, however, attention must be centered upon such literature as has established itself permanently in the affections of the race, the large and genuinely "typical" forms in which men's moods and fancies are accustomed to find expression.

<small>Minor Types</small>

This method of approach to English literature is open to criticism of various sorts. We are assured that creative artists do not think in terms of types; that these are artificial classes with artificial distinctions, set up by critics who follow in the wake of creation and classify the product of this creation as a pretense of explaining it. But this is true only in part. It is not a high type of creative mind that undertakes to produce a masterpiece according to a programme or code of technique. The great craftsman in letters probably cannot define in advance the exact design his imagination will take when the mood is on him. But he knows whether he is at work on a lyric poem or a short story, a play or a novel. Furthermore, he knows the finer technical points regarding the construction of this form, and consciously or unconsciously shapes his product to

**Writers Are Conscious of Types**

conform to them. The poet needs a fine frenzy, an "esemplastic" imagination—as Coleridge would say—that enables him to see the end of his task in the beginning. Investigation usually shows that the best of poets have given no little time and energy to the problem of effectiveness in selecting, massing, and phrasing details.

A more valid objection lies in the fact that there is a constant tendency to blend and confuse the so-called typical forms of literature, just as there is to confuse certain of the fine arts, and that many of our most worthy documents of literature are products of such fusion and defy classification. Only critics who are most severely classical array themselves against such methods, while minds of a highly romantic turn take particular delight in them. It is merely the old problem of the comic scenes in tragedy brought down to date, and Shakespeare is emphatically on the side of the romantics. Probably if alive today he would approve freely of plays that sacrifice structure and action to cleverly phrased "ideas," or of essays that are short stories with an intellectual point to them.

*The Fusion of Types*

It is by no means the purpose of this book to oppose such procedure. But it is clear enough that literary expression, in a series of centuries, has evolved these various forms, each with its particular selection of technical elements arranged in particular relations to each other, and that these forms represent the natural gamut of utterance from which the literary artist may choose. To object that a particular piece "falls between two stools" and is part lyric, part dramatic, may be as absurd as to complain of the sharps and flats in music. It is at least desirable, though, that the student or the

*Knowledge of Types Fundamental*

"gentle reader" should be able with assurance to pronounce a piece "part lyric, part dramatic," and to know what he is talking about when he does so. These typical forms are not likely to be overthrown by romantic fusions any more than music, scene painting, and poetry have lost their identity and general interest since they have been successfully blended into opera.

## BOOKS OF REFERENCE

### I. History of Critical Thought

J. W. H. Atkins, *English Criticism* (*Channels of English Literature*). New York (Dutton & Co ), 1912.

S. H. Butcher, *Aristotle's Theory of Poetry and Fine Art*. New York and London (Macmillan), 1907. (Originally published 1895.)

A. S. Cook, *The Art of Poetry* Boston and New York (Ginn & Co.), 1892. (The critical treatises of Horace, Vida, and Boileau )

Lane Cooper, *Methods and Aims in the Study of Literature*. A series of extracts and illustrations. Boston and New York (Ginn & Co.), 1915

Lane Cooper, *Aristotle on the Art of Poetry*. Boston and New York (Ginn & Co.), 1916.

Charles M. Gayley and Fred N Scott, *An Introduction to the Materials and Methods of Literary Criticism* Boston and New York (Ginn & Co.), 1901.

George E. Saintsbury, *A History of Criticism and Literary Taste in Europe*. 3 vols. New York (Dodd, Mead & Co ), 1902.

George E. Saintsbury, *Loci Critici* Boston and New York (Ginn & Co.), 1903.

### II. Critical Theory

Irving Babbitt, *The New Laokoon*. An essay on the confusion of the arts. Boston and New York (Houghton Mifflin Co.), 1910

W. C. Brownell, *Criticism*. New York (Scribner's Sons), 1914.

Ferdinand Brunetière, *L'Évolution des Genres dans l'Histoire de la Littérature française* Paris, 1890.

P. P. Howe, *Criticism (The Art and Craft of Letters)*. New York (Doran & Co ).
C. T. Winchester, *Some Principles of Literary Criticism* New York (Macmillan), 1900.
W. Basil Worsfold, *The Principles of Criticism*. An introduction to the study of literature. New York (Longmans, Green & Co.), 1902.

### III. Interpretation of Literature

*Counsel upon the Reading of Books.* Boston and New York (Houghton Mifflin Co.). (Essays by Henry Van Dyke, H. Morse Stephens, Agnes Repplier, Arthur T. Hadley, Brander Matthews, Bliss Perry, and Hamilton Wright Mabie.)
Hiram Corson, *The Aims of Literary Study.* New York (Macmillan), 1894.
W. H. Crawshaw, *The Interpretation of Literature.* New York (Macmillan), 1896.
W. H. Hudson, *An Introduction to the Study of Literature.* Boston and New York (Heath & Co.).
Richard G. Moulton, *The Modern Study of Literature.* An introduction to literary theory and interpretation. Chicago (University Press), 1915
F. V. N. Painter, *Elementary Guide to Literary Criticism.* Boston (Ginn & Co.), 1903.
P. H. Pearson, *The Study of Literature.* Chicago (McClurg), 1913.
W. H. Sheran, *A Handbook of Literary Criticism.* An analysis of literary forms in verse and prose. New York (Hinds, Noble & Eldredge), 1905.
Edwin L. Shuman, *How to Judge a Book.* A handy method of criticism for the general reader. Boston and New York (Houghton Mifflin Co.), 1910.
G. E. Woodberry, *The Appreciation of Literature.* New York (Baker & Taylor), 1907.

### IV. Type-Studies in Series

*The Art and Craft of Letters.* London (Hodder & Stoughton); New York (George H Doran & Co.). Volumes on Satire, Epic, History, Comedy, Ballad, Essay, Parody, Criticism. Others in preparation.
*Channels of English Literature.* Edited by Oliphant Smeaton. London (Dent & Sons); New York (Dutton & Co.). Volumes

on Epic and Heroic Poetry, Lyric Poetry, Elegiac, Didactic, and Religious Poetry, Dramatic Poetry, Satiric and Humorous Literature, Philosophers and Schools of Philosophy, Essay and Essayists, Novel, Historians and Schools of History, Criticism.

*The Types of English Literature.* Edited by W. A. Neiison. Boston and New York (Houghton Mifflin & Co.). Volumes on Popular Ballad, Literature of Roguery, Tragedy, Lyric, Saint's Legend. Others in preparation.

*The Warwick Library of English Literature.* Edited by C. H. Herford London (Blackie & Son); New York (Scribner's Sons). Volumes of critical discussion and selections on Pastorals, Literary Criticism, Essays, Lyric Poetry, Satires, Tales in Verse, Masques, Historians.

## V. Chronology

Frederick Ryland, *Chronological Outlines of English Literature.* London and New York (Macmillan), 1910. (First printed 1890.)

## II

## THE POPULAR BALLAD

### *History*

  THE popular ballad, though still a vital force in English literature, belongs essentially to a period of oral transmission, before literary productions took written or printed form. It is true that long after the cultured classes were reading printed books, balladry remained a cherished possession of the simple folk. But it was held in memory among them, and imparted by singing or recitation at the fireside. Gradually, as the plain people of England and Scotland ceased to be a primitive folk, these precious verse-traditions were seized upon by the more or less reverent hands of collectors and publishers, to thrill more learned readers, to tantalize investigators, and to inspire new and self-conscious verse-makers. Folk-poetry, as a creative phenomenon, is done, except as one may happen upon some isolated group of people, simple-minded, emotional, and homogeneous, as were the march-troopers of old.

**Introductory**

  Of various working definitions proposed for this literary type, that of Professor Gummere is perhaps most comprehensive and accurate: "a poem meant for singing, quite impersonal in manner, narrative in material, probably connected in its origins with the communal dance, but submitted to a process of oral tradition among people who

**Definition**

are free from literary influences and fairly homogeneous in character."[1] This represents what Professor Gummere himself calls the "definition by origins." And origins, elusive as they are, are sure to demand a large share of attention in any study of the popular ballad. It is now generally accepted that primitive social groups, under stress of a common emotion, expressed that emotion by the rhythmic movements of a tribal dance, accompanied by the chanting of crudely appropriate words. Frequently, no doubt, this singing, dancing throng was broken into two rival divisions, answering responsively to each other. Evidences of such practices are scattered far and wide, from "Saul hath slain his thousands, and David his ten thousands,"[2] which greeted the Israelites after their success against the Philistines, to the ceremonial dances of savage tribes, or the rhythmic games of children. It is reasonable enough to suppose that responses of this sort were impromptu, the improvisations of the group as a unit. Out of these, afterwards fixed and conventionalized, came the refrains of later balladry.

**Communal Lyric**

At times, however, these people would have assembled all aglow with the recollection of some striking incident of the day's experience,—a bride-stealing, a heroic rescue, or a miraculous escape from danger,—essentially the material for a narrative. It is not inconceivable that this too might have taken verse form to the dance-music, in dramatic stanzas, full of dialogue, progressing slowly because of much repetition, but improvised throughout the group rather than by any

**Communal Narrative**

[1] *The Popular Ballad*, p. 2. Cf. also pp. 13-14.
[2] I. Samuel xviii, 7. Cf. Exodus xv, and Judges xi.

distinct individual. Such practice of communal authorship could not, of course, be extended indefinitely. At some point in the process—long indeed before the creation of any ballad that has come down to us—the individual author emerged from the homogeneous throng. But he was still of the throng, in impression, and mood, and utterance, and the stanzas he improvised were of the impersonal, crudely dramatic sort already fixed upon by his fellows.

Primitive ballads are in certain respects like the legends of folk-lore. Both appear to have been the common property of practically all peoples in the dawn of their civilization. Various nations, indeed, enjoyed and developed the same ballad themes, just as they circulated the same folk-tales. But this development took place so long ago, and extant ballad versions are so elusive and in most cases so recent, that we can be sure of nothing in the way of transmission from one nation to another. Usually the oldest ballad themes are so simple that mere coincidence will account for their appearance in several countries at the same time.

*Ballad Circulation*

Approached with this point of view, the history of the English ballad falls naturally into several distinct periods.

I. The period of the simple ballad, usually concerned with domestic relations and showing traces of communal authorship.

*Periods of Ballad History*

II. The period of the adventure ballad, including both the outlaw ballads and the border ballads. To this period correspond too the heroic ballads, best exemplified in Denmark.

III. The period of the journalistic ballad,—the broadside or " ballad in print."

IV. The period of scholarly revival and artistic imitation.

Ballads selected by experts as a heritage from the good old times indicated in the first period are not necessarily found in the earliest written or printed versions. They may indeed have no connection with the primitive period, except that they have been constructed on the model of ballads that had such a history. Ballad antiquity is indicated not by external, but by internal evidence,—the substance and form of the ballad itself. Thus the simple ballad is built upon one situation or incident; a series of incidents, when introduced, being so closely connected that they are practically one. This situation, or group of related incidents, is presented dramatically, with the employment of striking dialogue, and often in stanzas rendered more effective by a system of repetition which alters only a line—or even a word—each time to advance the story. This is the "incremental repetition" spoken of by ballad scholars.

**The Primitive Form**

"He's taken the second ane by the hand,
And he's turned her round and made her stand,

'It's whether will ye be a rank robber's wife,
Or will ye die by my wee pen-knife?'

'I'll not be a rank robber's wife,
But I'll rather die by your wee pen-knife.'

He's killed this may, and he's laid her by,
For to bear the red rose company.

He's taken the youngest ane by the hand,
And he's turned her round and made her stand,

Says, 'Will ye be a rank robber's wife,
Or will ye die by my wee pen-knife?'

'I'll not be a rank robber's wife,
Nor will I die by your wee pen-knife.

'For I hae a brother in this wood,
An' gin ye kill me, it's he'll kill thee.'"

The lines above, from "Babylon, or the Bonnie Banks o' Fordie," a ballad rich in suggestion of public rendition with dance accompaniment, afford an excellent example of the way this repetition with incremental change was managed. These two stanza-groups, preceded by another introducing the "first sister," present in dramatic fashion the undivided central situation of this tragic theme. "Babylon" suggests primitive balladry too in its stanzas of two lines each, with alternating refrain lines. The first of the stanzas quoted were really delivered thus:

"He's taken the second ane by the hand,
*Eh vow bonnie,*

And he's turned her round and made her stand,
*By the bonnie banks o' Fordie.*

It's whether will ye be a rank robber's wife,
*Eh vow bonnie,*

Or will ye die by my wee pen-knife?
*By the bonnie banks o' Fordie.*"

This arrangement was continued throughout the ballad.

**The Developed Form**

In what seems to be a second, somewhat later development of the simple type of ballad, the central situation breaks up into several closely related incidents, presented like separate dramatic scenes in miniature, and at times connected by a stanza or two of transition.

The arrangement of lines in couplets gives way to a series of four-line stanzas, with alternate lines of eight and six syllables, the second and fourth lines in rhyme. A refrain, with these ballads, is the exception rather than the rule.

All the ballads in this first division, whatever their form, have the common theme of domestic interests, passions, and adventures. False wives and **Domestic Themes** false lovers, illicit love and its consequences, cruel brothers and stern parents who thwart the course of true affection, murder and suicide and incest,—these are characteristic features. When supernatural beings enter the action, it is to carry off earthly lovers, or to visit in ghostly form the objects of earlier devotion. The family is the largest unit considered, apparently; the community is only a much-interested observer.

In the second period of English balladry, much of this was changed. The earlier ballad of domestic tragedy continued to be circulated with little **Period of Adventure Ballads** modification, and was occasionally imitated as new material was afforded. But the folk had at length become conscious of itself, chiefly through the necessities of resistance: resistance to encroaching statutes that would interfere with certain privileges of poaching and the like, traditional through many generations; resistance —particularly along the English and Scottish border—to bold neighboring settlements that raided cattle, and killed from ambush, and obeyed an alien king. The community made other kinds of ballads now, in which it was vitally concerned and often played a part. Thus arose the ballad of border conflict, and the various groups of outlaw ballads culminating in Robin Hood.

In actual time the outlaw ballad was considerably earlier than the border ballad. While all attempts to identify a real Robin Hood have failed, ample evidence has been found that he and other outlaw-figures were widely celebrated in popular verse by the fourteenth century.[1] Most of the earliest of such verse has perished, leaving to us more elaborate and artistic specimens— best seen in the *Little Gest*—representing a late stage in the development of an early form, and contemporary with various cruder specimens of the border product. Border ballads, like border conflict, flourished in the two centuries or so from Chaucer's time to the awakening of the Renaissance in England. Many of these, like the adventures they celebrated, were very precious to the people, and were jealously confined within the limits of their own territory, where ballad collectors found them little changed.

*Outlaw Ballads Earlier*

A few of these border ballads display the primitive features of form, which always suggest somehow a singing, dancing throng. But they are usually specimens in which the simple domestic themes play an equally large part with those of strife and feudal vengeance, as in "Bonnie George Campbell" and "The Baron of Brackley," and "Captain Carr," with its haunting stanza of refrain. The larger number employ a structure already developed by the ballads of outlawry. This involves the gradual extension of the epic or narrative part at the expense of dramatic dialogue and incremental repetition. An accumulation of details, many of them unimportant, replaces the severely selective method of the more simple ballad. Clear-cut scenes disappear as

*Structure of the Border Ballads*

---

[1] E. g, the boast of Sloth in *Piers Plowman* (Passus v, about 1375): "But I can [know] rymes of Robyn Hood and Randolf Erle of Chestre."

transitions are amplified, and names of places and people are repeated, evidently to serve a patriotic purpose. In short, the style is that of the garrulous narrator, analogous to the minstrel of the verse romances.

All early ballads were fond of tragic situations, involving or at least suggesting physical prowess and adventure. Willie killed all the king's lifeguards on his way to Lady Maisry's bower,[1] and Earl Brand was stabbed from behind by one of the king's best men, after disposing of the fourteen others man to man.[2] Still, this sort of adventure was at first largely incidental to the domestic tragedy at the heart of the ballad. In the second period of ballad history, manly prowess and heroic adventure became themselves the essential features. Border feud and outlaw freedom made heroes, and the greatest of these was Robin Hood.

**Adventure Themes**

It is significant of these ballad heroes that they were thoroughly representative. Percy embodies the spirit of all English march-men, as truly as the doughty Douglas does that of the Scots. The eternal challenge of feud-vengeance rings in that conventional stanza ascribed to several popular leaders:[3]

**Representative Heroes**

> "— Fight on, my merry men all,
> I am a little hurt, but I am not slain;
> I will lay me down for to bleed a while,
> Then I'll rise and fight with you again"

Robin Hood has been often discussed as representing all the typical folk-virtues of his time: manly prowess,

---

[1] "Willie and Lady Maisry."
[2] "Earl Brand."
[3] "Johnie Armstrong," B, 18; "Sir Andrew Barton," 65.

shrewdness, piety, courtesy, loyalty in friendship, even adoration for the person of the king. His only crimes were poaching on game-preserves that had once been open to the peasantry, and levying tribute upon prelate or merchant who enjoyed more wealth than he deserved.

Consideration of this supreme outlaw hero, Robin Hood, suggests another characteristic feature of these adventure ballads, their tendency to **Adaptable** transfer themselves and their adventures **Adventures** bodily to the experience of some already popular figure, who eventually becomes the center of a mass of verse-tradition organized into crudely epic form. Thus the *Little Gest of Robin Hood* carries Robin through a closely related series of adventures, dignified enough in the eyes of the people and representative of their best ideals, and brings him to a hero's death at the close. Yet the poem may be dissected into a number of separate units, undoubtedly at one time independent, and likely enough to have been ascribed to various personages in widely different localities. There is much justification for the familiar statement that the *Little Gest* is a genuine folk-epic.

To this second period, also, belong the few specimens to be found in English of what may be called the heroic ballads, a class best represented in the **The Heroic** ballad literature of Denmark. There **Ballad** they seem to have been cultivated for and by the higher circles of society, and delivered before audiences familiar at first hand with the doughty deeds and courtly trappings that were always prominent features. The English specimens seem rather to be adaptations or pale reflections of the current romances, in which court circles for several centuries had found delight, until the tarnished fabric had descended, like well-worn garments of fashion, to the lower classes of society. The folk-product might assume either the accepted primitive manner, as in " Hind Horn ":

> "In Scotland there was a babie born,
>   Lill lal, etc.
> And his name it was called young Hind Horn.
>   With a fal lal, etc."

or the obvious signs of minstrel rendering to be found in " King Estmere ":

> "Hearken to me, gentlemen,
>   Come and you shall heare;
> Ile tell you of two of the boldest brether
>   That ever borne were."

In either case the matter is of kings and princes, of the hard-won love of princesses that are brave and fair, of marvelous achievements in lists and battlefields. The outlook on life is no longer provincial; the more conscious motives of friendship and honor play an important part; and plots are strengthened by a conflict of motives, as in " Bewick and Grahame."

With the introduction of the printing press into England, the popular ballad entered upon a third stage of existence. People craved the sight of their ballads in print, and newsdealers were not slow to satisfy the craving. These " broadsides," as they came to be called, were arranged in two double-column pages on the same side of a folio sheet, usually with a crude wood-cut surmounting the first page. Broadside ballads may be variously classified. The ballad minstrels had often referred to their performance as " saying and singing," a double term that seemed to indicate that eventually some

**Broadside Ballads**

ballads would be recited, others sung. But this possible distinction was lost entirely in this period. For while there were ballads more essentially lyric side by side with the great array of narrative material, all specimens of both types were thought of first as songs. A number of easy, catchy, and adaptable ballad tunes grew up, did service for one set of stanzas after another, and eventually became themselves traditional. This method of procedure resulted somewhat later in the "ballad opera," known best today through the success of Gay's *Beggar's Opera*, in 1728.

A better classification of broadsides would rest upon their real age: whether they represent good old ballad stuff, vulgarized somewhat for the penny press, or some current adventure or nine-days wonder, served up to a gaping populace before the time of novelty was done. The broadside ballad was the people's yellow journal, as will appear from a handful of the long-drawn-out titles of the sixteenth century:

**Their Journalistic Character**

"The true description of a monsterous Chylde, borne in the Ile of Wight, in this present yeare of oure Lord God MDlxiiij, the month of October."

"A briefe sonet declaring the lamentation of Beckels, a Market Towne in Suffolke, which was in the great winde upon S. Andrewes eve pitifully burned with fire, to the value by estimation of twentie thousande pounds, and to the number of fourscore dwelling houses, besides a great number of other houses, 1586."

"The West-Country Damosel's Complaint, or The Faithful Lover's Last Farewel: Being the relation of a young Maid, who pined herself to death for the love of a Young-man, who, after he had notice of it, dyed, likewise, for grief."

A prominent type of broadside ballad, sometimes carrying on very old traditions, but always directed at existing

## 24 THE TYPICAL FORMS OF ENGLISH LITERATURE

conditions, was the satirical ballad, aimed at certain much maligned classes, such as women and priests, or at recent developments in church and state.

**Satirical Ballads**  Political ballads in particular enjoyed an immense vogue between the closing of the theaters (1642) and the Restoration, and again toward the end of the seventeenth century. They had indeed an unbroken history down to the "Election Ballads" of Robert Burns.

Various Elizabethan documents furnish valuable evidence concerning the interest of the populace in printed ballads.

**Popularity of the Broadsides**  Falstaff and Bottom alike intend to have ballads made, to serve their purpose of revenge or pride.[1] Autolycus with his peasant audience and his pack of marvels not a month old gives Shakespeare a royal chance to poke fun at these journalistic extravagances.[2] Chettle's *Kind-Harts Dreame* shows us a family of ballad-venders in Essex busy in their booth singing lustily the selections they have on sale. Captain Cox is described in Robert Langham's *Letter from Kenilworth* (1575) as having over a hundred broadside ballads old and new, "fair wrapt up in parchment." Izaak Walton tells of an honest alehouse with "twenty ballads stuck about the wall," and a milk-woman who sang "Chevy Chase" and "Johny Armstrong." Various small printers made a business of publishing current ballads, and certain minor writers of Elizabeth's time composed great numbers of these. William Elderton, Thomas Deloney, and Anthony Munday were particularly active.

Poetically many of these productions were beneath

[1] *Henry IV*, part I, II, ii; *Midsummer Night's Dream*, IV, i.
[2] *Winter's Tale*. IV. iv.

contempt. Even the famous old ballad traditions had a way of collapsing into doggerel in their printed versions, and the new attempts limped badly and had neither rhyme nor reason. Many of them were hopelessly unpoetic in subject and in phrasing and marked by frequent crimes against good taste. They were notably *bourgeois* in their material interests, their class-pride, and their smug-faced morality. It was a sore trial for the old folk-ballads to pass through such a medium. Many of them, fortunately, did not have to.

<small>Crude in Form</small>

By the middle of the seventeenth century, the ballad came to the attention of the amateur collector. It was not enough that mine host treasured them to adorn the walls of his tap-room. There appeared genuine virtuosos in balladry, like the first possessor of Bishop Percy's Folio Manuscript, or the famous diarist Samuel Pepys. Editors like Tom Durfey, with his *Pills to Purge Melancholy*, and Allan Ramsay, with his *Evergreen* and *Tea-Table Miscellany*, blending old and new, genuine and spurious, with little thought of distinctions, at least kept traditional ballads before the English reading public. Then in 1765 came Bishop Percy's *Reliques of Ancient English Poetry*, built about the famous Folio Manuscript of ballads found in Humphrey Pitt's kitchen, where it served the cook in lighting the fires.

<small>Collectors and Collections</small>

This activity came at the very threshold of the English Romantic Movement, as a notable feature of the medieval interest upon which this movement was largely founded. The time was ripe for it, in Germany as well as in England. The reading public of both countries was satiated with the monotonous formality, self-consciousness, and artificiality of prevailing efforts at poetry, and in a search for genuineness in emotion and imagination was turning for relief to the obscure past,—a much-idealized Middle Age which it viewed through amber glasses. As in the Renaissance, the leaders of this new activity were scholars as well as enthusiasts, and they worked seriously and systematically.

**Ballads and Romanticism**

In England ballad scholarship was represented in Bishop Percy; in Joseph Ritson, with his numerous collections of old songs and his combative prefaces; in Sir Walter Scott, whose diligence as a collector made possible his *Minstrelsy of the Scottish Border;* as well as in numerous less-known men, such as David Herd, Motherwell, and Jamieson. None of these was averse to supplying gaps in manuscripts or printed texts with the product of his own pen, but Scott alone attained any skill as a ballad imitator. Ballad collecting has continued, and scholarly attention to the subject has increased down to our own day, especially since the appearance of the monumental collection of *English and Scottish Popular Ballads,* edited by Professor Francis James Child, of Harvard, and published in 1882-1898.

**Scholarship**

Ballad imitation of various sorts has thrived equally well during the nineteenth century. In Germany, where Percy's *Reliques* had an immediate vogue as notable as that in England, collectors and imitators at once began working side by side. Herder revived and published the folk-songs of his people, while Bürger was moved to the weaving of new ballads out of old traditions, imparting to his creations a somewhat mechanical and grisly supernaturalism. These ballads by Bürger reacted in turn upon

**Imitation**

England, slightly affecting Scott in his youth,[1] and exercising a large influence on Matthew Gregory Lewis, editor and very largely author of the *Tales of Terror and Wonder*. Interest in the fleshly horrible soon ceased, however, and later imitation of ballads has taken various more artistic forms, which perhaps may best be illustrated by certain fairly well-known poems: (1) "The Eve of St. John," by Scott; (2) "The White Ship," by Dante Gabriel Rossetti; (3) Kipling's "Danny Deever"; and (4) "The Admiral's Ghost," by Alfred Noyes.

The first of these is naturally nearest to real balladry, celebrating a theme of domestic infidelity and death and spectral visitation, with a richness of ballad conventionalities that only the author had at command. Scott yields to the taste for internal rhyme, and in various other ways marks the poem with his own individuality, but it is at least nearer the norm than most of the "Tales of Terror" among which it appeared. The second poem is a first-rate specimen of the revival of refrain lines, made as suggestive as possible, which marked certain verse-writing of the mid-Victorian period. Rossetti, trained to realize the emotional and imaginative possibilities of legendary adventure, did some of his best work in those ballad narratives with their compelling refrains, his aim being not to create the illusion of a popular ballad, but to raise the ballad to the level of art.

<small>Scott and Rossetti</small>

Most modern poets seem to appreciate best the dramatic crispness of the shorter, more conversational ballad—the form usually regarded as primitive. Kipling's presentation of the execution-scene of Danny Deever is entirely in conversation, with repetition that is

<small>Recent Attempts</small>

[1] See Lockhart's *Life of Sir Walter Scott*, chap. VII.

obviously incremental and with a striking use of refrain. It has of course various artistic touches. "The Admiral's Ghost" might be criticised as hardly related to balladry at all. Yet if removed from the framework that introduces a modern, rather than an ancient mariner as narrator, it closely resembles the ghost tales of the old ballads, leaps and lingers as they do, and gets its best effects, like them, by a few suggestive touches.

One final manifestation of the popular ballad must be mentioned. This is the prevalence of certain songs, closely approximating the old ballads, among certain homogeneous classes in our own country, particularly the cowboys of the West, and the negroes on the Southern plantations. A number of American scholars have made collections of this material, the largest being those of Professor John A. Lomax of Texas. On investigation, these negro and cowboy ballads show a surprisingly large number of the usual ballad characteristics. They are anonymous in origin, omnipresent in circulation, and have depended entirely on oral transmission. They are chiefly narrative, are frequently tragic, and are partial to the exploits of outlaws.

**Cowboy and Negro Ballads**

> "Jesse had a wife, the pride of his life,
> His children they were brave,
> But the dirty little coward that shot Mr. Howard,
> He laid Jesse James in his grave."

In form they display considerable variety, but the old alternation of eight syllables and six forms the basic structure of many specimens, while others display the familiar couplet with alternating refrain. Details are crude, and much of the poetry is mere doggerel, but the same thing may be said of most old ballads at various stages of their history. Ballad students may learn much from these natural utterances of our best modern specimens of a homogeneous, singing folk.

### Technique of the Ballad [1]

The simple ballad, apparently the earliest to develop, affords the most interesting study of technique. As has been noted, it is concerned chiefly with personal or domestic relations, frequently tragic in outcome or involving the matter-of-fact introduction of supernatural personages. The motives are affection of some sort—or the bitterness that comes from thwarted affection—and physical courage and prowess. These may appear in conjunction, but rarely in conflict. Conflict of emotions seems to belong with heroic or aristocratic traditions.

**The Simple Ballad— Themes**

The characters are largely from the ranks of the people, or from noble families resident among the people. There are occasional references to royalty, it is true, but in no case is there any great regard for caste distinction. The ballad is little concerned with identifying its characters or even with characterizing them with any thoroughness. Comparison of ballad characters with those found in Chaucer, for example, will make this clear, particularly in a specific case like the ballad "Sir Hugh" and the Prioress's Tale. Such characterizing touches as do appear in the ballads are likely to be mere convention,—"sweet," "bonny," "well-fared," and the like.

**Characterization**

[1] See Walter M. Hart, *Ballad and Epic*, for a more detailed analysis of ballad technique.

The setting of these ballads is refreshingly vague. Time is defined only so far as to meet some requirement of the story: Hallowe'en in "Tam Lin"; **Setting** "about Yule" in "Young Waters." Usually there is no time indication at all. References to place are more common but little more illuminating. Rarely a town is named; more frequently we hear merely of highlands or lowlands or "north countree." Details of place description are notably lacking. There is a garden or a wood, perhaps at best a "green garden" or a "silver wood," and there is an end of it. This lack of dependence on setting to create "atmosphere" is most striking in supernatural accounts, where we of today are accustomed to expect a wealth of detail,—the subconscious detail of realism, or the studied detail to rouse the imagination.

The simple ballad is at heart a situation or incident, which is presented concisely and vividly, and with as little attendant explanation as possible. In **Organization** most cases the situation breaks naturally into two or more closely related incidents or scenes, with or without transition-stanzas. In any case there is usually a brief conclusion. This may be merely a narrative stanza or two; or, in the frequent tragic conditions, may include a testament or a lament. The organization of these ballads thus anticipates in many ways the modern short story, and like it depends on the methods of the dramatist. Analysis of a simple ballad will usually show this arrangement:

I. Narrative Introduction.

II. One or more dramatic scenes, connected scenes usually involving transitions.

III. Conclusion, possibly including testament and lament.

The exact boundaries of these divisions will not always be clear and certainly not beyond dispute.

In the individual scenes of these ballads, the method is naïvely dramatic. Dialogue is regularly present and is as direct as possible, with so little explanation that a mere reader is often confused. In the scenes, too, incremental repetition is most prominent, suggesting the peculiar adaptability of these dramatic parts to the choral dance. The conclusion of the ballad is likely also to be dramatic in effect, either through the testament device, which is in dialogue form, as in "The Cruel Brother," or "Edward," or through the appealing lament, presumably the utterance of the chief mourner, or representing a bereaved community:

**Dramatic Effects**

> "My meadow lies green,
>     and my corn is unshorn,
> My barn is to build,
>     and my babe is unborn."
>         ("Bonnie George Campbell.")

Mere narrative conclusions are likely to fall into conventional forms and suggest later additions, like the familiar

> "Lord Thomas was buried without kirk-wa,
>     Fair Annet within the quiere,
> And o the tane thair grew a birk,
>     The other a bonny briere."

But all these details do not explain the charm of balladry. There is still the difference underlying Dr. Samuel Johnson's parody on "The Children in the Wood," nor is the case weakened by the fact that the Doctor selected a rather modern ballad. It was one thing to say with the ballad-singer:

**Imaginative Appeal**

> "These pretty babes, with hand in hand,
> Went wandering up and down;
> But never more could see the man
> Approaching from the town."

It was quite another to remark with Dr. Johnson:

> "I put my hat upon my head,
> And walked into the Strand,
> And there I met another man
> Whose hat was in his hand."

The difference of imaginative appeal is not simply a matter of suggested archaism; for an archaism of spelling as extreme as that of Dr. Johnson's contemporary Chatterton[1] would make this second stanza nothing more than grotesquely commonplace. The real distinction of great balladry is the distinction of much great literature in other forms, the expression in simplest terms of things deeply tragic or pathetic, yet so general in their appeal as to awaken sympathy in an extended circle of hearers or readers. Hat or no hat in the Strand is a problem of no emotion and little imagination; no human being who loves little children and realizes their helplessness can miss the appeal of those last lines of "The Children in the Wood." Not all balladry has this element of imaginative power. A surprisingly large amount, however, reveals at least a flash of it.

In the adventure ballads of border conflict or outlawry these vivid suggestions of tragic fact or poignant experience are not so much in evidence. In the organization of plots the narrative introductions and connections

---

[1] Thomas Chatterton composed a number of archaic-looking poems, which he represented as drawn from manuscripts of an early English poet named Rowley.

have been expanded from their subordinate place in the simple ballads to be the dominating elements in these later forms. These ballads belong to the professional minstrel who still relies occasionally on dialogue and incremental repetition and suggestion, but prefers to hold attention by telling everything and heaping up concrete details. There are long introductions, because the adventure he is to relate grows out of another of some significance; there are long transitions because these tales of raid and rescue emphasize the journeying from place to place that formerly needed only a line or two. Time is no more definite than before; place is now mentioned in some detail. Adventures such as these are important in themselves, not because they reflect experiences of all time; and such adventures must be distinctly localized. The scattered references to nature and scenery crystallize finally in the Robin Hood cycle, where they undertake to express the joyous spirit of the greenwood.

**Narrative Ballads of Adventure**

Theme and characterization keep developing throughout the balladry of this second stage. The interest still divides between experience of the emotions and men's delight in courage and physical prowess. In the border ballads this physical heroism is at its height, though even there such emotional factors as clan pride, devotion of retainer to his chief, and touches of piety enter in. In the best outlaw ballads, the hero is an object of reverence among his men and deserves it by the graciousness and shrewdness that supplement his native strength. None of these ballads has much to do with conflict of emotions. That belongs to the romances and to the few heroic ballads, such as "Bewick and Grahame," that have filtered down from aristocratic sources.

**Themes**

Adventure ballads are fairly packed with characters. There are numerous muster-rolls of heroic names that must have aroused patriotic response in the hearts of listeners. The heroes portrayed have become distinctively representative: in the border ballads, of clan or vaguely even of nation; in the outlaw stories, of the oppressed common-folk as against tyranny and its immediate instruments. Only in the latter case, however, do these heroic figures take on any complete characterization, and this is found only in the person of one man—in the courteous, pious, and resourceful Robin Hood. The others are "bold" and "doughty," but little more. The Robin Hood ballads are likewise the only ones that show any particular attempt to group characters for purposes of contrast or parallel. Indeed, the literary effectiveness of Robin's cabinet of chief retainers appears only on perusal of a number of the ballads, or the collected product in the *Little Gest*.

**Characterization**

Such changes as the popular broadsides of the sixteenth century brought into balladry are too few and insignificant to require attention. The popular ballad reached its artistic climax in the period of oral tradition.

*Subjects for Study*

1. Comparison of "Sir Hugh" with Chaucer's "Prioress's Tale."
2. Recasting of some supernatural ballad ("The Wife of Usher's Well," "Sweet William's Ghost," "Tam Lin") as a prose tale.
3. Development of Robin Hood as a folk-hero.
4. Comparison of "Hind Horn" with the related romance *King Horn*.
5. Comparison of "Thomas Rymer" with the related romance.

6. Comparison of "Thomas Rymer" with Keats's "La belle Dame sans Merci."
7. Historical account of ballad scholarship.
8. Comparison of "Sweet William's Ghost" with Bürger's "Lenore."
9. Comparison of "Sir Patrick Spens" with Rossetti's "The White Ship."
10. Characteristics of the popular ballad in the *Cowboy Songs* collected by Professor Lomax.

## Collections

*The Book of British Ballads.* Selected by R. Brimley Johnson. Everyman's Library: Dutton & Co. Cloth, 40 cents.

An extensive and convenient collection of the ballads of the English people, not restricted to the more primitive forms.

*English and Scottish Ballads.* Selected and edited by R. Adelaide Witham. Riverside Literature Series: Houghton Mifflin Co. Cloth, 50 cents.

An excellent but limited selection, with a helpful introductory sketch.

*A Collection of Ballads.* Edited with introduction and notes by Andrew Lang. Chapman & Hall. Fifty-five representative ballads with appreciative introductory sketch.

*Old English Ballads.* Selected and edited by Francis B. Gummere. Athenæum Press Series: Ginn & Co. Cloth, 80 cents.

An admirable selection grouped according to themes. Includes the complete "Gest of Robin Hood." The scholarly introduction is too much concerned with theories of ballad origin to be of great service to beginners.

*The Oxford Book of Ballads.* Chosen and edited by Sir Arthur Quiller-Couch. Oxford University Press. Cloth, $2.

A thoroughly representative collection arranged in seven divisions, according to theme.

*English and Scottish Ballads.* Edited by Helen Child Sargent and George L. Kittredge. Students' Cambridge Edition: Houghton Mifflin Co. Cloth, $2.25.

Based on Prof. Child's collection and containing one version of each of the three hundred and five ballads there printed. A sound and illuminating introduction by Prof. Kittredge.

*The English and Scottish Popular Ballads.* Edited by Francis James Child. 5 vols. Houghton Mifflin Co.

## 36   THE TYPICAL FORMS OF ENGLISH LITERATURE

The monumental collection, as complete as can be made. Other collections are based on this of Prof. Child, just as all ballad scholars are inspired by his various notes and introductions.

*Cowboy Songs.* Collected and edited by John A. Lomax. Sturgis & Walton. Revised edition in 1916.
A first-hand accumulation of genuine popular balladry of our own day.

*Folk-Ballads of Southern Europe.* Translated into English Verse by Sophie Jewett. G. P. Putnam's Sons.
An interesting collection of continental folk-songs analogous to the English and Scottish popular ballads.

### Critical Discussions[1]

#### I

Joseph Addison, *The Spectator,* Nos. 70 and 74 (1711).
An appreciation of "Chevy Chase" in terms of heroic poetry.
*A Collection of Old Ballads* (1723-25).
Valuable prefaces and introductions.
Bishop Thomas Percy, *Reliques of Ancient English Poetry* (1765).
Significant preface, introductions and critical essays, particularly the "Essay on the Ancient Minstrels."
Joseph Ritson, *Ancient Songs and Ballads* (1790).
Includes "Observations on the Minstrels" and "Dissertation on Ancient Songs and Music."
Joseph Ritson, *Robin Hood* (1795).
Critical and biographical introduction. Misleading.
Walter Scott, *Minstrelsy of the Scottish Border.* 3 vols. (1802-03).
Critical notes and introductions; also the "Essay on the Imitation of Popular Poetry."
William Motherwell, *Minstrelsy Ancient and Modern* (1827).
Hales and Furnivall, *Bishop Percy's Folio Manuscript.* 3 vols. and supplement (1867-68).

[1] Wherever practicable the list of Critical Discussions will be divided into two parts, the first tracing the history of critical opinion, the second confined to the present day.

## II

Francis James Child, Article on "Ballad Poetry" in *Universal Cyclopedia* (1892,—revised from earlier edition).

F. B. Gummere, *The Beginnings of Poetry*. The Macmillan Co., 1901.

F. B. Gummere, *The Popular Ballad* (*Types of English Literature*). Houghton Mifflin Co., 1907.

F. B Gummere, Chapter on "Ballads" in *Cambridge History of English Literature*, Vol. II (1908).

Walter M. Hart, *Ballad and Epic* (*Harvard Studies and Notes*, Vol. XI). Ginn & Co., 1907.

Andrew Lang, Article on "The Ballad" in *Encyclopedia Britannica* (1910).

Andrew Lang, *Sir Walter Scott and the Border Minstrelsy*. Longmans, Green & Co., 1910.

T. F. Henderson, *The Ballad in Literature* (*Cambridge Manuals*). Cambridge University Press, 1912.

Frank E. Bryant, *A History of English Balladry*. Richard G. Badger, 1913.

J. C. H. R. Steenstrup, *The Medieval Popular Ballad*. Translated from the Danish by E. G. Cox. Ginn & Co., 1914.

Frank Sidgwick, *The Ballad* (*The Art and Craft of Letters*). Doran & Co., 1915.

## III

## THE LYRIC

*History*

THE Greeks were accustomed to divide their song into two great classes: *melic* or *lyric* poetry, which was the expression of an individual singer's emotion, to the accompaniment of the lyre; and *choric* poetry, which represented some strong communal feeling and was composed for choral singing, supplemented by instrumental harmony and possibly appropriate dance-movements. Out of the first of these have been evolved our modern conceptions, none too distinct, of lyric quality and lyric form in verse,—conceptions in which the original significance of the word "lyric" has been lost completely. In the process the second or choric class has been found to have all the essential qualities of the first, and the entirely superficial distinction between one singer and a homogeneous chorus has been broken down.

**Original Significance**

A good Greek lyric had in it all the possibilities of later developments, as appears from examination of—for example—a song of Sappho.

**Greek Lyric**

"Blest as the immortal gods is he,
The youth whose eyes may look on thee,
Whose ears thy tongue's sweet melody
    May still devour.
Thou smilest too?—sweet smile, whose charm
Has struck my soul with wild alarm,
And, when I see thee, bids disarm
    Each vital power

## THE LYRIC

> Speechless I gaze: the flame within
> Runs swift o'er all my quivering skin;
> My eyeballs swim; with dizzy din
>   My brain reels round;
> And cold drops fall; and tremblings frail
> Seize every limb; and grassy pale
> I grow; and then—together fail
>   Both sight and sound."[1]

This is clearly the expression of an emotion rising in the heart of the singer, yet common to hosts of lovers who lack the power of phrasing it. In this case vividness is secured by aid of the imagination, but there is comparative simplicity of thought, and the brevity of the poem permits distinct unity of impression. Even in translation it is apparent that words and music were intended to supplement and balance each other. The poem was written to be sung, though the poet's work was done first.

In the process of evolution several things have happened. The subjective, introspective element has been greatly intensified, so as often to lift the lyric entirely out of popular comprehension and limit its appreciation to the elect. Subjectivity, indeed, has become the chief lyric characteristic. Imagination has at times made overfree with lyric verse, and is expected to be at all times present. Unity of impression has been maintained, even in longer and more complex lyric forms, such as the ode.

**Increased Subjectivity**

The balance of words and music, however, has come to be well-nigh disregarded, except in a few conspicuous instances, such as the best hymns. In some cases lyrics have developed such abstruseness or complexity of thought that their message cannot be conveyed in song to the ordinary ear. We are surprised, for example, to

[1] A translation by John H. Merivale, 1833. The original is regarded as not quite complete.

learn that certain contemplative Elizabethan sonnets had musical settings. Another type of lyric has undertaken to dispense with the complement of music by making the verses themselves musical in effect, by striving after the verbal melodies that seem, as we often say, to sing themselves. This tendency in lyric poetry was first prominent in the Elizabethan period, when the love of melody fairly outran the possibilities of musical composition. It prevailed again at various stages of the 'Romantic Movement, from Shelley and Keats to Swinburne. Indeed it has perennial support in the well-known fondness of romanticists for a fusion of the arts, against which critics are constantly contending.[1] Today we rather expect good lyric to abound in this verbal melody, as do the shorter poems of Yeats and Masefield and Noyes, but the songs we really sing rarely occur to us as lyrics at all, even when announced as such on the bills of our musical comedies.

*Less Dependence on Music*

The printing press, undoubtedly, has played havoc with our conceptions of lyric poetry. To pass from the notion of poetry that is sung to that of poetry recited is one thing; to pass on to the notion of poetry merely conned from the printed page is quite another. In this way has arisen much of the insistence on the poet's subjectivity, on the prime value of his mood or message, and the corresponding emptiness of mere form. In this way poets have felt ever greater need for forcing sheer beauty of sound upon the reader's attention. In this way too has come the increasing disregard for poetry among the thinking, reading people, who naturally enough fail to

*Poetry in Print*

[1] E. g., the German critic Lessing, in his *Laokoon*, 1766, and Irving Babbitt, *The New Laokoon*, 1910.

get the thrill they demand from lines of varying length, each beginning with a capital letter. Yet these same people demand no thrills from a page of printed music and never condemn a song unsung.

Lyric poetry came to the Anglo-Saxons as a part of their Germanic birthright. Yet during the Anglo-Saxon period we hear much more *about* their
**Anglo-Saxon** lyrics than we hear *of* them. Such poems
**Lyric** as have been preserved indicate that individuals gave expression in this form chiefly to the gloom and resignation to fate that marked the race. The poems are uniformly elegiac,—laments real and imaginary. The dramatic device of an imaginary sufferer is also characteristic of Anglo-Saxon lyric, leaving the problem of personal revelation sometimes as difficult as in Elizabethan sonnet sequences. Again, little of the verse is purely emotional, being taken up largely with narrative, description, or moralizing. Probably the best lyric of the period is *Deor's Lament,* the complaint of the scop or minstrel, whose beloved master has deposed him for a rival. The original poem is in the usual four-stressed alliterative lines of Anglo-Saxon verse. It approximates, however, a stanzaic arrangement with an effective refrain. The last of these stanzas, as translated by Professor Gummere, follows:

"To say of myself the story now,
I was singer erewhile to sons-of-Heoden,
dear to my master. Deor my name.
Long were the winters my lord was kind;
I was happy with clansmen; till Heorrenda now
by grace of his lays has gained the land
which the haven-of-heroes erewhile gave me.
That he surmounted: so this may I."[1]

[1] *The Oldest English Epic,* p. 178.

The first outside influence upon early English song came probably from Latin hymns of the Christian church. These hymns were as much inclined to lamentation as the Anglo-Saxon poems, but in the way of form had much to offer, —verse-harmonies, end-rhyme, and regular metrical structure. They became popular in England, as did Latin drinking songs from the continent somewhat later. After the Norman Conquest England was soon full of song, song that was facile and beautiful and rich in coloring, but it was all in French. Nearly two centuries were required for the English language to come into its own again, but when it did, it was quick to appropriate much that was good from this foreign verse-music still echoing over woodland and moor.

**Latin and French Influences**

To this time belong what are usually regarded as the first love-lyric and the first spring song in the English tongue,—the "Blow, northern wind" and "Sumer is icumen in." These two motives are combined in the somewhat more elaborate "Alysoun," preserved with "Blow, northern wind" in a manuscript anthology of about 1310.

**Early Specimens**

"Bytuene Mersh and Averil,
  When spray biginneth to springe,
The lutel foul hath hire wyl
  On hyre lud to synge.
Ich libbe in love longinge
For semlokest of alle thinge.
He may me blisse bringe,
Icham in hire baundoun.
An hendy hap ichabbe yhent,
Ichot from hevene it is me sent,
From alle wymmen mi love is lent
And lyht on Alysoun."

THE LYRIC 43

Of the one hundred and seventeen poems in this manuscript there are about forty in English, showing considerable native freshness under the formative influences of France.

The fourteenth century brings the contrasting figures of Lawrence Minot and Geoffrey Chaucer, the first narrow in his vision, native English in his
**Minot and Chaucer** literary impulses, and strongly partisan in his sympathies; the second liberal in his views and thoroughly eclectic in his literary relationships. The twelve battle-songs of Minot that are preserved to us celebrate English victory in rough and simple meter suggestive of the popular narrative ballads of those and later days. Chaucer, while not primarily a lyric poet, affords the student first-rate models in English of various metrical forms then popular in France, particularly the ballade and roundel. That he was amply able to vitalize these foreign forms and make them his own, is shown by the poetic dignity of his "Flee fro the presse," and the genuine delight in nature expressed in the roundel sung by the birds in the *Parlement of Foules:*

> "Now welcom somer, with thy sonne softe,
> That hast this wintres weders over-shake,
> And driven awey the longe nightes blake."

Current folk-song finds no place in Chaucer's own compositions; he was essentially a poet of the court. But
**Only French Forms** in the detailed account of his pilgrims en route to Canterbury there is abundant evidence of the prevalence of such amusement. Who does not know the yellow-haired, shrill-voiced Pardoner, who sang

> "Come hider love to me"

and the pimply Summoner who in deep tones "bore to him a stiff burdoun"? The surprising thing is not that Chaucer wrote no folk-song, but rather that with so much knowledge of the new poetry of Italy, perhaps even a personal acquaintance with his "master Petrarch," as he calls him, his only employment of Italian lyric is in a paraphrase of one sonnet of Petrarch in the midst of *Troilus and Cressida.*

All these preliminaries have brought us only to the threshold of a genuinely lyric England. French troubadour forms never took firm root in English soil, and withered and died with Chaucer's uninspired imitators. The important contribution of these French forms to English poetry was an indirect one. Even before their influence manifested itself in Chaucer's lyrics, they had crossed the Alps into Italy and attracted the attention of poets there. Certain Italian verse-forms, notably the sonnet and the strambotto, seem to be indebted to models furnished by the troubadours, not only in general plan, but in the refinements and imagery with which they were conceived.

**The Italian Tradition**

It is customary to date the beginning of Renaissance lyric from the Italian poet Petrarch, and to recognize Petrarch as the creator and master of the sonnet. This exquisite verse unit of fourteen lines lends itself so completely to degrees and shades of emotion that it can no longer be considered the possession of one nation or tongue. In the fourteenth and fifteenth centuries, however, the sonnet grew and thrived in Italy alone, under the influence of Petrarch's series or sequence of sonnets to his lady Laura. Before the fashion extended into other countries, imitation had developed greater and

**Petrarch and the Sonnet**

greater artificiality and extravagance until a group of "purists" had arisen in reaction against these extremes. Thus foreign nations adopting the sonnet form were at liberty to choose how far they would deviate from the Petrarchian model in the light of Italy's own experimentation.

It was some time after 1500 before first France and then England took up the fashion of sonnets in the manner of the Italians. Indeed England to **Wyatt and** some degree learned the fashion from **Surrey** French poets and continued to follow their immediate examples. Thomas Wyatt and Henry Howard, Earl of Surrey, who first seriously attempted transplanting the sonnet into the English court, had been impressed with the interest French court poets were taking just then in Italian verse as a means of refining their own language and giving it ease and grace and fluency. The English language was needing these qualities still more. So Wyatt and Surrey, fresh from the actual life of French and Italian courts, each in turn tried writing sonnets and other Italian forms in English words.

The historical value of the result is far out of proportion to the actual poetic value. The popularity of these poems, circulated for years in manuscript **Their** or finally printed in *Tottel's Miscellany*, **Influence** 1559, can be accounted for only by the dearth of genuine poetic conceptions and the harmonious phrasing of them at the accession of Queen Elizabeth. The immediate successors of Wyatt and Surrey attempted to follow in their footsteps, but added nothing to the growth of the English lyric.

The actual lyric outburst of Elizabethan England may be traced to a small coterie of brilliant young men, ex-

46 THE TYPICAL FORMS OF ENGLISH LITERATURE

perimenting in 1579 with the possibilities of English as a medium of poetic expression. They first tried to subjugate it to the old quantitative methods of Greek and Latin verse. One of them, Philip Sidney, has left numerous of these classic experiments scattered through his prose romance, the *Arcadia*. But like various reformers in the English Renaissance, these men theorized about classic models and in actual practice turned to more immediate Italian ones. Sidney's sonnet-sequence, *Astrophel and Stella*, deservedly set the fashion of Elizabethan sonnets. Edmund Spenser, another young man of the group, survived Sidney and made a rich and sincere contribution to the vogue with his *Amoretti* sonnets. Samuel Daniel, another friend of Sidney, paid tribute to Sidney's sister, the Countess of Pembroke, in a series of sonnets to *Delia*. Shakespeare alone ranks with Sidney in the skill with which he attained the effect of sincerity in expressing passions that may have been real or have been only well imagined.

Sidney and His Friends

Some consideration of *Astrophel and Stella* will serve to illustrate the essential features of Elizabethan sonnets in sequence. This series is concerned with a delayed and unsuccessful wooing, which despite its apparent failure represents a spiritual victory for both parties. Astrophel (Sidney) is portrayed as betrothed in youth to Stella (Penelope Devereux) with little affection on either side until the match is broken off and she becomes the wife of Lord Rich. Then begins Astrophel's protestation and soliciting of favors from Stella, which apparently she would be glad to grant if she could do so with honor. Her virtue is triumphant over his desire, however, and he achieves only a solitary kiss, after which their rela-

"Astrophel and Stella"

tions are completely severed. The actual steps in this uneventful experience are indicated in perhaps a dozen sonnets and a few of the songs accompanying the collection. Sonnet XXXIII is the most illuminating of all.

> "I might!—unhappy word—O me, I might,
> And then would not, or could not, see my bliss;
> Till now wrapt in a most infernal night,
> I find how heav'nly day, wretch! I did miss.
> Heart, rent thyself, thou dost thyself but right;
> No lovely Paris made thy Helen his:
> No force, no fraud robb'd thee of thy delight,
> Nor Fortune of thy fortune author is;
> But to myself myself did give the blow,
> While too much wit, forsooth, so troubled me,
> That I respects for both our sakes must show:
> And yet could not, by rising morn foresee
> How fair a day was near: O punish'd eyes,
> That I had been more foolish, or more wise!"

There are a number of sonnets based on slight experiences that are only incidental to the plot:—Stella appeared walking without a sunshade (XXII); **Themes and Devices** Sidney's friends expressed wonder at his abstraction (XXVII); he won one tournament (XLI) and retired ingloriously from another (LIII). A still greater number attempt the expression of a mood or develop a more or less fantastic idea, from punning on Lord Rich's name—

> "But that rich fool, who by blind fortune's lot
> The richest gem of love and life enjoys,
> And can with foul abuse such beauties blot;
> Let him, depriv'd of sweet but unfelt joys,
> Exil'd for aye from those high treasures which
> He knows not, grow in only folly Rich!" (XXIV)

to all the strained and artificial images that have always tempted sonneteers:

> "The windows now, through which this heavenly guest
> Looks over the world, and can find nothing such,
> Which dare claim from those lights the name of best,
> Of touch they are, that without touch do touch,
> Which Cupid's self, from Beauty's mine did draw:
> Of touch they are, and poor I am their straw." (IX) [1]

The most emotional of these little poems take occasion to analyze and quibble over their passions, while the larger part of the series would be classed as intellectual exercises in verse rather than as frank outbursts of simple feeling. This is illustrated by Sidney's frequent analysis of the conflict of Virtue and Desire, in their relations to Reason. The ordinary Elizabethan, familiar enough with the idiomatic speech of his day, must have found many of the lines packed with thought and difficult to follow. Even though we know that various sonnets of the period had musical settings, we feel assured that typical Elizabethan sonnets were for the artist of fine phrases in the drawing-room, not for the singer in the market place.

**Intricacy of Thought**

Most of the stock features of the sonnet-sequence may be found in *Astrophel and Stella*. There are frequent indications of imitative work, even including the assurances of originality.

**Conventional Features**

"I am no pickpurse of another's wit,"

asserts Sidney at several times. There is the insistence that this is genuine passion,—a point that only outside evidence can determine. There is the organization of material after the manner of

---

[1] Poets were fond of describing the head, and indeed the entire body, as a castle, the dwelling place of the soul. The eyes were the windows, the teeth the warders of the gate, etc. Cf. Spenser's "House of Alma" in the *Faerie Queene*, Book II, Canto IX; and Phineas Fletcher's *Purple Island*. The word "touch" above is

classic tragedy,—hope rising by degrees to a climax only to sink into despair or spiritual victory over the baser self. The verse is the customary iambic pentameter, with only an occasional sonnet built of Alexandrine lines. The fourteen lines do not usually divide into the octave and sestette of Italian and many French sonnets, but follow the English method of three quatrains and a final couplet, the latter frequently involving surprise or epigrammatic sting.

These Italianate sonnets, though produced in legions from *Tottel's Miscellany* (1559) until about 1610, had to contend for popular favor with lighter and less circumscribed lyric forms. Both in form and in content these latter were better adapted to musical settings and had thus a twofold appeal to the music-loving public. " Songs and sonnets " had been the composite title of the first edition of *Tottel's Miscellany;* the songs preserved with *Astrophel and Stella* brighten and clarify the whole progress of that sequence; the sweet music that ripples through the plays of Shakespeare has brought him closer to us than the mystery of the false friend and the woman colored ill celebrated in his sonnets. Indeed the lyric qualities we are inclined to recognize as distinctively Elizabethan are almost always found in songs.

**Elizabethan Song**

Elizabethan songs were of three general classes: the simple melody, as illustrated in popular music of the day, such as the ballads set to tunes; the short Italianate madrigal forms, highly regarded by the best musicians; and the " airs," developed later, and brought to perfec-

first used for a species of black marble representing Stella's black eyes that *affect* those they behold without actual *contact.* They are later spoken of as *touch-wood,* or fine kindling used with straw in building fires—here the fire of love.

tion by Thomas Campion. The madrigal had grown up abroad in an attempt to adapt secular themes to a certain system of church music. This involved several voices, often as many as four or five, not harmonized in one prevailing melody but taking up the theme one after another, in the method of the old-time part-song or "round." Most of us, at one time or another, have helped perform "Three Blind Mice" or "The Animal Fair" after this manner. Italian lyrics of six, eight, or ten lines were arranged for such rendition, and at first were translated syllable for syllable into English form. Later, English poets found this a perfect medium for the little verse epigrams Wyatt had taught them to compose, and cultivated the form vigorously. We know it best in Shakespeare's "Take, O take those lips away," or "Hark, hark, the lark."

**Melodies, Madrigals, and Airs**

The "air" was usually a group of stanzas to repeat a melody, harmony being obtained from other voices or from one or more musical instruments. It was so closely related to folk-song that expert musicians were slow in accepting it. The development of the lute and other instruments forced the vogue upon them, and after 1600 these airs of three or more stanzas soon supplanted madrigals in the song books that were appearing so frequently. Campion, who represents Elizabethan song-writing at its best, was as much musician as poet, and in many instances was particularly happy in producing songs that read as well today as they sang well on the lips of his contemporaries. The themes of these songs varied with the tastes of their composers, but by the time of Campion the prevailing themes of all English lyric were shifting somewhat to correspond with the

**Airs the Most Popular**

decline of Petrarchian sonnets and the coming of a fresh classical impulse. In matters of this sort refined distinctions are unsafe. The qualities we may select as classical, or Anacreontic, or whatever name we give them, may appear in poetry that is entirely Italian or French in its origin. There are pagans, as well as Puritans, about us today. But there is something in Renaissance verse of the sixteenth century that seems to separate it from Petrarch and his more immediate followers, and to class it with the poetry of Catullus and Horace and the verse that these Elizabethans attributed to the Greek poet Anacreon. Then, soon after 1600, appeared certain poets like Ben Jonson and Herrick, avowed imitators of the classical authors, and they produced lyrics with these same qualities of mood and theme.

These Greek and Latin poets, like Petrarch, sang of love; but they preferred to dwell upon the present delights of love and the visible, almost tangible charms of their ladies. "*Carpe diem igitur,*" the famous dictum of Horace, taught many a poet of the Renaissance to urge present delights because beauty is short-lived and ugly death not far away. Women, wine, and flowers, the contemplation of beautiful, delicate, and graceful things and experiences, perfect harmony of sense impressions perfectly phrased—all these are in that self-conscious Greek and Latin lyric, polished till it shows no mark of the tools and seems spontaneous. The poems are little bits of genre painting in words, cross-sections of life caught at its beautiful moments for the thrill of artistic satisfaction they may afford.

*Classical Art-Lyrics*

English poets of Elizabeth's day had caught the glow and fervor of these ancient models from time to time. The seventeenth century, minus the youthful enthusiasm of the previous generation, did two things. Sometimes it took the imaginative excesses of that generation and forced them into bold and unmeaning extravagance. At others it elevated the themes of this classical poetry to the highest level of artistic verse-form. The first method is illustrated by men like Cowley and Crashaw, to whom the conceits or vagaries of thought and expression become ends in themselves. The results of the new movement toward Greek and Latin models need no comment for the multitudes who know Jonson's " Drink to me only with thine eyes " or Herrick's " Gather ye rosebuds " and his " Daffodils."

**The Seventeenth Century**

In the gamut between extravagance and elegance, men composed much verse in this century, except during the period of the Civil Wars. Most of it was the work of courtiers, who attained unusual facility in poetic numbers. Shortly before the Restoration of 1660, certain poets—notably Denham and Waller—" refined " English poetry by the introduction of the heroic couplet, which by its influence soon crowded less regular and more involved forms into obscurity and helped to make the eighteenth a century barren of lyric. Not entirely barren, however. The poet Cowley, with considerable versatility, had brought to England some knowledge of the Pindaric ode, the varied and elaborate choral composition with dance accompaniment that had once celebrated victory in the Grecian games. The Italian poet Chiabrera had been imitating this form abroad, and Cowley attempted the same thing in English. He was successful enough to attract a following. The Pindaric ode came to be the only exception to the general rule of absolute regularity in verse. Many people assumed that irregu-

**Couplets and " Pindarics "**

THE LYRIC 53

larity, then, was the chief requirement of the Pindaric type. Really capable poets, like Dryden before 1700 and Gray and Collins afterward, produced great odes, full of dignity of conception and power of execution. Crowds of inferior rhymesters ground out what they called " Pindarics," full of broken lines and artificial phrasings, and as regards emotion signifying nothing.

The early eighteenth century was, for various reasons, not a lyric period. Life centered in the city and was valued there not for the romantic possi-
**Eighteenth** bilities that later poets and story-tellers
**Century** have discovered, but for its material com-
**"Reasonable-** forts, its fellowship and interchange of
**ness"** opinions, its emphasis on rules and fashions in matters of taste. Reasonableness and restraint took the place of vigorous emotion, which was under a cloud since the Puritan outburst. Science, politics, and the *philosophy* of religion stifled imagination in English minds. Self-consciousness brought ridicule into literature with renewed power, to deride individuality and extravagance by way of burlesque and comedy, formal satire and biting epigram. Poetry came to mean the treatment of any subject, no matter how dull or unimaginative, in machine-like stanzas or a long procession of mechanically constructed heroic couplets with language that was beautifully vague and unreal.

Such extremes, as a rule, only prepare the way for a hostile reaction, which often begins by
**The** imitating the very things against which
**Romantic** these extremes reacted. The reasonable-
**Reaction** ness of the eighteenth century scorned and ignored the imaginative exuberance of medieval France and Elizabethan England, and was

much concerned with the problem of "methodizing" Nature. The "Romantic Revival" that followed was initiated by a revival of interest in a "middle age" that was vaguely regarded as reaching somewhere from the dawn of Christianity to the days of Cromwell, and a worshipful return to primal Nature untouched by the hand of man. With the Romantic Revival came imagination and deep, genuine emotion, and with these came lyric poetry once more.

There is no place here to linger on attractive transition figures, who combine much of the old spirit with varying degrees of the new. Thompson, Shenstone, Gray, Collins, Blake,—all are interesting and repay the general reader as well as the literary historian. Even a material-minded public cannot entirely forget Gray's "Elegy" or "How sleep the brave." Robert Burns is peculiarly significant in a study like this. For one thing, he is so widely known and so easy to appreciate. For another, it is through him that Scottish folksong, kept alive and beautiful through so many years of obscurity, emerged once more to teach all England how to sing. Better still, we may find in him another of those rare song-poets in whose brain words fit themselves over and over again to the lilt of a tune until at last the perfect phrase is found for what the melody has already been able to utter. The poetic result is no longer the rude doggerel previously sung to these old airs, nor is it laden and enriched with imagery and conceit no vocal rendering can make effective.

Burns died in 1796, just as day was breaking upon modern lyric poetry. Two years later appeared the collection of *Lyrical Ballads,* containing Coleridge's "Ancient Mariner" and nineteen poems by Wordsworth.

In 1796, too, Scott published his translations of Bürger, and by 1805 inaugurated his series of verse romances with *The Lay of the Last Minstrel.* Byron in 1807 printed his collection of juvenile poems, *Hours of Idleness,* at the same time that Keats and Shelley, in cottage and castle, were maturing toward the privileges of man's estate.

**The Larger Freedom**

The poetic output of this marvelously gifted group, diverse as it was in many particulars, was to have one great dominating fact, the effort after a larger freedom. The hackneyed themes and trite imagery of three generations, the tawdry paraphrases of expression, the endless tramp of precise and monotonous couplets, these things had had their day and should enslave men no more. The Revolution in France, whatever its material success, had set Englishmen thinking and saying things they had hardly dared to approach before. There would always be conservatives, in letters as in politics. But for the time being, English poets were to be emphatically liberal.

Walter Scott in the lyric of his battle songs and coronachs, as well as in his extensive narrative verse, loosed the imagination among the achievements of the legendary heroes of the Scottish clans; Coleridge, also treating narrative material lyrically, sought imaginative courses over uncharted seas traversed by ghostly barks, or along the banks of sacred Oriental rivers decked with royal pleasure-domes.

**Freedom of Imagination**

Scott awakened thrills of patriotism; but Wordsworth, with the simple-mindedness of an ancient mystic, taught men to open their eyes and see into the very heart of nature, where was God. In the *Lyrical Ballads,* he was already reminding men—

## 56  THE TYPICAL FORMS OF ENGLISH LITERATURE

> "Of something far more deeply interfused,
> Whose dwelling is the light of setting suns,
> And the round ocean and the living air,
> And the blue sky, and in the mind of man:
> A motion and a spirit, that impels
> All thinking things, all objects of all thought,
> And rolls through all things."

**Freedom as a Gospel**

The second group made of their "liberties" the programme of a crusade. The times were out of joint, conduct and thought were in bondage to outworn traditions, life as men lived it was far from being worth while. Moreover, the public, governed by conservative critics, failed—as no doubt it did—to appreciate young and protesting genius. Young Germany was busily breaking its outworn shackles. Why should not England do likewise? Hence Byron, passionately fond of beauty and reveling to surfeit in the pleasure of sense-impressions, lamented the futility of life and managed to place something misanthropic in almost every poem. Shelley began his protests in college, and left academic halls for a frenzied pursuit of imperfectly conceived ideals. But in their imperfections these ideals were very beautiful, and the pursuit of them was a series of beautiful adventures for which we are very grateful. The spirit of his poetry may be described by the lyric apostrophe to Asia, bride of his own Prometheus:

> "Lamp of Earth! where'er thou movest
> Its dim shapes are clad with brightness,
> And the souls of whom thou lovest
> Walk upon the winds with lightness,
> Till they fail, as I am failing,
> Dizzy, lost, yet unbewailing!"

Keats, if he can be thought of as a propagandist, was the pathetically cheerful apostle of beauty, giving his brief life gladly to imparting the pleasure that all richness of beauty gave him. Beauty of image and of harmony, of Attic carving, or of old romance,—he only prayed that he might be spared to do them justice:

**Delight in Beauty**

> "As she was wont, th' imagination
> Into most lovely labyrinths will be gone,
> And they shall be accounted poet kings
> Who simply tell the most heart-easing things.
> O may these joys be ripe before I die."

Whatever their specific interest, these poets all had something to impart, to them so vital and significant that it intruded upon description and narrative and made them also lyric. With Scott it is the patriotism that breaks, in the midst of *The Lay of the Last Minstrel*, into the emotional " Breathes there a man with soul so dead." " Life of Life," the hymn to Asia already mentioned, is a lyric in Shelley's poetic drama, *Prometheus Unbound*. When men hold strong convictions, they easily become lyric in expressing them, no matter what literary form they have undertaken. Conversely, their avowed lyric attempts are affected by the zeal to pass these convictions on to others, and too often become didactic and argumentative. This is a factor in English romantic verse. The reflection that concludes Wordsworth's best lyrics is likely to become too coldly intellectual, while Byron and Shelley are constantly preaching their doctrines of liberation, however effective their phrasing.

**Poetry and Strong Convictions**

In any case the strongest appeal of the romantic poets was to the imagination, with its " esemplestic " function— as Coleridge called it—of flashing one white beam of appreciation into the very heart of a scene or situation and grasping the thing in its organic completeness. This flash of genius was the common bond between genuine critic and creative artist. Applied to Nature, the "living garment of God," this constructive or recreative imagination penetrated to the very soul of the universe, so that the creative artist who in words or colors brought back the message of eternity—the artist-critic, even, who interpreted his message for a duller world—became a veritable prophet or priest of the Most High. Thus Art, subordinated at first by these romanticists to be the handmaid of Nature, came gradually, as men thought their way through the mystery, to rival Nature in significance, and at last to outrank her. For if Nature merely contained the divine message, writ large for any who possessed the key, was not he greater who provided the key and read the message for a waiting world? To all this, German writers developed a corollary that English poets touched very slightly. Each artist-interpreter reads his own message for the world from Nature and from life. They are not all the same. Does not their chief value as messages lie in their individuality, their distinctness? Hence the justification of poetic fantasy and whimsicality, of ghosts and fairies, of Tieck's "doppelgänger" and Chamisso's man who sold his shadow to the Devil.

**Nature and Art**

With so difficult a road to travel, these English poets ventured to take liberties also with the vehicle in which they journeyed. They tried all sorts of experiments with the form of their verse. The sonnet, discarded by Ben Jonson and almost untouched since Milton, was reinstated by Wordsworth in its Miltonic dignity; made to

**Freedom in Verse Forms**

pay tribute to this master whose "soul was like a star, and dwelt apart"; and utilized again and again for memorable utterances. Since Wordsworth, indeed, the sonnet form has kept its popularity consistently. Tom Moore brought back to favor the measures of Anacreontic lyrics. Coleridge wove beauties never dreamed of into the verses of old romance; Byron and Keats obtained distinctive effects from the Spenserian stanza; Shelley roamed at will among the old verse-treasures of England, France, and Italy, and everything he touched was new and beautiful. Practically all these poets made use of the ode, both in its simpler hymn-like form—a mere extended lyric—and in the complicated structure of Pindaric tradition. They interpreted it delicately, with subtle variations and refinements; but when they wished, obtained power and intensity from it as well. The great odes of this period make an impressive list: Wordsworth's "Intimations of Immortality," Coleridge's "Ode to Dejection," Shelley's "Ode to Liberty," and "Ode to the West Wind," and Keats's "Ode to Autumn," "Ode to a Nightingale," and "Ode on a Grecian Urn."

**Irregularity Made Effective**

It is not enough to speak of the freedom of these men in their choice of meters. There is a greater freedom in the way they used them. The old Elizabethan device of verbal melody returned to England in this romantic revival, resulting in line after line that would be precious for its music of phrasing if one could not understand a word of its meaning. More than this, Shelley in particular began a freer manipulation of the measures themselves, of the stresses and pauses, bringing into verse effects more akin to music than ever had been achieved before. To the pedantic critic of words and syllables in his own day, Shelley's lyrics must have seemed intolerable in their strained scansion. To us, who have the benefit of a century of experiment with his methods, the poems are still rich in musical beauty. The distinction is plain enough if we compare with the clear-cut measures of the seventeenth century stanzas like these:

> (a) "Swiftly walk over the western wave,
>     Spirit of Night!
> Out of the misty eastern cave
> Where, all the long and lone daylight,
> Thou wovest dreams of joy and fear
> Which make thee terrible and dear,—
> Swift be thy flight!"
>
> (b) "When the lamp is shatter'd
> The light in the dust lies dead—
> When the cloud is scatter'd
> The rainbow's glory is shed.
> When the lute is broken,
> Sweet tones are remember'd not;
> When the lips have spoken,
> Loved accents are soon forgot."

**American Romanticists** The activities of these English romanticists served as an inspiration to various American poets whose lyrics are common property. The most scholarly figure is that of Emerson, whose devotion to romantic individualism and interest in Nature placed him at the head of a group of New England transcendentalists. His numerous poems sacrifice warmth and beauty to his intellectual leanings. Whittier, a rigorously orthodox Quaker, is likewise a poet of Nature, but in the simple, unmannered fashion of Wordsworth, or better still of Cowper. The verse of Edgar Allan Poe is marked by the romantic melancholy so prominent also in his prose.

He has a bold, almost grotesque imagination that suggests Coleridge or the Germans, a wealth of color and imagery somewhat in the manner of Keats and Shelley, and like the latter he is constantly awake to the musical possibilities of his haunting verses. Some of his methods he has explained in detail in his account of the composition of "The Raven."[1]

**An Unproductive Interval**

The rich flowering of English romantic poetry brought no worthy fruit. Song-writing, begun so spontaneously by Burns, and carried on less successfully by Tom Moore and "Barry Cornwall," found no skilled artist to cultivate it farther. Revolutionary passion sank back again to the sympathy with want and suffering that poets had been expressing a generation before and novelists were busily appropriating as their theme. Thomas Hood's "Bridge of Sighs" and "Song of the Shirt" are the familiar humanitarian poems of the period. After Shelley and Keats verse-makers became more cautious once more in attempting irregular things with their rhymes and measures. For a few years England was practically without notable poets; then about the middle of the century appeared Tennyson, the Brownings, Arnold, the Pre-Raphaelite group, and the various lesser figures that help to make the reign of Victoria significant in letters as in material achievement.

It is somewhat the fashion of late to ridicule Victorian England for such things as the prudery of its morals, the unctuousness of its sentiment, the inadequacy of its thought on vital matters, and its smug satisfaction with the politely commonplace. But England was not hurt by its morals, and it is safer to remain conservative and even commonplace in a period of adjustment such

[1] "The Philosophy of Composition."

as that was. As for sentiment, the border line between true and deep emotion and sentimentalism is an uncertain thing and critics often fix it for themselves. Anyhow there is a taste for the sentimental in all English-speaking people, particularly the great middle classes. At remote extremes, Gray's " Elegy " and modern fiction may base their popularity in part on an appeal to this taste.

*The Victorian Period*

The great lyric poets of the period, it must be insisted, were neither maudlin nor shallow. They were large-minded, great-hearted, thoroughly informed. They looked the varied problems of the day squarely in the face, and they drew upon all available resources of verse to give utterance to their convictions on them. Arnold, classic in his inspirations, thoroughly Greek in his imagery and clear-cut verse form, found himself disturbed in his thinking and out of harmony with material developments about him, but assumed a tone of scholarly resignation. Browning, dramatic, vigorous, individual, found joy in the welter and strife of things, pleasure in the contemplation of great characters at great moments, and assurance of ultimate triumph of the right, so long as " God's in his heaven." Mrs. Browning, deeply concerned in the various phases of outside life, deeply moved by her own inner experiences, was equally optimistic in her own way. Tennyson is probably the most comprehensive and representative figure of them all. He touched, with no feeble hand, all the great questions of the day. He was successful in mastering all moods of verse but the dramatic and made many serious attempts at that. He echoed the harmonies of the whole honor-roll of English poets. Eminently patriotic, he had no

*Representative Poets*

patience with destructive whim or revolutionary caprice, but celebrated an England that should go on from strength to strength in strict conformity to law and system. In religious unrest, he frankly had his doubts and longed to know the truth, but never flinched till his mind had carried him through to satisfying assurances.

Tennyson's lyrics have kept their place extremely near to the hearts of his people. Part of their secret lies in their mastery of technique. He began as **The Lyrics of Tennyson** a technician rather than a reformer, and by early experiments with the pure "art-lyric," dependent upon its own mechanical beauty, equipped himself to express moods and emotions when they should come. As these came he phrased them with the mature artist's perfect balance of passion and restraint, of form and content. The lyrics scattered through *The Princess* are more than adequate to illustrate these gems of verse-composition, whether we select one purely artistic like "Blow, bugle, blow," or those of mood and sentiment, such as "Sweet and low" or "Tears, idle tears." Tennyson had capacity too for deeper, nobler things. Except for differences of form, "In Memoriam" could be called a deeply contemplative sonnet-sequence on grief, portraying a progress through despair and gloom to the light of renewed assurance as definitely as *Astrophel and Stella* is a drama of spiritual victory. The "Ode on the Death of the Duke of Wellington" reveals at its best the simple majesty that in modern time has taken the place of earlier extravagances in the "Pindaric." It is significant that at the recent death of Lord Kitchener all English-speaking people turned instinctively to this ode as the best expression of national bereavement.

Tennyson's lyric themes are various, and his exquisite

phrasing of this form is of a kind with his work in all types of poetry. Browning's comparatively few lyrics are generally love-poems and display a smoothness and sweetness of tone rarely found in his other poetry. One feature of Browning's art these lyric poems of his retain,—the richness of suggestion that throughout his verse makes it difficult for all his wealth of words to keep pace with his thought and feeling. This quality is found, for instance, in " Prospice " and Pippa's song, and in the one stanza of " Parting at Morning " :

Browning

> "Round the cape of a sudden came the sea,
> And the sun looked over the mountain's rim:
> And straight was a path of gold for him,
> And the need of a world of men for me."

Mrs. Browning's temperament naturally found expression in lyric form, but the expression of her moods was frequently carried too far to be effective. Occasionally some poem, such as " The Musical Instrument," is developed directly to its natural conclusion, and shows her capable of great things. Her *Sonnets from the Portuguese,* where the unit of form kept her in check, are delightful poetic revelations of a love that was little short of worship. Matthew Arnold's lyric moods were those of contemplation, not of passion. To express them he had such dignified beauty of verse at his command that men come back to him after much reading and rejoice in his sweet reasonableness. He was particularly successful in the dirge, the most solemn type of ode, and has produced in " Thyrsis " and " The Scholar Gypsy " two specimens that rank among the highest.

Mrs. Browning—Arnold

America's typical early Victorian is her still-popular

Longfellow, whose versatility, breadth of interest, and appeal to the general reader remind one most of Tennyson. He seldom shows intensity of feeling or depth of thought; he is by no means the master of harmonies that Tennyson was; he is not national in his interests, nor concerned with national problems. But he portrays emotional moods the people can understand, paints imaginative pictures within the scope of their fancy, possesses a sweetly facile lyric style. There is genuine sentiment and enduring form in lyrics like "The Day is Done," "The Bridge," and "The Psalm of Life."

**Longfellow**

The Pre-Raphaelites are a particularly interesting product of this period in England. The name has no literary significance, but was chosen by a small group of very youthful artists to express their conviction that since Raphael painting had become more and more enslaved by rules and traditions, and was to be revitalized—which they purposed to do for it—by reverting to the ruder technique of those who painted at the very dawn of the Renaissance, before Raphael. This was only a belated application of the Romantic revolt to painting, the last of the fine arts to feel its effects. It was based once more on an attempt to revive the medieval, but an attempt this time made with a rare richness of pictorial imagination and a naïve but keen sense of artistic values. It happened that one of the members of this group, Dante Gabriel Rossetti, had poetic talents at least equal to his abilities in color. A little later William Morris brought to the circle of friendship a more productive pen. The romantic spirit is always prone to break down barriers between the arts. Hence from this Pre-Raphaelite Brotherhood came a close affilia-

**The Pre-Raphaelite Brotherhood**

tion of art and song,—paintings that illustrated poems, and verses that described in terms of painted canvas. A painting *in* the frame and an appropriate sonnet inscribed upon it; that was Rossetti's programme.

**Rossetti**

Rossetti brought back from the Middle Ages all the beauty and color Keats had found there, but he experienced from this a sensuous pleasure equal to that of Shelley. Other things he found there too: a passion for the heaping up of detail, a love of symbolism,—the " blessed damozel "

"had three lilies in her hand,
"And the stars in her hair were seven,"—

the absorption and unworldliness of a mystic, even an appreciation of the possibilities of old-time verse devices, such as the refrain in " The White Ship " and " Sister Helen." Next to " The Blessed Damozel " he is known best in lyric for his sonnet-sequence, *The House of Life.* This is a composite performance, some sonnets written early in life, others late,—some indeed buried for years in his wife's coffin,—and the whole arranged finally in an organic unity. The sonnets are jewels of verse, fit memorials—as he wished them to be—of " dead deathless hours." Like his art, they anticipate the present time in their truth to life and Nature as the artist saw it, which is for him truth enough. For many readers they are oversensuous and dwell too much on long throats, full lips, and veils of golden hair. Since their day, however, this type of verse has never ceased to be.

Of all the friends of Rossetti, the one whose area of influence was widest was William Morris. He was another apostle of beauty to an all too sordid world, his chief desire being to bring the beauty of medieval architecture and decoration into the everyday surroundings of the nineteenth century. His reverence for the Middle Ages seen with an artist's pictorial imagination led him also to produce much rich and harmonious verse and prose, marred somewhat by the medieval fault of effusiveness. As a result he has given us few good lyric poems. But his long narrative pieces, and particularly the shorter accounts of great dramatic moments, are rich in coloring and abound in suggestions of tense emotions. He also made capital out of ballad refrains, which by this time were frequently expanded so much as to lose their effectiveness.

*William Morris*

The best exemplification of this ideal of "life as seen through the artist's eyes" is found in the work of Swinburne. His early associations were with the Pre-Raphaelites, and with them he indulged to the full a vividly pictorial imagination and a fondness for suggestions from the remote Middle Ages. Like Rossetti, he reveled in details of sensuous gratification, including long throats and lips for kissing. Like him, too, he had a limited range of subjects and images and tended toward symbolism in his treatment of these. His greatness is in none of these things. He was not content that poetry and painting should play complementary parts in his verse; from the first line of the first chorus in his early *Atalanta in Calydon* he adds the resources of a third of the fine arts—music—to produce a movement that only Shelley had anticipated.

*Swinburne*

> "When the hounds of spring are on winter's traces,
> The mother of months in meadow or plain
> Fills the shadows and windy places
> With lisp of leaves and ripple of rain."

68 THE TYPICAL FORMS OF ENGLISH LITERATURE

Swinburne thought and felt more deeply than the Pre-Raphaelites. The delight of sensuous experiences grew upon him until even pain was an exquisite reminiscence, to be celebrated in verse. This beauty-worship, he came to see, was not consistent with Christian faith and traditions, as the Brotherhood had tried to keep it, but was essentially pagan. So Swinburne renounced orthodox faith and lamented the banished gods. Then came realization of the emptiness of life and its pleasures, with no hope beyond except perchance a pagan underworld of rest, the " Garden of Proserpine ":

**His Ideas**

> " Then star nor sun shall waken,
> Nor any change of light:
> Nor sound of waters shaken,
> Nor any sound or sight:
> Nor wintry leaves or vernal
> Nor days nor things diurnal;
> Only the sleep eternal
> In an eternal night."

This does not mean that Swinburne was generally despondent or pessimistic. He celebrated force and heroism, loved Nature in her simple elements, particularly the sea, had a place in his heart for child-life and the English home. Above all he loved his art, for which he did so much.

The last generation of English poets is both versatile and prolific, their product increasing in volume down to the present year. There may be few really great singers or great songs represented among them. But in the multitude of verses scattered through English and American magazines, the flood of books of verse pouring from the presses of both countries, there is a thousand times more of pleasure and thrill and uplift than

**Contemporary Poets**

the casual reader ever imagines. In the midst of this abundance it is almost as hard to distinguish dominating interests and tendencies as it is to point out the poems that will be admired at the end of the century. Certain features have such prominence, however, that they cannot be ignored, and the consideration of them will help to brighten the student's pathway if he must still be led reluctantly to the reading of verse.

For one thing there has been a marked leaning toward the bright, clever, often epigrammatic verse of social intercourse and urban life, for which we have borrowed the French name *vers de société*. This is easy to do moderately well, but its perfect grace requires a master hand. It has flourished whenever conditions were ripe for it and has generally been built on classic or on French forms. Old forms like the rondeau and ballade have particularly marked its recent appearance. Back in the days of Queen Anne, men like Gay and Prior were the leaders in verse of this kind; early in the nineteenth century it was maintained in its cleverness by Thomas Hood, Thackeray, and Winthrop M. Praed; of late we have it in all degrees of seriousness, from the poignant emotional tone given it by William E. Henley, through the delicacy and facility of Austin Dobson and Andrew Lang, to the careless jesting of American column-writers.

Vers de Société

The models of verse-making set up by Shelley and Swinburne have continued to attract a following. Some of our contemporaries have emphasized their richness of imagery and phrasing, paying tribute at the same time to Keats and his master Spenser. Thus the problem of the art-lyric is still with us: whether such riot and abandon of mental and verbal conceits can be con-

Verse Embroidery

sistent with genuine feeling; whether, for example, pages of Francis Thompson can get to the heart so grippingly as one stanza of the "Ballad of Reading Gaol." At least we admit that we enjoy verbal embroideries and heaped sweetness within reasonable limits, and so austere a poet as Milton taught us the power of mere words long before Alfred Noyes experimented with

"Apes and ivory, skulls and roses, in junks of old Hong-Kong,
    Gliding over a sea of dreams to a haunted shore of song."

A more notable tendency at present is to develop the musical values of verse that Shelley and Swinburne had discovered. Sometimes this is indicated **Verse** in a happy combination of melodious **Melody** phrases and tripping measures, with assonance and internal rhyme, as in Noyes's "Song of England":

"There is a song of England that none shall ever sing;
    So sweet it is and fleet it is
That none whose words are not as fleet as birds upon the wing,
    And regal as her mountains
    And radiant as the fountains
Of rainbow-colored sea-spray that every wave can fling
Against the cliffs of England, the sturdy cliffs of England,
    Could more than seem to dream of it,
    Or catch one flying gleam of it,
Above the seas of England that never cease to sing."

Other poems approximate music rather in their time, their meter being distinctly quantitative, not like classic verse, but with the swing of modern song. A suggestion of this may be found in John Masefield's familiar poem "The West Wind":

"It's a warm wind, the west wind, full of birds' cries;
I never hear the west wind but tears are in my eyes.

For it comes from the west lands, the old brown hills
And April's in the west wind, and daffodils."

Perhaps the most subtle verse melodies, as well as the most haunting imaginative suggestions, have come to our recent poetry from the new Irish school of poets, seeking to phrase in such cadences as fall naturally from Celtic lips the world-old joy of their people in the mystic other-world of the fairy folk, the traditions of their story-tellers, and the patriotic longings of their race. William Butler Yeats has become best known among this group, though it includes various other sweet singers.

**The Irish Poets**

In verse as in story, our age is still fond of realism; and this is the first time when English poets have dared to be as fully and frankly realistic as they pleased. Part of this verse is a mere ripening of the fruit of socialistic literature, maturing all through the nineteenth century and now grown almost offensive in its detail of miseries. Some of it is in dialect, a form that even Tennyson attempted with some success, and that we know from *Barrack-Room Ballads* and *Songs of a Sourdough*. Some associates itself with the celebration of the strenuous delights of sea-roving, as set forth by Kipling and Masefield. The best of it does not stop with the details themselves and lose itself in their sordidness, or make them the reason for vigorous moralizing, but finds the thrill or the joy or even the artistic beauty these things possess and dwells upon it. One man looks out over a city stifling under the smoke from soft coal and shudders at the grime of it. Another thinks through to the industry throbbing beneath, or remarks, "How like an etching of Whistler!"

**Realism in Verse**

Along with this freedom in its expression, verse has

today a freedom in its technique that it never enjoyed before. The tyranny of meters **Free Verse** is relaxed, not merely when there are song effects to be attempted, but whenever the poet—or rather certain poets—please. *Vers libre* came into its own with Walt Whitman, and after a considerable struggle has just found a rather wide following. It lends itself well enough to dramatic monologue, as Browning knew some years ago, and for the longer verse-compositions, even those lyric in their impulses, it may be done with no little charm. It is in line too with certain ultra-modern and revolutionary tendencies in art. Still there is abundant place in our appreciation for poetry that has maturity and restraint, and in simple regular meters expresses a deep-souled message bearing on the vital things of life. While this chapter is being written it is still a matter of wonder that the Great War has produced so few great or even adequate poems. Perhaps the English Muse has been trained to lighter measures so long that she must experiment awhile with solemn things.

For American students the significant feature of this new movement in poetry is the part our own country has chosen to play in it. Not only do the **American Verse of Today** regular magazines give added attention to verse; new periodicals, entirely for verse and the criticism of it, have sprung up in all parts of the land, and there is no lack of poetic talent to fill all their pages. Most of the poets and periodicals proclaim themselves as devoted to the "new poetry," by which they mean freedom from restraint and conventionality in message and in form, moods and visions inspired by the everyday world about us, but in every sense the poet's own. Mr. William

THE LYRIC 73

Stanley Braithwaite is now issuing an annual *Anthology of Magazine Verse*, compiled entirely from American periodicals. Comparison of the poems in recent issues of this book with the poetic product of any period in the history of English literature will do more than anything else to indicate the rare versatility and variety of the American verse of today. It will serve likewise to familiarize students with the names of some of the large array of capable American poets impossible to enumerate here.

*Technique of the Lyric*

Introductory

While it is not possible to go into all the varieties and refinements of lyric verse, or to state in terms of a formula the impalpable something that distinguishes really great poetry, it is worth while to indicate certain obvious features, which the student may expect to find throughout his reading. After centuries of discussion the essentials of lyric organization are still little known to the general reader. Not long since, they were presented in simple, easily intelligible form by Professor John Erskine, in his book *The Elizabethan Lyric*.[1] His statements there will be followed rather closely in this account.

Transference of Emotions

Lyric verse, like every other art product, is concerned with emotional moods, the feeling being aroused directly by experiences or thoughts, or indirectly through activity of the imagination. The poet who experiences this mood, in which he may be unique or the representative of a considerable group, attempts to convey it to his audience, to create in them indeed the identical experience of his own heart. His medium of expression is the

[1] Columbia University Press, New York, 1905. See Chap. I.

language of his audience, shaped into lines of more or less metrical regularity, whose cadences fall upon the ear with an effect that is pleasing in itself as well as consistent with the mood to be conveyed. As already suggested, verse should at least be read aloud, if not intoned, to get a just appreciation of the poet's art.

A lyric unit is the result of a single emotional impulse, and is of necessity brief, being limited to the duration of effect from this single impulse. A longer lyric, such as the ode in its various types, may be constructed by developing a series of emotional impulses organically related to one another. While the lyric mood is entirely a subjective experience, the impetus or impulse that arouses it may come entirely from the outside, as in Tennyson's "Flower in the crannied wall," or Sidney's sonnet beginning:

**The Emotional Impulse**

> "Having this day my horse, my hand, my lance
> Guided so well that I obtain'd the prize."

It may on the other hand be itself a subjective thing,— an idea or a flash of realization brought into the mind by circumstances or associations having in themselves no value for the poet's purposes. Various familiar poems are initiated in this manner, Wordsworth's sonnet, "The world is too much with us," being an excellent example. More frequently still, the lyric impetus is probably a combination of objective and subjective, an experience or sense-impression plus the idea it at once arouses in the mind. This process may easily be observed in such a lyric as Shakespeare's "Blow, blow, thou winter wind," from *As You Like It*.

The lyric, of course, is a peculiarly personal and intimate thing, often so much so as to be obscure and uninteresting to the general public. So the stimulus is in most cases represented as coming to the poet himself. For all practical purposes, though, it may be a community, a nation, or any unified throng, for which the poet serves as spokesman. There is also what might be called the "dramatic lyric," in which the poet creates an imaginary character, whose artistic experience is developed before us, without any introduction of the author's personality at all. The Elizabethans were particularly fond of this type of lyric, though we have an admirable example in Keats's "La Belle Dame sans Merci."

**Subjectivity**

In the normal lyric unit the course of development is as follows: The initial impetus is first brought to the reader's attention, by direct statement or suggestion. The immediate effect of this on the poet is usually emotional and this emotion in turn is portrayed again directly or by implication. Then follows an intellectual reaction, the reflective powers, the judgment, or the will being brought into play for a time. The entire experience is then brought to a close with a settled conviction, a resolution, or a calmer and more permanent emotional state. Wordsworth's lyric "The Solitary Reaper" may be taken as an illustration. The first of the four stanzas directs attention to the picture that has served as a stimulus to the poet's art.

**The Complete Lyric Unit**

> "Behold her, single in the field,
> Yon solitary Highland Lass!
> Reaping and singing by herself;
> Stop here, or gently pass!
> Alone she cuts and binds the grain,
> And sings a melancholy strain;

O listen! for the vale profound
Is overflowing with the sound."

The thrill the poet received from the song is imparted to the reader in the second stanza, by direct assertion and striking comparison.

"No nightingale did ever chaunt
More welcome notes to weary bands
Of travellers in some shady haunt,
Among Arabian sands:
A voice so thrilling ne'er was heard
In spring-time from the cuckoo bird,
Breaking the silence of the seas
Among the fairest Hebrides."

This thrill of emotion is succeeded by an intellectual process,—curiosity as to the possible subject of song like this.

"Will no one tell me what she sings?—
Perhaps the plaintive numbers flow
For old, unhappy, far-off things,
And battles long ago:
Or is it some more humble lay,
Familiar matter of today?
Some natural sorrow, loss, or pain
That has been, and may be again?"

This curiosity too subsides and the poet is content with the emotional impression of the solitary singer,—something to carry in his heart for days to come.

"Whate'er the theme, the maiden sang
As if her song would have no ending;
I saw her singing at her work,
And o'er the sickle bending;—
I listen'd, motionless and still;
And, as I mounted up the hill,
The music in my heart I bore
Long after it was heard no more."

It will be observed in this poem that the entire development, through sense-impression, emotion, and curiosity, to the conclusion, is held together by the initial impulse and takes its tone from this. Thus it does not exceed the limits of one lyric unit.

This poem by Wordsworth has been a particularly favorable example. By no means all good lyrics present all of these distinct elements so admirably fused together, and very few show them so equally dividing the poem. Some poems are chiefly concerned with the initial picture, and elaborate that with such wealth of imagery that they are imaginative studies and little else. It is also possible to present these details so effectively as to imply and impart intense emotion in the mere description, or to set in motion and sustain a train of thought that has impressed the poet. Mrs. Browning's "A Musical Instrument" gives all but the last two stanzas to the initial picture, and Swinburne's spring chorus from *Atalanta in Calydon* seems at first view to be all description. It is as easily possible to leave the initial impetus to the slightest suggestion and pass directly into an expression of the emotion.

<small>The Relation of Parts</small>

The reflective or contemplative lyric may of course spring from an outside impulse, but is very likely to be introduced by some striking thought that has occurred to the poet for the first time in this particular form. The poem may be developed to its conclusion without a single division that might be called purely emotional. Yet if it is a good lyric, the thoughts expressed will be so vital or impressive, the mood of contemplation will so far outweigh the substance of the reverie, that the real impression from the verse unit will be upon the feelings.

<small>Contemplative Lyrics</small>

The climactic or epigrammatic effect that concludes so many sonnets only serves to drive such impression home.

This organic unity of development is of course not all of lyric. Its other essential—the perfect expression of its mood within the limits of its particular vehicle—it shares with all other poetry, and indeed with all art. Fancy pours from her pictured urn not only "thoughts that breathe," but also "words that burn." Poetry makes of its subjects at least three technical requirements simple enough to state, but difficult enough to pronounce upon. Their achievement is so doubly difficult that it serves to separate the poet from the mere dabbler in verses, the artist from the tyro. These are (1) finality of phrasing; (2) appropriateness of verse-form, including meter and stanzaic arrangement; (3) the charm of verse melody.

*Poetic Expression*

By the first of these we mean the almost inspired choice of words and their fortuitous grouping into phrases that not only convey thought with clearness, but illuminate and vitalize the conception in all its imaginative richness, as it seems that no other combination of words could. Such phrasings are not necessarily of the striking, memory-passage variety, although many of them linger in our recollection like a fine fragrance. That is the more exquisite lyric in which all portions are of such perfection as satisfies without calling attention to itself. The problem of appropriate meters is simple enough in its larger relations. The slow movement of iambic combinations suggests serious and reflective moods, as the tripping anapest leads to mirth and movement. In the middle ground, however, there is an infinite variety of effects obtained by various substitutions for

*Phrasing and Meter*

the prevailing measure, and the appropriateness of these to their themes must be determined by the trained taste. The formal charm of lyric verse depends only in part on the metrical arrangement of single lines. More significant is the combination of lines—
The Stanza often of varying lengths—in recurring stanzas held together by rhyme-scheme. These stanzas are supposed to correspond to successive stages in the development of thought and emotion, as in "The Solitary Reaper," but the principle is not always observed. For any poem that an author is moved to write, he has an almost infinite choice of stanzas, offering the most subtle variations of effect by their differences of rhythm and rhyme. Closely related to the more delicate impressions a master-craftsman may secure by his choice of stanza are the effects of verse-melody, the harmonies and cadences we all feel in verse like that of Shelley or Swinburne, but find little rational explanation for. Dr. Johnson made sport of those who would adapt sound to sense. "Sound," he declared, "can resemble nothing but sound, and time can measure nothing but motion and duration." But this objection is based on a literal sort of imitation that does not enter into the case at all. Harshness or liquid smoothness of utterance, slowness or rapidity of verse-movement, alliteration and unobtrusive internal rhyme, haunting cadences and refrains, even studied irregularity, somehow get their hold upon our imaginations and intensify our appreciation and enjoyment of poetry.

*Subjects for Study*

1. The influence of the sonnets of Petrarch during the Renaissance.
2. Reasons for the lyric activity of the Elizabethan period.
3. Relation of poetry and music in: (a) Elizabethan airs

and madrigals; (b) the songs of Burns; (c) modern popular song.

4. A study of lyric themes: (a) Elizabethan period; (b) romantic period; (c) today.

5. Essentials of current *vers libre*.

6. Formulation of a series of lyric themes from actual initial impulses.

7. Exercises in composing sonnet, song, and *vers de société* from themes in (6).

8. Specimen of original lyric based on some essay by John Galsworthy.

9. Lyric based on some Pre-Raphaelite painting.

10. Lyric based on some short story of atmosphere: Kipling's "They" or Edward Everett Hale's "The Man Without a Country."

### Collections

*The Golden Treasury* of the best songs and lyrical poems in the English language. Selected and arranged with notes by Francis Turner Palgrave.

Originally compiled with the advice and assistance of Tennyson, and published in 1861. Revised editions by Professor Palgrave in 1883, 1890, 1891. The Second Series, also edited by Professor Palgrave, and composed of lyrics from the second half of the nineteenth century, published 1897. These collections have not been superseded. They may be had in various cheap editions, such as the following:

Macmillan Company—Popular Classics, cloth, 25 cents; Miniature Series, both parts, $1.00 each.

Dutton & Co.—Everyman's Library, cloth, 40 cents; Temple Classics, 45 cents; Muses' Library, 50 cents.

Oxford University Press—First Series with additional poems, World's Classics, cloth, 35 cents; Oxford edition, 60 cents.

Dodge Company—First and Second Series in one volume, cloth, 75 cents; in two volumes, each, 50 cents.

Crowell & Co.—Various editions, 35 cents to $2.00.

*With the Poets.* A selection of choice English poetry. Edited by Dean Frederick W. Farrar. Funk & Wagnalls. Cloth, $1.00; paper, 25 cents.

A convenient and cheap collection, chiefly of lyric poems.

*Choice of English Lyrics.*

*Six Centuries of English Poetry.* Both edited by J. Baldwin. Silver, Burdett & Co. Each, cloth, 50 cents.

Adequate, well-selected anthologies, provided with good editorial apparatus.

## The Lyric

*The Cambridge Book of Poetry and Song.* Selected from English and American authors, by Charlotte Fiske Bates. Crowell & Co. Cloth, 60 cents.

A miscellaneous collection, chiefly of lyrics, arranged alphabetically by authors. Not very convenient for class use.

*Lyrical Forms in English.* Edited by Norman Hepple. Cambridge University Press. Cloth, 75 cents.

A carefully organized collection with good critical material.

*English Lyric Poetry, 1500-1700.* Edited with an introduction by Frederick I. Carpenter. Warwick Library: Charles Scribner's Sons. Cloth, $1.00.

*Lyrical Verse.* Vol. I, 1558-1685. Vol. II, 1685-1846. Selected and edited by Oswald Crawford. Chapman & Hall (London).

*English Songs.* Edited by Edward Arber. In ten volumes: I, The Dunbar Anthology; II, Surrey and Wyatt; III, Spenser; IV, Shakespeare; V, Jonson; VI, Milton; VII, Dryden; VIII, Pope; IX, Goldsmith; X, Cowper. Oxford University Press.

*Sonnets.* Selected from English and American authors by Laura E. Lockwood. Riverside Literature Series. Houghton Mifflin Co.

*English Sonnets.* Edited with introduction and notes by A. T. Quiller-Couch. Chapman & Hall.

*The Golden Book of English Sonnets.* Edited by William Robertson. Lippincott Co.

. . . . . . . .

A wide range of lyric specimens will be found in all the general anthologies of English poetry. The following may be noted:

*The Pageant of English Poetry.* Compiled by R. M. Leonard. Oxford edition, Oxford University Press. Cloth, 60 cents.

*Five Centuries of English Verse.* Edited by W. Stebbing. Oxford edition, Oxford University Press. Two volumes, each, 60 cents.

*The Oxford Book of English Verse.* Chosen and edited by Sir Arthur Quiller-Couch. Oxford University Press. Cloth, $2.00.

. . . . . . .

*The Lyric Year.* One hundred poems, edited by Ferdinand Earle. Mitchell Kennerley.

## 82　THE TYPICAL FORMS OF ENGLISH LITERATURE

*Georgian Poetry, 1911-1912.*
*Georgian Poetry, 1913-1915.*
Both volumes published by The Poetry Bookshop. New York, G. P. Putnam's Sons.
*Anthology of Magazine Verse.* Edited by William Stanley Braithwaite. Published annually by Gomme & Marshall.
*The Little Book of American Poets.*
*The Little Book of Modern Verse.*
Both volumes edited by Jessie B. Rittenhouse. Houghton Mifflin Co.
*Some Imagist Poets.* (*New Poetry Series.*) Houghton Mifflin Co.

### Critical Discussions [1]

I

Sir Philip Sidney, *The Defense of Poesy.* 1595. (Written before 1585.)
George Puttenham (?), *The Arte of English Poesie.* 1589.
Thomas Campion, *Observations on the Art of English Poesy.* 1602.
Samuel Daniel, *A Defence of Rhyme.* 1603.
Sir William Temple, *Of Poetry.* 1690.
William Congreve, *Treatise on the Pindaric Ode.* 1706.
Alexander Pope, *Essay on Criticism.* 1711.
Joseph Warton, *On the Genius and Writings of Pope.* 1756.
Edmund Burke, *Essay on the Sublime and the Beautiful.* 1756.
Thomas Gray, *Metrum.* 1760-61 (?).
Thomas Warton, *History of English Poetry.* 1774-78.
Samuel Johnson, *Lives of the Poets.* 1779-81.
William Wordsworth, Preface to the *Lyrical Ballads,* second edition. 1800.
Samuel Taylor Coleridge, *Biographia Literaria.* 1817.
William Hazlitt, *Lectures on the English Poets.* 1818.
Percy Bysshe Shelley, *Defence of Poetry.* 1821.
David Masson, *Essays Biographical and Critical: Chiefly on English Poets.* 1856.
Matthew Arnold, *Essays in Criticism.* 1865.

II

Raymond M. Alden, *An Introduction to Poetry.* New York (Holt & Co.), 1909.

[1] See page 36, note.

## THE LYRIC

A. C. Bradley, *Oxford Lectures on Poetry*. London and New York (Macmillan), 1909.

R. P. Cowl, *The Theory of Poetry in England*. London and New York (Macmillan), 1914.

F. St. John Corbett, *A History of British Poetry*. London (Gay & Bird), 1904.

W. J. Courthope, *A History of English Poetry*. 5 vols. New York (Macmillan), 1895.

Max Eastman, *The Enjoyment of Poetry*. New York (Scribner's Sons), 1913.

John Erskine, *The Elizabethan Lyric*. New York (Columbia University Press), 1905.

W. A. Neilson, *The Essentials of Poetry*. Boston and New York (Houghton Mifflin Co.), 1912.

Sir Arthur Quiller-Couch, *Poetry*. New York (Dutton & Co.), 1915.

Edward B. Reed, *English Lyrical Poetry*. From its origins to the present time. New Haven (Yale University Press), 1912.

Ernest Rhys, *Lyric Poetry* (*Channels of English Literature*). New York (Dutton & Co.), 1913.

Felix E. Schelling, *The English Lyric* (*Types of English Literature*). Boston and New York (Houghton Mifflin Co.), 1913.

## IV

## THE EPIC

*History*

Beginnings
of Poetry

As it happens, epic poetry is one of the oldest forms that has come down to us, both in general literature and in that of our own race. Yet we feel reasonably sure that before these epic-structures were produced, there were various smaller poetic units, independently created and later fused to form these more extended national poems. By general agreement poems like the Greek *Iliad* and *Odyssey*, the Germanic *Nibelungenlied*, and the old English *Beowulf* are classed as popular or folk-epics, for just this reason of composite origin and growth. Their authors are either entirely unknown or are shadowy personages who may just as probably have been only amalgamaters and organizers. In various instances scholars have come across poetic fragments practically identical with portions of some recognized folk-epic, yet giving evidence of an earlier independent existence; bits of such raw material, no doubt, as later went to make up a finished whole. In studying the *Little Gest of Robin Hood* it was possible to compare this with numerous real and hypothetical Robin Hood ballads and thus to observe a comparatively recent folk-epic in the making.

The Old English poem *Beowulf*, clearly a folk-epic in the process of its growth, displays a virility of spirit, a freedom of imagination, and a comprehensive unity in the character of its hero that represent rare literary quality. Beowulf himself, nephew of his sovereign Hygelac, as Roland was of Charlemagne, gives us a high opinion of heroic ideals among the Anglo-Saxons. He had the strength of thirty men in his hand-grip, the courage in youth to plunge into the gruesome, demon-haunted mere and in old age to stalk alone into the barrow of the fire-dragon, the unselfishness to risk life for a royal neighbor in trouble or to maintain a youthful prince on a throne he might have had himself for claiming it.

*"Beowulf" and Its Hero*

Historically Beowulf appears to have been the doughty young kinsman of a Scandinavian king who made a disastrous raid on the Franks about 520 A.D. Various details in the poem seem to refer to this and similar natural enough experiences,—a swimming match for instance with a certain Breca. But the main adventures of the poem, the slaying of the monster Grendel and his mother and the conflict with the fire-dragon, are not only separated by more than fifty years of the hero's life, but are essentially the vague supernatural stuff cherished in folk-tradition from a very early time. Here it has been adapted to an extremely human and well-authenticated hero in a vivid setting of realistic manners and surroundings. Moreover, somewhere in the four hundred years before our only manuscript of the poem was written, numerous references to Christian faith and bible story were incorporated into what had been originally pagan adventures. Thus Hrothgar's men offer heathen sacrifices against Grendel, a monster of "Cain's kin," and the poet apologizes:

*As a Popular Epic*

"Such was their custom,
Hope of the heathen: hell they remembered
In their mind's thoughts: the Creator they knew not,
Judge of their deeds."

Beowulf, on the other hand, freely acknowledges the power and grace of God, but his remains are disposed of with anything but Christian ceremonies.

The history of the epic form down through the centuries is concerned not so much with folk-epic as with the art-epic, the creation of a known poet, according to gradually formulated ideals and principles of technique. For our own purposes this process may be regarded as beginning just before the Christian era, when the Latin poet Virgil composed his *Æneid* in emulation of the two Homeric poems. Virgil was a serious-minded patriotic poet and a master-craftsman in verse, so that it is well that the chances of literary history have made his poem a model for all time, not only in its essential features, but in many incidental matters of no real artistic importance. English attempts at the epic, for example, have never been inspired or even affected by the *Beowulf*. But every one of them is in many respects Virgilian.

The Art-Epic

Virgil, in composing this first significant art-epic, clearly set the fashion of imitation, with the *Iliad* and the *Odyssey* constantly before him. Just as these were appeals to Greek national pride through the development of episodes of the Trojan War, Virgil worked out the favorite Roman tradition of descent from the Trojans by way of a heroic refugee (Æneas) from fallen Ilium. The *Iliad* was concerned with the actual conflict about the walls of Troy; the *Odyssey* with the adventures of the Greek prince Ulysses (Odysseus) in returning

The Methods of Virgil

home after the conflict. The *Æneid* combines the wandering and the strife in one poem, devoting the first half to the journey of Æneas to Italy, the second to his experiences there in establishing his race. In all three poems the supernatural relations are of great importance, the human figures being almost puppets controlled by jealous-hearted, bickering gods and goddesses. Each of the Homeric poems had contained twenty-four books. Virgil reduced his epic to exactly half that number. He followed his models, however, in beginning the first book with a plunge into the midst of the action,[1] after a conventional statement of theme and the invocation of a muse. Later Æneas is given occasion to narrate his earlier adventures to Dido as Ulysses did at the court of Antinous. All three poems are highly oratorical, introducing numerous councils and formal speeches. Virgil even carries his imitation to minor tricks of style, most notable being the long-drawn-out epic simile.

Virgil's dependence upon these models is fully as evident in the details of his story. The second book of the *Iliad* contains a catalogue of the Greek and Trojan troops, with their commanders; a similar muster-roll of the forces of Latium appears in the *Æneid*, book seven. The shield made by Vulcan for Achilles at the request of the latter's mother, Thetis, affords a passage of beautiful description in the eighteenth book of the *Iliad*. In the *Æneid*, book eight, is a similar description of the shield Venus secured for her son Æneas. As Achilles ordained funeral games for Patroclus (*Iliad*, book twenty-three), Æneas did for his

Imitation
in the
"Æneid"

---

[1] Horace's phrase, *in medias res*, by which he describes this process in his *De Arte Poetica*, has become a commonplace of criticism.

father Anchises (book five). The journey of Ulysses was retarded by a long sojourn with the nymph Calypso, experiences with the Cyclops, Circe, and the monsters Scylla and Charybdis, and a visit to the infernal regions. Æneas lingered in Carthage and won the heart of Queen Dido, just escaped Scylla and Charybdis and the Cyclops, and paid a very similar visit to Hades.

The most obvious thing about the whole history of epic poetry is this careful economy of invention for which Virgil has thus set the standard. Indeed, the danger is that students, seeing so much of this mechanical sort of imitation, will undervalue the qualities that go to make an epic poem great. It is both easy and popular to cry "Homer and Humbug,"[1] and scholarship must needs defend itself in these utilitarian days. These early epic poems flashed a white light of imagination across certain obscure national traditions. They gave them glamour without making them improbable, dignity without making them prosy, concrete detail without making them garrulous. In the unfolding of these mighty destinies, there is constant emphasis upon patriotic ideals, particularly in the work of Virgil. "Pius Æneas"—where piety means loyalty to one's family line—dared all the violences prompted by jealous gods that he might find a resting-place for his household gods and establish what became the Roman nation.[2] The exploits of the heroes, the muster of the troops, the coöperation of the im-

**Real Greatness**

---

[1] See Stephen Leacock's *Behind the Beyond*.
[2] " . . . Multum ille et terris iactatus et alto
vi superum, saevae memorem Iunonis ob iram,
multa quoque et bello passus, dum conderet urbem
inferretque deos Latio, genus unde Latinum
Albanique patres atque altae moenia Romae."
—*Æneid*, I, 3-7.

THE EPIC 89

mortals, all these were as direct appeals to a patriotic audience as they are in Europe today. All this, too, is presented with a wealth of poetic beauty which it is impossible to appreciate through the medium of translation. It has endured the test of time, and its greatness as art is not a myth but a splendid reality.

Before classic culture gave way to the obscurity of the early Middle Ages, there were several Latin epics presenting great historical events according to the programme established by Virgil. Best known of these are the *Pharsalia* of Lucan and the *Thebaid* of Statius. Shortly after appeared the first of the romances, which were to supply the demand for long narratives of adventure until the epic was restored to Europe in the Renaissance. These romances have so many bearings upon the history of epic poetry that they must receive consideration here. They fall into two distinct and widely separated groups: the Greek prose romances of about the fourth century, A.D., and the chivalric romances of the late Middle Ages, first in verse and later in prose. The first group was produced in the period of late Greek culture centering in Byzantium and Alexandria. Much of it is known only by fragments and traditions, but there are complete specimens in the *Ethiopica* (or *Theagenes and Chariclea*) of Bishop Heliodorus, *Daphnis and Chloe*, by Longus, and *The Loves of Clitophon and Leucippe* by Achilles Tatius.[1] The chivalric romances were the common property of

The Greek and Chivalric Romances

[1] These are outlined in Dunlop's *History of Fiction* and published entire in a convenient edition in Bohn's Libraries. Cf. F. M. Warren, *History of the Novel Previous to the Seventeenth Century*, and S. L. Wolff, *The Greek Romances and Elizabethan Prose Fiction*.

Europe in the twelfth and thirteenth centuries and have been preserved in numerous manuscript versions. They evolved or grouped themselves in so-called "cycles," most important being the Troy cycle, the Alexander cycle, the Charlemagne cycle, and the cycle of King Arthur. These names suggest the common subject of each group of stories.[1] Most of them took shape in France and a large number were circulated in England in French versions. There were numerous translations into English and a few native English contributions.

The relation of these groups of romances to the type of epic established by the *Æneid* may be outlined in brief.

Adventure in Epic and Romance
"*Arma virumque cano,*" Virgil had declared in his opening line: that is, martial adventures and the exploits of a wandering national hero fulfilling his destiny, were to be his theme. Action played a large part in the content of the *Æneid*, and that action, as we have seen, about equally divided between a much disturbed journey over seas and the warfare necessary to establish a state. The Greek romances enlarge upon wandering adventure and shun warfare, being concerned chiefly with such experiences as shipwrecks and pirate combats. The chivalric group is set forth once more against the larger background of war, conducted according to the code of medieval chivalry, and wandering adventure is kept in prominence. In the epic the larger experiences, while not presented as historically accurate, approximated history, and were reasonable enough in the judgment of the public. The adventures in the Greek romances were realistic enough in themselves,—almost

---

[1] See the discussion of these and the bibliographies in W. H. Schofield's *English Literature from the Norman Conquest to Chaucer*, and C. S. Baldwin's *English Medieval Literature*.

sordidly so at times,—but they were spun in an interminable succession that was almost fantastic. Finally realism of detail gave way also until the chivalric quest led knight and squire straight into a no-man's-land of the idealizing imagination. Yet it must not be forgotten that both epic and romance of chivalry, each in its own way, were founded upon history.

To the constructive imagination of Virgil, unity was the supreme consideration. General unity of effect could be obtained only through unity of plot.
**Unity of Action** That is, each experience, each adventure, however inclined to run off at a tangent, must be shown to be an essential part of a large and organically constructed chain of events leading to the high destiny of the hero. With romances came the type of plot known all too well today: take a man and woman, just married or about to be, separate them by surprise and accident, and keep them separated by a succession of accidents until patience or ingenuity is exhausted. As soon as they are brought together the story ends. This method of technique, once accepted, soon puts a premium on surprise and variety at the expense of unity.

In the treatment of character there was a similar development. The constant intervention of divine beings, which seems a highly imaginative feature
**Character** to the readers of today, was a matter of current acceptance under classic mythology, where gods were only men writ large. In fact, considerably more of imagination went into the appreciation of the details of magic and enchantment that the romances substituted for this supernatural machinery of epic poetry. Likewise the conception of Æneas as a lover was one that probably occurred to Virgil and his public

no more pointedly than that of Ulysses and his passion for Calypso did to the Greeks. But the fact remained that the amour of Æneas and Dido was related with no little detail, occupied some three books of the *Æneid* and was ready to be unduly emphasized whenever it met the attention of an audience that was so minded. So what was merely an episode in epic structure became essential to romance. The hero must be a lover and the central motive must be love. Not love merely, but romantic love; and romantic love is ordinary love much idealized until it is practically a sort of worship. When love like this dominates the being of a man and woman and they pass unscathed through a devious course of adventures for the sake of it, we have reached the core of the earlier romances. Later ones added to the hero the characteristic of magnanimity and he thus became complete. It must be added that these heroes of romance were so much alike in their prowess and passion that stories were readily transferred from one to the other; what was Gawain's on one day was told to the glory of Launcelot on another.

After considerable development in France the romance cycles, particularly that of Charlemagne and his peers, passed over into Italy, and there in course of time, around the person of Charlemagne's nephew Roland, grew up poetry that gave to the world a new form, the romantic epic. In the *Song of Roland*, a typical French poem of about 1100 A.D., this young hero is represented as meeting death through the treacherous cutting-off of Charlemagne's rear-guard, which he was commanding. There is no mention of love except a mere statement at the end that when news of Roland's fate reached the city of Aix, Aude the Fair died of grief. Yet the first of these Italian romantic epics to catch our

**Italian Romantic Epics**

THE EPIC 93

attention is Boiardo's *Orlando Innamorato* ("Roland in love"), and the next is Ariosto's more pretentious *Orlando Furioso* with its famous legend of Roland's madness for love.

These two poems appeared just about 1500, exactly at the time when critics, under the impulse of the Renaissance, were turning their eyes to the epic
Their poem as the most exalted form of poetry
Dependence and to the *Æneid* as the model epic of all
on Virgil time. Vida's *Ars Poetica*, for example, outlined the precepts of epic verse as Horace had those of drama, and based all these precepts on Virgil. Now it is true that the *Orlando* poems followed the *Æneid* in many minor details of form. They began with theme and invocation; they used formal speeches and formal descriptions and formal similes; they had an abundance of supernatural machinery. But in certain fundamental things they were exactly the opposite of this classical masterpiece, and they were popular notwithstanding this.

For one thing they greatly overemphasized the love motive. Prowess in arms and patriotic significance were
still maintained, but the heroic figures
Their were lovers first of all, and then doughty
Distinctive warriors that they might please their
Features ladies. Events were vastly more crowded and complicated, with numerous episodes leading nowhere in particular, underplots entangled with the main issue, and so many characters of importance that it is difficult to fix upon a real hero at all. Whereas the classical epic was confined to one action of one man, this new poetry, said the critics, admits many actions of many men, and unity of action is no more. Probability in a form like the epic, which encourages

supernatural machinery, is always a doubtful and rather personal matter; but these romantic poems were far more improbable than the *Æneid* could be to anybody. Finally, the romantic epics departed entirely from the traditions of Virgilian verse, and were composed in stanzas.

The controversy over Virgilian epic and romantic epic went on in Italy for almost a hundred years. Men wrote in both forms, and while severer critics condemned the modern type, the public persisted in finding it more pleasing. At length it occurred to scholars to attempt a reconciliation, and Torquato Tasso set about this in his *Discourses on Poetry* (*Discorsi dell' Arte Poetica*) and enforced his opinions by a new epic, *Jerusalem Delivered*, completed in 1574. Into this splendid story of the crusades Tasso wove two other features for which he contended vigorously as a critic,—the celebration of the true religion and an abundance of moral instruction. In other respects this was a typical romantic epic, with all the movement, color, and passion of its predecessors. Tasso made one serious mistake with it. He submitted the manuscript to the judgment of his fellow-critics, and the faults they found with it postponed publication for years and helped to drive the author to a madhouse.

Tasso and the Critics

These Italian romantic epics were the immediate inspiration of England's first great attempt at any form of art-epic, the *Faerie Queene* of Edmund Spenser, published in part in 1590, the uncompleted remainder in 1596. This poem carried the idea of a moral or didactic purpose farther than even Tasso had contemplated in writing his *Jerusalem Delivered*. This purpose is explained in the prefatory letter that accompanied the first three books as being "to fashion a gentleman or

Spenser's Programme

THE EPIC 95

noble person in vertuous and gentle discipline." The scheme of twelve books, into which the *Faerie Queene* was to be divided, we may recognize as a sacred heritage from the *Æneid*. Just as Tasso's moral intentions were developed under the so-called Catholic Reaction,—the purifying of the Church from within,—so Spenser was dominated by the rapidly-growing Puritanism of England, so that he complicated his allegory of culture and gentility by various allusions to the religious controversy of his day. Double allegory is a frequent device.[1] Unity of effect is further destroyed by the freedom with which Spenser inserted episodes and elaborated descriptions, all of them interesting and beautiful, and justifying themselves abundantly to everyone except the severest critics. His unity, indeed, was little more than a unity of programme and this is shattered by the fact that less than half of the original scheme was ever completed.

The setting of the *Faerie Queene* is legendary, but the legends are drawn from English romance and English folk-lore, with no little patriotic appeal. Certain episodes are notable for their national feeling, such as the succession of English sovereigns in Book III, Canto III, and the topographical descriptions connected with the marriage of the Medway and the Thames (Book IV, Canto XI). Everywhere Spenser finds occasion to improve upon the movement and color that Italian readers had enjoyed so much in their own poems. Sensuous gratification is carried a bit too far, perhaps, to accord with a document of Puritanism, but the exquisite grace and

His Originality

---

[1] See the Prefatory Letter again: "In that Faerie Queene I meane glory in my generall intention, but in my particular I conceive the most excellent and glorious person of our sovereine the Queene."

charm of Spenser's art refines and justifies everything he touches. His melodious verse is arranged in stanzas,—stanzas of his own invention, so rich and varied in their possibilities that they promptly found a place among the great and permanent verse-forms of our poetry.

If, as we like to believe, the *Faerie Queene* was one of Spenser's contributions to a somewhat concerted effort to try out the various literary possibilities of the English tongue, we look in vain for any specimen of classical epic, produced within or without his group, and worthy to rank with its products. The nearest approach is to be found in *The Civil Wars of York and Lancaster*, by Samuel Daniel. This employs many devices of epic form, but follows too closely the detailed facts of history to be classed as genuine epic in its conception. Indeed it is versified history rather than poetry at all. Another approximation came to England in translation from France and attained an immense popularity in the early years of the seventeenth century. This was Joshua Sylvester's translation of the *Semaines* of Du Bartas, published in English as *The Divine Weeks and Works*. The *Semaines* were long biblical paraphrases, the first presenting the week of Creation, the second designed to cover all later history. The bare outline of narrative was embellished with a wealth of detailed information and no end of extravagance, and except for certain mechanical devices, there was again little that could be called epic poetry.

The fusion programme for epic construction, as set down by Tasso, seems to have exercised its largest influence in France, in the first half of the seventeenth century. During nearly fifty years, every Frenchman of any literary consequence felt called upon to compose an epic—or as

*Other English Attempts*

he called it, a heroic poem. According to Tasso's code these specimens were based upon French history or legend, at a period not too recent or too remote. They had to do with Christianity, the true religion, and they introduced some kind of supernatural machinery. They had a complexity of incidents, but reverted to the Virgilian method of emphasizing the exploits of a dominating hero. This hero, by the way, was now a magnanimous lover as well as a mighty warrior, and still held in his destiny the fate of the nation. Mechanical details of form were scrupulously observed, but genuine poetic inspiration was in most cases sadly lacking.

*French Heroic Poetry*

There is no need to list the titles of these epics today. They are of interest now only to the literary historian, who regards them as one of several manifestations of the "heroic" impulse felt so strongly in that century by France, and somewhat by England under French influence. This means the exaltation of mighty figures—the supermen of history and tradition—until their exploits reach superlatives; then devising for each one a romantic love-passion for which he would gladly sacrifice all material things; finally making him courteous, urbane, condescending, and all the other things involved in the word "magnanimous." There were heroic prose romances as well as heroic poems, and authors soon discovered the dramatic possibilities also present in men like these. Davenant, as we shall see, constructed his poem *Gondibert* on the plan of a five-act drama, and Dryden transferred the themes and methods of these poems to his "heroic plays."

*Its Relations and Effect*

Davenant's *Gondibert* (1651) marks the first appearance of this heroic type of epic poem in English. Not only is it written to programme, but the "Gondibert" author attached to it a critical letter by way of preface, explaining just where he did or did not conform to custom. The places where he did not conform are comparatively few. His is not a national poem, the scene being laid in the courts and camps of Italy rather than in an earlier England. He has no patience with the supernatural extravagances of most heroic poems. His friend Cowley declared to him:

"Thou, like some worthy knight, with sacred arms
Dost drive the monsters hence, and end the charms."

He organizes his poem in five books corresponding to the five acts of a tragic drama, with subdivisions into cantos in the manner of scenes. Finally he adopts a stanza that is all his own, thus protesting against the couplet rhymes that had taken the place of the Italian and Spenserian stanzaic arrangements. Certainly Davenant deserves credit for the originality he displayed where originality was rare. He deserves credit too for the sound morality, the historical interest, and the energy of movement he put into this production. But Cowley said more than he meant in the commendation just quoted. When Davenant wrote, his poem probably did not suffer greatly from the exclusion of the monsters, but he certainly did manage to "end the charms."

We wonder indeed what charms there should be in these heroic poems, or what prompted readers of that day to discover charms in them, as we turn to the writings of Sir Richard Blackmore. He was easily the most prolific of English epic poets, as is witnessed by his *Prince Arthur*, 1695; *King Arthur*, 1697; *Eliza*,

1705. The leading critics of the day were arrayed against him, and very justly so. Yet for a time at least he had an indulgent and even approving public that was willing to invest freely in his lengthy commonplaces.

The one really great English poet in the tradition of the Virgilian epic stood entirely apart from this French heroic school and from the court that cultivated it. He went back of this vogue to the Italian and Latin masters from whom it had developed; he worked in poverty and obscurity; and he was slow to be recognized by either critics or public. Milton's *Paradise Lost* was published in 1667, his *Paradise Regained* in 1671, but it was not until Addison's papers on *Paradise Lost* in the *Spectator*, during 1712, that a reasonable appreciation was accorded to these poems. These papers, for all their formal reserve, still serve as an admirable commentary on the poem, for it is only as we approach Milton's work through them or by a historical path such as this chapter follows, that we realize how thoroughly he was dominated, in spite of all his genius, by the traditions of classical form.

*Milton's Classical Epics*

In *Paradise Lost*, deservedly the better known of the two poems, we find a unity of construction comparable only to that of Milton's model, the *Æneid*. This unity, with the end for which it is conceived, is expressly stated in the customary theme, accompanying the invocation:

*Unity of Construction*

"Of Man's first disobedience, and the fruit
Of that forbidden tree, whose mortal taste
Brought Death into the world, and all our woe,
With loss of Eden, till one greater Man
Restore us, and regain the blissful seat,
Sing Heavenly Muse, . . .

... what in me is dark
Illumine, what is low raise and support;
That to the highth of this great argument
I may assert Eternal Providence,
And justify the ways of God to men."

In this subject, as Milton conceived it, there is likewise immense complexity and a majesty that approaches the sublime. For at one stroke he achieved these virtues and solved the vexed problem of supernatural machinery in Christian poems by setting Eden before a background of the eternities, and repeating in the fall of man the conflict that resulted in the fall of Lucifer. Adam and Eve are enticed to their sin in pursuance of Satan's scheme of revenge upon the Almighty: through the ultimate triumph of Christ, son of God and man, the seed of the woman is to bruise the serpent's head. This is more than material for a national poem; it should concern all of Christendom, and ultimately the entire human race. It rings with echoes from the memorable passages of scripture; traverses the secret places of heaven and hell; ransacks ancient myths for marvelous abstractions like Sin and Death. Of a truth such song as this soars with no middle flight, and pursues

"Things unattempted yet in prose or rime."

In his organization of this material, however, Milton is in strict accord with the rules. The poem, first cast in ten books, was afterward rearranged so that there were twelve,—the number in the *Æneid*. The reader is plunged *in medias res*, and the preliminary conflict in heaven is related to Adam by Raphael in the fifth and sixth books. Rhetorical and fairly dramatic speeches are very much in evidence, though their effectiveness is dulled considerably by an over-formal logic, the result of the author's training and diplomatic experience. Even some of the traditional episodes of classical epic are retained, such as the muster of Satan's forces, in the first book.

Much interesting discussion has centered about the hero of this poem. *Paradise Lost* is certainly not heroic poetry at all, said critics of the seventeenth cen-
**Problem of** tury, or else we are mistaken in looking
**the Hero** to Adam as a hero. Dryden contended that Satan is the real hero of the poem. Addison rather waived the question as irrelevant, but suggested the Messiah. But *Paradise Lost* could be good and consistent classical epic without at all being heroic poetry as the seventeenth century understood this. It is true that Adam is not a mighty warrior or a passionate lover or a magnanimous conqueror. He falls an easy victim to temptation, and is departing from the Garden, "with wand'ring steps and slow," as the poem ends. He was pitted, though, against immortals, and as the sole representatives of mankind, he and Eve were instruments employed by the Messiah and his enemies in working out their conflict for supremacy. At the same time these solitary mortals, under the will of higher powers, were accomplishing the destiny not of one nation, but of their race. Does Æneas or Ulysses do more? The best their manhood can achieve is weak and paltry work compared to the storms and tempests, the impervious shields and clouds of invisibility with which the gods through them manipulate their celestial strife. It is true that Ulysses routs the suitors and Æneas establishes his race in Latium before their stories close. But the promise of Michael brightens the pathway out of Eden and points

to ultimate victory. Satan is splendid in his indomitable spirit of revenge, but he is neither victorious nor a hero. To the general reader *Paradise Lost* is not significant because of the care with which it observes classical traditions. It is a great poem to us because

**A Work of Art** it develops in artistic unity one great imaginative conception, and abounds throughout its course in daring flights of fancy into unknown and unknowable regions. In this respect it is always to be classed with Dante's *Divine Comedy*, with which the young Macaulay compared it in a suggestive, if somewhat inaccurate, fashion, in his well-known essay on Milton. Milton too succeeded as few English poets have in mastering a vehicle entirely adequate for his lofty message. There was a day when English critics, notably Dr. Samuel Johnson, disparaged the verse of *Paradise Lost* as rude and inharmonious, but the verdict of time has been that its cadences are the most majestic and beautiful that have fallen upon English ears.

There is an old-time commonplace that it is an easy step from the sublime to the ridiculous. Heroic poetry, by its constant striving after lofty heights,

**Burlesque and Mock-Heroic** was always perilously near exaggeration, and this in turn was a great encouragement to burlesque. In Italy there was a vogue of burlesque verse in the earliest days of the romantic epics, and the richest period of French heroic poetry produced mock-heroic verse that has long outlived the thing it satirized. While there are countless variations, this mocking poetry abroad fell into two fairly distinct classes. The simpler of these, the travesty, or burlesque proper, presents a dignified subject, worthy of epic treatment, in a flippant, disrespectful manner, in a short, choppy sort of verse, packed with slang and vulgarity and unnatural rhymes. The other, the mock-heroic, has all the epic dignity of form and idiom of which the author is capable, but celebrates some hopelessly trivial subject. The first of these, while extremely popular among the Restoration wits and always more or less in evidence since, has rarely been admitted into polite society. Any serious literary form can be thus burlesqued, and it happens that burlesque plays, like *The Rehearsal* or *The Knight of the Burning Pestle,* are much easier to point out than burlesque epics.

The mock-heroic has a more distinguished lineage. It begins in Italy with Tassoni's poem *La Secchia Rapita* (The Stolen Bucket) and extends through Boileau's poem of a church divided over the location of the reading-desk (*"Le Lutrin"*) to Pope's delightful fantasy, *The Rape of the Lock.* This last is one of the finest specimens of mock-heroic poetry in our language. Its theme—the theft of a curl from the head of the fair Belinda—has of course neither epic dignity nor the occasion for epic action. The jest lies in treating it as if it had.

"The Rape of the Lock"

Particular care is given to the introduction of as many epic devices as possible,—some of them managed with extreme cleverness. The reader is not plunged *in medias res,* but is provided with the customary theme:

Its Epic Devices

"What dire offence from amorous causes springs,
What mighty contests rise from trivial things,
I sing."

The sylphs, spirits of the air, borrowed by Pope from the doctrines of the Rosicrucians, furnish the chief supernatural machinery, though there are also dreams and portents and a grisly visit to the Cave of Spleen. There are conventionally formal speeches inserted in the much-expanded action; a game of cards supplies a muster of the troops; and there is a thrilling heroic combat in which metaphors and ladies' frowns are the most fatal weapons. The poem abounds in satire on the society of the day, driven home by Pope's favorite trick of grouping the serious and the trivial in unexpected combinations:

> "Some dire disaster, or by force, or slight;
> But what or where, the Fates have wrapp'd in night.
> Whether the nymph shall break Diana's law,
> Or some frail China-jar receive a flaw:
> Or stain her honour, or her new brocade;
> Forget her prayers, or miss a masquerade;
> Or lose her heart, or necklace at a ball."

This suggests the purpose for which these mock-heroic poems were commonly used. They did not satirize extravagances in the literary type; they were not critical documents. Rather they satirized general conditions, social, religious, or literary, and thus became powerful weapons directed against the weaknesses or abuses of the day. The most conspicuous instance of such employment is seen in Samuel Butler's poem *Hudibras*, published just after the Restoration to satirize defeated Puritanism. Technically it is a mixed form, combining the structure and extravagant spirit of mock-heroic with the verse and vocabulary of ordinary burlesque. Various features of the popular romances were utilized, Sir Hudibras himself and his man Ralpho being borrowed in great part from the hero and his attendant squire in Cervantes's famous mock-romance *Don Quixote*. Few readers of to-day are able to find Hudibras attractive. In its own century, however, it established a type and fixed a standard in England that aroused hosts of imitators who wished in this way to pay old scores against persons and institutions. Like their model, these attempts have lost interest as their thrusts and allusions have become meaningless.

    The formal epic, on severely classical lines, remained more or less a popular model during the eighteenth century, but no results of permanent value were attained. Glover's *Leonidas*, 1737, was the most widely read of the new poems, and having been adopted for a time as a sort of political document, acquired a fame that it does not seem to deserve. It is stiff and artificial, and has its chief critical interest in the fact that the author dispensed intentionally with all supernatural machinery. As the romantic reaction grew, there came a considerable interest in long narrative poems, but these were romantic in spirit and treatment, and under medieval rather than classical influences. Medieval interest also brought into prominence the old folk-epics of various peoples, finding them rich in romantic possibilities. The Homeric poems, always regarded as more romantic than the *Æneid*, clearly surpassed the latter in popular favor, and have continued to attract scholars and translators down to our own day. Thus the pathways of epic and romance, never far removed from each other, were apparently merged into one in the early years of the nineteenth century.

*The Fusion of Epic and Romance*

    This fusion of classical epic and old romance is most apparent in Tennyson's poetic rendering of the Arthurian cycle, which he has called not the "*Arthuriad*," but the "*Idylls of the King.*" For all his origin in medieval romance, Arthur might well have served as the hero of a great national epic. For years Milton con-

"The Idylls of the King"

templated such a treatment of him, and Blackmore's ill-fated attempts in no way disqualified him. To Tennyson he appeared as a great spiritual leader of his people, rescuing them from Roman and barbarian, and organizing them into statehood on a system of loyalty, self-sacrifice, and service. Structural unity is obtained by opening the action with the coronation and marriage of the king, and extending it through the perfection of the Round Table to the final dissolution of the order and the "passing" of Arthur,—a process of tragic conflict between the noble principles of chivalry and the selfish appetites and passions that are always in the world. This moral interpretation, as well as the national significance of the hero, is recognized by Tennyson, when he speaks of—

"this old imperfect tale,
New-old, and shadowing Sense at war with Soul
Rather than that gray king, whose name, a ghost,
Streams like a cloud, man-shaped, from mountain peak,
And cleaves to cairn and cromlech still."

**Supernatural Machinery**

Supernatural machinery, the common property of epic and romance, is admirably managed throughout the poem. Arthur moves before a background of divine Providence, from his mysterious birth to his mysterious voyage to Avalon. The hand that lifts Excalibur above the waves seizes it again from Sir Bedivere. Merlin, descended straight from heathen superstition, prepares the "siege perilous" to receive the stainless Christian knight Sir Galahad, who is to quest successfully for a vision of the holy grail. Such methods at once suggest the supernatural treatment in the romantic epics, but with greater dignity and reverence.

THE EPIC 107

We look in vain, however, for the technical features of either classical or romantic epic. The unity just discussed is a unity of framework rather than an organic unity of all the parts. The *Idylls* are really idylls,—separate pictures of episodes in and about the court of Arthur,—rather than books or cantos of a single poem. Each has its independent beginning and in no respect prepares for that which follows. There is scarcely one of the traditional devices we have come to associate with epic form,—the formal theme, the plunge *in medias res* with a later narrative exposition, the catalogue of forces, or the epic simile. There is blank verse, it is true, as in *Paradise Lost,* but it is not Miltonic blank verse. Classical ideals are upheld in the artistry and precision with which the flowing verses are made rich and beautiful, but the spirit is that of slightly ennobled and purified romance.

Absence of Epic Features

Tennyson's first draft of the *Idylls,* containing only four of them, appeared in 1859. The year before, William Morris had ventured to publish his first book of poetry, *The Defence of Guinevere and Other Poems,* in which he approached Arthurian legend in a very different manner. It was all extremely real and vivid to Morris, the experiences of passionate, warm-blooded men and women, living—as he lived in imagination—in the great and beautiful "Middle Ages" that romantic poets conceived of. Soon after, he turned to the sagas and epics of a still earlier time, visualized them amid the same civilization, and began translating them with the same pictorial power. He turned the *Æneid* into English verse, but was too much of a story-teller to get the best results out of so studied a composition. His *Sigurd*

William Morris

108  THE TYPICAL FORMS OF ENGLISH LITERATURE

*the Volsung* (1877), based on Icelandic folk-epic, deals with material better adapted to his talents. For it he chose a swinging line of six stresses, rhyming in couplets, which he managed with rare skill. Still later came his rendering of the *Odyssey,* catching much of the realism of the original and made more convincing than many more scholarly versions.

In 1908 Thomas Hardy completed what is nominally a poetic drama in three parts, entitled *The Dynasts.* But

Thomas Hardy's "The Dynasts"

the author intended it only for "mental performance" or at most a solemn recitation of the speeches by figures behind a gauze curtain. The nineteen acts and more than a hundred scenes, the rapid alternation of the most realistic episodes of court or camp with the poetic debate of supreme intelligences, the constant insistence on viewing from the heavens pygmy armies crawling like worms across the earth below,—such pageantry as this is for no theater man's hand can construct. It seems better to regard this as a great dramatic epic, its theme the rise and overthrow of the ambition of Napoleon, considered as a manifestation of the great World Will which for Hardy takes the place of God or the Fates. The interpreters of the action are the Spirit and Chorus of the Years, the Spirit and Chorus of the Pities, the Spirits Sinister and Ironic, and various other supernatural figures. The narrative is indicated by a series of dumb-shows connecting the significant bits of action and dialogue that serve as scenes. The characters are the entire *dramatis personae* of the Napoleonic Wars.

Even today the spirit of epic is not dead among us. The great American epic is as yet unwritten. But a young and patriotic poet of England—Alfred Noyes—has recently celebrated in his *Drake* the achievements of the hero who first won for that nation the mastery of the seas. It is a striking coincidence that almost immediately that mastery was challenged in a world war, and threatened by tiny craft that bore to her dreadnaughts much the relation of Drake's black barks to stately Spanish galleons. As for the poem, it is almost heavy at times with the imagery and ornament of Spenserian romance, but in all essentials it is epic that returns close to the Virgilian norm. The theme, as clearly stated in the beginning, is the glory of the man who made one little isle "queen of the earth and sea," at the same time that he fought for the new faiths and for the soul's freedom. The material is arranged in twelve books, the first concerned with Drake's wanderings on his privateering voyage around the world, the remainder with his exploits as England's admiral. The rapid, thrilling narrative still introduces elegantly formal speeches, though there is considerable dialogue that is crisp and realistic. Drake's own career is well under way when the poem opens, and its earlier experiences are related by him on board his ship, *The Golden Hynde*.

Drake himself is the typical national hero, achieving the destiny of his race under divine Providence. Prayer and devotion color the entire story, but there is little actual machinery of the supernatural,—the storm before Doughty's mutiny and flight, or the cannon shot that interrupted Bess's wedding. For the hero Drake is also a lover, whose loyalty to a village sweetheart purifies and ennobles his character without making him the sighing sentimentalist of romance.

"Old ocean was his Nile, his mighty queen
An English maiden purer than the dawn,
His cause the cause of Freedom, his reward
The glory of England."

The conventionality of all classical epic is still better illustrated by the employment of such details as a muster of Drake's pygmy fleet as it sets out to round the world, or the occasional epic similes, like this one:

**Conventions of Epic**

"Strange as in some dark cave the first fierce gleam
Of pirate gold to some forlorn maroon
Who tiptoes to the heap and glances round
Askance, and dreads to hear what erst he longed
To hear—some voice to break the hush; but bathes
Both hands with childish laughter in the gold,
And lets it trickle through his fevered palms,
And begins counting half a hundred times
And loses count each time for sheer delight
And wonder in it; meantime, if he knew,
Passing the cave-mouth, far away, beyond
The still lagoon, the coral reef, the foam
And the white fluttering chatter of the birds,
A sail that might have saved him comes and goes
Unseen across the blue Pacific sea."

## Technique of the Epic

With the exception of the drama, no literary form has had more critical discussion than the epic poem. Aristotle in his *Poetics* and Horace in his *Art of Poetry* both gave it a consideration secondary to that of tragedy. Vida's treatise, modeled on Horace, substituted the epic for tragedy in the place of first importance. The seventeenth century carried the discussion to the last extreme of artificiality, although the English treatises that followed are fairly reasonable and appreciative. Best

**Critical Documents**

known of these are Dryden's critical prefaces and Addison's papers in the *Spectator* on *Paradise Lost*. This mass of material, and the comparative infrequency of the form in English, dispenses with the necessity of any detailed discussion here.

The theme of epic narrative, usually expressed compactly in the first few lines, is primarily the organic succession of martial exploits through which **Theme and** a chosen hero fulfills national destiny. **Purpose** To this, in the case of the romantic epic, is added the celebration of a supreme love-passion, while the "heroic" poem commonly adds the glorification of the true faith. Epic poetry, like drama, is an imitation of life, and aims to please, as well as to thrill and inspire a widely scattered public with the fruits of the author's imagination. Many critics have argued for a moral or didactic purpose in epic; some have gone so far as to suppose that the poet first selected an abstract moral truth, and then sought through history for a plot to drive it home. But however true it is that epic poems convey ethical truths and sometimes even insist upon this moral purpose,—like Milton's

"assert eternal Providence
And justify the ways of God to men,"—

the fact remains that we must consider them first as works of art, or pieces of literary technique.

The plot of an epic poem, then, is characterized by greatness of scope and majesty of incident. It is allowed a latitude in time that is denied to **Plot** tragedy, its only limit in this respect being the power of the human imagination to grasp it as a connected and completed development. From the account must be excluded all such incidents as are merely trivial. Yet the smallest details may be admitted provided there is indication of their real significance in the great scheme of things. Even the pique of Achilles over a captive maiden is a matter of small importance, except as the changing fortunes of the Trojan War are made to hang upon it.

Both these considerations suggest the ideal of unity, a very precious principle since the days of Aristotle.

**The Ideal of Unity**

There must be one organic action, in epic as in tragedy, distinctly arising out of the apparent dead level of the commonplace, moving irresistibly through its curve of progress, and sinking once more into placidity at the end,—the "beginning, middle, and end" of Aristotle's theories. In classical epic this great single action may introduce innumerable episodes so long as they are made relevant, but it must concern itself with one dominating figure of a hero ("one action of one man"). Certain romantic epics made a limited period of historical action the unifying principle and admitted various prominent characters ("many actions of many men"). Both of them, in order to suggest rapidity and keep connections more distinct, used the device of plunging midway into the action, as the dramatist often does ("*in medias res*"), and leaving the exposition to be drawn later.

The exaltation that belongs to events in epic poetry is transferred also to the characters. The human beings are of noble birth and lofty station, just as

**Characters**

the action lies always in courts and camps. While consistent with character-types of which we know, they must be enlarged and magnified in their passions and experiences, to suggest the fit subjects of divine supervision. Such requirements make it extremely likely that epic characters will lose variety and individuality,—as they did among the uninspired French epics of the seventeenth century. The more worthy poems, however, present a considerable array of distinct and striking characters, grouped effectively for parallel and contrast. Even Milton, as Addison suggests, doubles his small possibilities by presenting Adam and Eve both before and after the fall.

Of varying significance is the concourse of immortal figures that at least survey the scenes from the clouds, or in most cases bestir themselves actively upon the terrestrial stage. At times it seems that the real plot is being enacted in the skies, and the mortals are mere pawns with which these divinities play out their game. At others, when Christian monotheism is supreme, Divine Providence alone directs the actions from on high. In any case supernatural personages should at least be consistent enough with the theology of the day so that this machinery is no mere empty mockery of form.

**Supernatural Personages**

Majestic characters like these mortals and immortals have of necessity lofty thoughts, and much of the skill of epic poets is employed in giving such thoughts adequate expression. At this point art comes to the aid of genius, for the inspiration that organizes at a flash the vast structure of the poem has need of a trained ability to weigh and select words and poetic measures. Too often the attempts at epic have been mere jugglings of conventional tricks of style that at a master's touch would have produced real poetry. It is enough to list a few of these devices once more. Oldest of all is the Homeric epithet, a highly-expressive compound term applied over and over again to some character or thing,—

**Matters of Form**

"Apollo, bearer-of-the-silver-bow" or "the loud-sounding sea." From Homer too come the extended epic similes, in which description becomes an end in itself and the comparison is almost forgotten. Various sorts of unidiomatic usages—archaisms, foreign expressions, and new coinages—have always been found to lend an air of remoteness and destroy triviality. The romantic poets developed the possibilities of the set pieces of luxurious description that we know best from Spenser. Meter has varied with the several periods and schools of poetry, but now that the place of Milton in English poetry is fully established, formal blank verse is generally accepted as the most effective epic medium in this language.

No one can read the critics on epic poetry without finding much discussion of "probability." All agree that an epic poem, like a drama, should have **Probability** probability, and that within its larger bounds and less realistic medium things less probable can be made to appear probable than is the case with dramatic pieces. But probability is a rather shadowy thing at best and extremely personal. For probable things are not necessarily facts, and it is required only that the things related might have happened, not that they really did. Indeed Aristotle makes an interesting comparison of "probable impossibilities" and "improbable possibilities," and finds the former proper enough for literary purposes. In this category would come the various supernatural manifestations that we refuse to accept as actual facts, but admit without hesitation in our poetry. Most of the incidents and characters in epic and drama are not only probable but possible, and it is rare in dealing with great literature that one pauses to reflect: "This could never have happened in real life."

# The Epic

### Subjects for Study

1. Technical comparison of the *Æneid* and *Beowulf*.
2. Comparison of Shakespeare's cycle of English history plays with Virgilian epic.
3. Consideration of Spenser's *Faerie Queene* as an epic poem.
4. Consideration of Tennyson's *Idylls of the King* as an epic.
5. Consideration of Thomas Hardy's *The Dynasts* as an epic.
6. Consideration of Alfred Noyes's *Drake* as an epic.
7. Reasons for the decline of epic creation.
8. Plan of an epic of King Arthur based on Malory's *Morte d'Arthur*.

### Texts

*Paradise Lost.*
Oxford University Press: World's Classics, cloth, 35 cents; Oxford edition, 60 cents.
Dutton & Co., Everyman's Library, cloth, 40 cents.
Houghton Mifflin Co., cloth, $1.00.
Crowell & Co., cloth, 60 and 75 cents.
*Faerie Queene.*
Oxford University Press, Oxford edition, cloth, 60 cents.
Dutton & Co., Everyman's Library, two volumes, cloth, 40 cents each.
Crowell & Co., cloth, 60 and 75 cents.

### Critical Discussions[1]

#### I

Sir Philip Sidney, *The Defense of Poesy*. 1595 (written before 1585).
Sir John Harington, Preface to the translation of *Orlando Furioso* 1591.
Sir William Davenant, Preface to *Gondibert*. 1650.
John Dryden, *An Essay of Heroic Plays*. 1672.
Thomas Rymer, Preface to the translation of Rapin's *Reflections on Aristotle's Treatise of Poesie*. 1674.
Thomas Hobbes, Preface to Homer's *Odysses*. 1675.
John Dryden, *Apology for Heroic Poetry and Poetic Licence*. 1677.
John Dryden, Dedication of the *Æneis*. 1697.
Jonathan Swift, *The Battle of the Books*. 1704 (written 1698).
Joseph Addison, *Spectator* papers on *Paradise Lost*. 1711.

[1] See page 36, note.

116 THE TYPICAL FORMS OF ENGLISH LITERATURE

Thomas Warton, *Observations on the Faery Queen.* 1754.
Thomas Carlyle, *Heroes and Hero-Worship.* 1841.
David Masson, *Essays Biographical and Critical, Chiefly on English Poets.* 1856.
Matthew Arnold, *On Translating Homer.* 1861.

II

Lascelles Abercrombie, *The Epic (The Art and Craft of Letters).* New York (Doran & Co.), 1914.
H. Munro Chadwick, *The Heroic Age.* Cambridge (University Press), 1912.
John Clark, *A History of Epic Poetry (post-Virgilian).* Edinburgh (Oliver & Boyd), 1900.
W. Macneile Dixon, *English Epic and Heroic Poetry (Channels of English Literature).* New York (Dutton & Co.), 1912.
S. H. Gurteen, *The Arthurian Epic.* New York (Putnam), 1895.
S. H. Gurteen, *The Epic of the Fall of Man.* New York (Putnam), 1896.
W. P. Ker, *Epic and Romance.* Essays on medieval literature. New York (Macmillan), 1897.
J. W. Mackail, *Lectures on Greek Poetry.* New York (Longmans, Green & Co.), 1911.
Howard Maynadier, *The Arthur of the English Poets.* Boston and New York (Houghton Mifflin Co.), 1907.
Gilbert Murray, *The Rise of the Greek Epic.* Oxford University Press, 1911.
E. N. S. Thompson, *Essays on Milton.* New Haven (Yale University Press), 1914.

# V

# THE PERSONAL ESSAY

## History

Origin of
the Type

THE essay is another of the literary forms revived during the Renaissance in imitation of classical usage. It was so little practiced by the Greeks and Romans, however, that it came to modern Europe with few worthy representatives and practically no fixed principles of structure. The form began apparently with the simple purpose of putting philosophical opinions and moral dicta into a prose that would hold the reader's interest as well as instruct him. It was not far from conversation written down, and might readily take the shape of semi-private correspondence. Both Cicero and Seneca, indeed, the first important authors who employed the essay form, addressed these more familiar discussions to individuals.

Latin Models

Cicero's essays are of considerable length, logically developed, and adorned with his customary flowers of rhetoric. Certain of them, because of their study by college classes, are widely known; his *De Amicitia, De Senectute,* and *De Officiis,* for example. Seneca wrote the same type of moral or philosophical letter-treatise, as represented by such titles as *De Providentia, De Tranquilitate Animi, De Brevitate Vitae.* But he wrote also a number of briefer and more familiar *Moral Epistles,* which come much nearer to the manner of modern essays.

With these two Latin authors it is necessary to associate one who wrote in Greek, but at a somewhat later period than either of the others. This was Plutarch, who in his obscure career at the end of the first Christian century, produced two books that were greatly admired by Europe during the Renaissance and were translated time and again for eager readers. The better known of these, *The Lives of the Eminent Greeks and Romans*, is a biographical work which need not concern us here. The other, the *Moralia*, is a collection of about sixty moral essays that come nearest of all classical writings in approximating the modern personal essay. Many of the subjects will become exceedingly familiar to the student: "Of Moral Virtue," "How a Man May Discern a Flatterer from a Friend," "Of Meekness," "Of the Tranquillity and Contentment of Mind," "Of the Natural Love or Kindness of Parents to Their Children." The essays are fairly positive but not always consistent in their statement of opinions, afford the reader considerable knowledge of the author's personality, proceed informally in a course that is generally logical, and illustrate their points freely from a long store of anecdote, such as a biographer must have had at his disposal. While hardly entertaining to the general reader, they are informal and colloquial, approaching very near to the later ideal of the essay,—conversation put in written form.

**Plutarch's "Moralia"**

Men are agreed that the modern essay begins with the French writer Montaigne, toward the end of the sixteenth century. He was a scholar rather than a man of the world, who at the age of thirty-eight took the opportunity afforded by the death of his father, to retire to the

**Montaigne**

ancestral estate and devote the remainder of his life to repose and study. Here he extended still further his already wide and desultory reading and indulged to the full his fondness for introspection and contemplation. He was temperamentally a skeptic, so that his method of procedure with the various questions that arose in his mind was to marshal all the evidence on all sides, to set forth all illustrations history afforded for this evidence, and then to leave the entire issue suspended in midair. He drew heavily upon the opinion and anecdote of earlier authors, but felt bound to accept nothing from them without question or challenge. Thus he stood midway between the medieval temper of mind, which blindly accepted " authority " as sufficient proof, and the modern skeptical attitude of mind, which makes a new and personal investigation of everything.

He was not interested merely in the subjects of his contemplation. He found an intense pleasure in studying himself during the several stages of this contemplation, and in recording his various reactions from the first sense impression through the entire train of thought or emotional experience thus started. He was not solving problems or completing discussions; he was rather breaking ground in them, or making " essays " at them, and finding satisfaction in the pursuit that he would never have obtained from the possession. In these " essays " of Montaigne it is first apparent why the personal essay, for all its vagaries, is a type of literature, and why in its informal prose it seems rather closely allied to poetry. In a lyric poem, for instance, some distinct impetus arouses in the poet an emotional mood with or without an accompanying reflection, and this thing peculiarly his own he attempts to convey to others through the medium of appropriate verse. The essayist is touched by a similar impulse, enters upon a course of meditation in which æsthetic pleasure is fully as important as the thought itself, and undertakes to record this unique mental experience in a form that is as pleasing as the content.

These informally attractive records of mental experiences correspond so closely to what the classical essayists had done, that one is not surprised **Montaigne's** to find that in the extensive list of Mon- **Indebtedness** taigne's reading, chief place is given to the writings of Seneca and Plutarch. Moreover these names appear almost constantly among his quotations, and receive in addition direct acknowledgments that leave no room for doubt. In the twenty-fifth essay of the first book there appears a statement that Florio has translated thus:

"I have not dealt or had commerce with any excellent booke, except Plutarke or Seneca, from whom (as the Danaides) I draw my water, uncessantly filling, and as fast emptying."

Two essays of the second book analyze and praise the writings of these two at considerable length. The first, Essay 10 ("Of Books") indicates Mon- **His Acknowl-** taigne's preference for the works al- **edgments** ready mentioned,—Plutarch's *Moralia* and Seneca's *Moral Epistles*. Essay 32 is entitled "A Defence of Seneca and Plutarke," and begins with this sentence:

"The familiarity I have with these two men, and the ayd they affoord me in my olde age, and my Booke meerely framed of their spoiles, bindeth me to wed and maintaine their honour."

The composition and publication of Montaigne's *Essays*

extended over the last twenty years of his life. Books I and II were printed in 1580, and reprinted for the fourth time, with numerous additions and an entirely new third book, in 1588. A posthumous edition in 1595 contained no new essays, but many revisions of the earlier ones. These frequent revisions were not so much recasting of the thought to secure better organization, but rather the insertion of new material as it occurred to the author,—and often at points where it hardly seems to fit. For organization and logical sequence did not greatly concern Montaigne; he certainly did not construct his essays with these in view. His method may better be described as that of "association of ideas," which means that each thought or image suggests a circle of other thoughts and images somehow related to this in our experiences. Something from this circle becomes the next center of our immediate interest, arouses in our mind a new circle of associations within which a new center is found, and so on. In Montaigne's use of this process the general subject of discussion is rarely lost sight of entirely, and is usually recalled to the reader at the end. An extreme example is his essay "Of Coaches" (Book III, No. 6). Mr. Arthur Tilley has analyzed its contents as follows:[1]

**His Methods**

"It is obvious, he begins, that great writers are wont to give several reasons for things besides the one which they believe to be the true one. For instance, what is the reason for blessing people when they sneeze? What is the cause of sea-sickness? He believes he has read in Plutarch that it is due to fear.

**An Essay in Outline**

[1] *The Literature of the French Renaissance*, II, pp. 172-3. Also printed in *Macmillan's Magazine*, 1890.

This he doubts from his own experience, for though he is often sea-sick, he is never in any fear at sea. Here follows a digression on the nature of fear. Riding in a coach or litter, especially a coach, affects him in the same way as being on board ship. Marc Antony was the first Roman to drive lions in a coach, and Elagabalus drove even stranger teams. The mention of these inventions suggests another observation, namely, that excessive expenditure shows weakness in a monarch. This leads to a somewhat long discussion on the difference between extravagance and true liberality in princes, followed by an account of the Roman Amphitheater, chiefly taken from the Seventh Eclogue of Calpurnius. Compared with the ancient world, our modern world shows signs of decrepitude and exhaustion. But a new and infant world, in no way inferior to ours in magnificence, has been discovered. This leads to a most eloquent description of the conquest of Peru and Mexico, full of sympathy for the conquered, and of indignation at the cruelty of the conquerors. *Retombons à nos coches.* In Peru they do not use coaches, but litters. The last king of Peru was being carried in a litter when he was captured in battle."

Such a discussion as this, on the subject of "Coaches," suggests at once the uncertain connection between Montaigne's material and his titles. Many of them, indeed, give little or no indication of what he is actually to treat of, but the majority will be found dependable enough. A brief consideration of these in any good edition will reveal most of the favorite topics to which, in one form or another, personal essays have kept returning from Montaigne's time to our own. Various of these had already been anticipated by Cicero, Seneca, and Plutarch.

**Titles of the Essays**

The length of Montaigne's essays varies greatly. In the main, his early productions are the shorter ones, some of them being little more than historical anecdotes slightly moralized. He was always fond of such anecdotes and had such an abundant supply that he never seemed to lack several apt and striking illustrations to give concreteness to his discussion. Almost as frequent were his quotations, drawn from a wide variety of authors, and adding further zest to his own utterances. He was never a stylist, as he frequently protested, but his manner of expression had all the naturalness, flexibility, and vivacity of the skilled conversationalist. He had a large vocabulary rich in colloquialisms, was a genius at metaphor, and dispensed with the cumbersome machinery of connectives as a rapid talker would.

Details of Style

Montaigne's essays in their original form were well known in England by 1600, and probably a dozen men were at work putting them into English. Only one complete translation was printed, that of John Florio in 1603, which has remained the standard ever since. More important still was the considerable number of imitations in English form that began at this time, definitely ushering the personal essay into being in England, as a form of literary prose. Only one English essayist has survived from this period, however, and he can scarcely be regarded as a disciple of Montaigne in any respect, unless it is that he too was prompted to put the contents of his commonplace books into print and call them "Essays."

Montaigne in England

The *Essays* of Francis Bacon appeared, like those of Montaigne, in several editions, each considerably revised and augmented. The first of these was published six years before Florio's Montaigne, but there is every reason to suppose that Bacon was well acquainted with the French original before he began to write. In various instances, the same subjects are treated by both authors, and there is frequent similarity in the opinions they express. Both draw upon a common fund of anecdote and quotation, so that resemblance is to be expected in such matters. Beyond this, however, their method of treatment is as distinct as can be. While it is clear that Bacon constantly speaks from experience, his interest is not in himself but in the results of his observations. These results take the form of clear-cut theories and convictions, not interesting uncertainties; and are organized into logically compact treatises which move irresistibly from beginning to conclusion. The sentences are crisp and often antithetic, and epigrams are so frequent that much of our proverbial wisdom of today is mere borrowing from Bacon's *Essays*. How often have we heard some of these:

"Prosperity is the blessing of the Old Testament; adversity is the blessing of the New."

"He that hath wife and children hath given hostages to fortune."

"A civil war indeed is like the heat of a fever, but a foreign war is like the heat of exercise, and serveth to keep the body in health."

"Virtue is like a rich stone, best plain set."

"Some books are to be tasted, others to be swallowed, and some few to be chewed and digested."

"Reading maketh a full man; conference a ready man; and writing an exact man."

The influence of Bacon did not lean much in the direction of the distinctly personal essay. Neither did that of such other English essayists as came to prominence during the course of the seventeenth century: Ben Jonson the jottings of whose *Timber* occasionally take first-class eassay form; Thomas Dekker, anticipating in the chapters of his satirical treatises the social satire of later periodicals; Abraham Cowley, in his *Discourses;* and Dryden and Sir William Temple, forerunners of the formal critical essayists of the nineteenth century.

**Other Seventeenth-Century Essayists**

The personal essay awaited the rise of English periodical literature, in the reign of Queen Anne, in order to assume its proper place before the public. With the appearance of the *Tatler* in 1709 and the *Spectator* in 1711, a new type of essayist came to light, a personage but not a person, a mere lay-figure radiating the genius of Steele, the wit of Pope, or the sympathy of Addison, and yet revealed to the reading public as one distinct, consistent, and thoroughly human individual. Resting upon this mysterious individual was the necessity, undreamed of by Montaigne, of completing one unit of literary production in every twenty-four or forty-eight hours, in a form that would please and attract a large and miscellaneous audience. But the periodical essay was built upon the foundations laid by Montaigne, while various contemporary literary fashions affected its superstructure.

**"Tatler" and "Spectator"**

The half century following the Stuart Restoration in England—urban, scientific, material-minded, and suspicious of emotional indulgence—was emphatically a *prose* period. The essay that developed was probably the least prosaic of its prose forms, and considerably less so than much of its so-called poetry. Among the prose forms there are several that deserve close scrutiny

**A Period of Prose**

for the effect they had in making the periodical essay the flexible and uniformly effective medium it soon became. All the forms of fiction then employed have a significance here. The moral tale, sometimes with a local setting, sometimes with a large display of supposed Orientalism, was then much in vogue, and was frequently taken over bodily in the periodical essays. The equally popular realistic tales came to be used more and more in essays during the century, but from the first may be supposed to have had no little influence in matters of technique They were closely connected with comedy, and certain of their characters were almost sure to be treated satirically and depicted as types,—that is, as individual representatives of larger groups of people sharing their weaknesses. Detailed satire of social customs and conditions was likely to be involved in these tales, for even when the scene was foreign, it was an easy implication that such things happened nearer home. Still more important for the essay was the skill these story-tellers displayed in massing their details for effect; their directness, their concreteness, and above all their simplicity.

**Contributing Forms— Tales**

From the long prose romances had descended two popular and realistic forms then much in use to satirize individuals as well as society in general. These were the *memoir* and the *roman à clef*. The first purported to be actual biography, and wandered as far as it pleased—or dared—into the field of satire and romancing. The second elaborated a medley of fact and fiction with various scandalous details of the day, 'and located it in some imaginary kingdom where people bore the stock names of the romances or were designated chiefly by

**Memoirs and Key-Novels**

consonants and dashes ("Lady M——h" or the "Duchess of C——s"). Eighteenth-century essays delighted in mysteries of identification, and no doubt secured a large part of their popularity through this tantalizing, half-veiled personal gossip. One need only note the number of times the *Spectator* pretends to be addressed by men and women who assume that they have been attacked. Satire of conditions in all strata of society made up the very fiber of these pseudo-romances, and passed easily from them to the essays. Characterization, developed in careful detail, passed over in the same manner, as did the employment of conversation and correspondence as a means of portraying individuality.

The prose forms just mentioned were all more or less under the influence of satirical comedy, or "comedy of manners," which was the most distinctive literary expression of the day. Congreve, Wycherley, Vanbrugh, finally Steele himself, all following the lead of Molière in France, had made attractive on the English stage the most biting of satire directed at the very leaders of society. The impulse from this reached the essay, directly as well as indirectly, and made itself felt in the growing tendency to present type characters for satire, many of them with appropriate names; in a recognition of the gain in reality that came from presenting these characters in action and conversation, as Goldsmith does his Beau Tibbs; in a finer subtlety of incidental and apparently unconscious criticism, such as marks the work of Addison; even in the use of familiar stage devices, such as the pet phrases that characters in the essays are constantly using.[1]

**Comedies of Manners**

[1] Cf. the favorite expressions of Beau Tibbs: "Let it go no farther!"—"A great secret!"

Character-satire had become familiar also through the "character-writings" of the period. These were analyses of familiar type characters,—
**Characters and Correspondence**
the lover, the miser, the braggart soldier, and the like,—and usually gave little suggestion of individuality. They prepared the way for the minute dissections of motives and impulses sometimes found in the essay. Correspondence, in its various forms, continued in close relationship with these personal essays. The romances and their kin, as we have seen, used quoted letters as a further means of advancing their stories and revealing character. Steele and Addison and all their following worked this method to exhaustion. From the time of the Greek satirist Lucian (125-200 A.D.), "imaginary letters" had been a safe way of satirizing one's neighbors, and a certain evil-minded Tom Brown was filling London with such things in Addison's time. Naturally some of this found its way to the periodicals. Indeed the periodical essay itself was only the printed extension of a sort of semi-public correspondence,—the gossipy "news-letters" sent out in manifold by professional scribes to subscribers in the country at every trip of the mail-coach. Little of the intimate and racy tone of these documents was lost when quill pens gave way to printing presses.

Another tradition from Lucian reached an importance at this time that cannot be ignored. This was a method of satire still in practice today and conveniently designated as the device of
**The Detached Observer**
"the detached observer." With Lucian this observer had been Charon, who ferried the souls of the dead across the Styx to Hades, and made observations of his prospective

patrons. The *Visions* of the Spanish satirist Quevedo, early in the seventeenth century, represented the author as variously conducted on a mad round of observation. Le Sage, only two years before the *Tatler*, published in France his *Diable Boiteux*, in which a little demon on crutches transports the author over the house-tops and permits him to see all that is passing below. This was promptly adopted by all of Europe, the English version taking the title, *The Devil on Two Sticks*. From omniscient observers like these it was easy enough to pass to such creations as the "Tatler," "Spectator," "Rambler," or "Connoisseur," or the more naïve creatures from foreign lands, like Montesquieu's "Persian" in France or Goldsmith's "Chinese Official" in England. Addison's "Spectator" was perhaps more clearly individualized than any other of these, preserving his curtain of mystery to the end, yet constantly revealed to us in his shyness, his silence, and his penetrating observation. He is the best instance available of impersonality made personal, and his offspring of today—Mr. Dooley and Hashimura Togo, for example—appear commonplace beside him.

It is not far amiss to regard the periodical essay of Steele and Addison as a resultant of all these forces: the familiar, rambling chat of Montaigne, the more formal and serious dicta of Bacon and Dryden, fiction in its several forms, comedy of manners, character-writing, correspondence, and *The Devil on Two Sticks*. Only on such an assumption does its infinite variety become not merely possible, but necessary. The public was responding to such things as these; all resources were necessary for authors who would hold the readers of London six times a week. Consequently the essayists adopted freely all the methods and devices that promised to serve their turn, and managed somehow to preserve a uniformity of spirit and point of view throughout.

It is impossible to generalize far regarding the *Tatler* and *Spectator* essays, particularly the latter. Neither is it possible to judge their comprehensiveness from any book of selections, made up largely of "Sir Roger de Coverley" papers. While the bulk of their material is social satire, concerned with England in all its possible phases, there are also to be found worthy specimens of philosophical discussion, criticism of music and letters, moral narrative and historical anecdote, running commentary on stage performances, and occasional dabblings in science. The current history and political controversy so prominent in the *Tatler* were judiciously omitted from the *Spectator*, and subsequent essayists did not restore them.

Contents

Addison has set down his principles of organization, in the *Spectator* for September 5, 1712. They seem to conform to his own practice and that of his successors:

Organization

"Among my daily Papers which I bestow on the Publick, there are some which are written with Regularity and Method, and others that run out into the Wilderness of those Compositions which go by the Name of *Essays*. As for the first, I have the whole Scheme of the Discourse in my Mind before I set Pen to Paper. In the other Kind of Writing, it is sufficient that I have several Thoughts on a Subject, without troubling myself to range them in such Order, that they may seem to grow out of one another, and be disposed under the proper Heads. *Seneca* and *Montaigne* are Patterns for Writing in this last Kind, as *Tully* and

*Aristotle* excel in the other. When I read an Author of Genius who writes without Method, I fancy myself in a Wood that abounds with a great many noble Objects, rising among one another in the greatest Confusion and Disorder. When I read a methodical discourse, I am in a regular Plantation, and can place myself in its several Centers, so as to take a View of all the Lines and Walks that are struck from them. You may ramble in the one a whole Day together, and every Moment discover something or other that is new to you; but when you have done you will have but a confused imperfect Notion of the Place: In the other, your Eye commands the whole Prospect, and gives you such an Idea of it as is not easily worn out of the Memory.

"Irregularity and Want of Method are only supportable in Men of great Learning or Genius, who are often too full to be exact, and therefore chuse to throw down their Pearls in Heaps before the Reader, rather than be at the Pains of stringing them."

Through the entire eighteenth century the periodical essay retained the popularity Steele and Addison had given it, and deviated little from the subjects and methods they had tried and found good. Of the vast number of such publications, a representative list was collected and reprinted by Alexander Chalmers in 1803 under the title of *The British Essayists*. In his volumes appear also:

**Eighteenth-Century Imitators**

| The Guardian | 1713 | Steele et al. |
|---|---|---|
| The Rambler | 1750-52 | Samuel Johnson |
| The Adventurer | 1752-54 | Dr. John Hawkesworth |
| The World | 1753-56 | Edward Moore et al. |
| The Connoisseur | 1754-56 | George Colman and Bonnel Thornton |

| | | |
|---|---|---|
| *The Idler | 1758-60 | Samuel Johnson |
| | (published in *Universal Chronicle*) |
| The Mirror | 1779-80 | A group of Edinburgh wits |
| The Lounger | 1785-87 | Edinburgh wits |
| The Looker-On | 1792-93 | William Roberts |

Of the product of the mid-eighteenth century, the most distinctive work is that of Dr. Samuel Johnson, and of Oliver Goldsmith, whose two series, *The Bee* (1759) and *The Citizen of the World* (1760), Dr. Chalmers saw fit to omit from his collection. If Dr. Johnson had any inclination to catch and hold the attention of the man of the streets and the lady of the drawing-room, he was sadly lacking in the adroitness, the grace, and the brilliancy requisite for such an effort. His mind gravitated to serious subjects in the fields of ethics and literary criticism, his social satire was over-blunt, and his wit was slow and ponderous. The good Doctor's conversation, as we judge from Boswell's records, was vigorous and entertaining, but it is only occasionally that he imparts the virility and point of his conversational style to his essays. Certain mannerisms in his writing stand out all too prominently,—his vague, abstract introductions to what is essentially concrete subject-matter, his lexicographer's vocabulary, and his peculiar balanced sentences, almost rhythmical in the regularity with which one clause answers to the other:

"The consciousness of my own abilities roused me from depression, and long familiarity with my subject enabled me to discourse with ease and volubility; but however I might please myself, I found very little added by my demonstrations to the satisfaction of the company; and my antagonist, who knew the laws of conversation too well to detain their attention long upon an

*Doctor Johnson*

unpleasing topic, after he had commended my acuteness and comprehension, dismissed the controversy, and resigned me to my former insignificance and perplexity."[1]

Goldsmith's sprightliness is in delightful contrast to the gravity of his friend and associate. He brought to his essays the sentiment and humor of a Celtic temperament, the imagination of a poet, and a power of vivid and concrete creation that was later to give him success in comedy and the novel. He alone, in his Beau Tibbs and "The Man in Black," produced anything worthy to compare with the Sir Roger de Coverley group developed by Steele and Addison. He presents these characters as the trained dramatist might, in action and conversation, amid a carefully constructed stage-setting, and makes them actually live and breathe before our eyes. He is fond of pathetic situations as well as comic, and all his satire is tempered with sympathy.

Goldsmith

The Romantic Revival, at the end of the eighteenth and beginning of the nineteenth century, affected the personal essay as it did practically every other literary form. In the first place, it placed a new value upon the personal element itself. The hundred years of periodical essay-writing just considered serve in a way to reveal personalities, but not entirely. As already noted, Tatler, Spectator, or Guardian is never really Dick Steele or Joseph Addison. He may be either of them in a given instance, or perhaps Pope or Arbuthnot. He is rather a shadowy embodiment of honest and well-balanced public opinion,

Effects of the Romantic Revival— Personality

[1] "The Scholar's Complaint of His Bashfulness," *The Rambler*, No. 57.

and his utterances win approval not because they are individual things, but because they conform so well to the ultimate opinion of the cultured class, when this has had time to take stock of itself. Goldsmith's sentimental concern with poverty and the lower classes anticipates later originality of ideas, but it was safeguarded by the approval of a rapidly-growing faction of humanitarians. It remained for Lamb to interest people in thought and expression because it was *his own*.

The favorite subjects of the romanticists found their way into the personal essays of this period. Lamb gave medievalism a new application in his fondness for the old folio editions of Elizabethan and still earlier writers.

**Romantic Subjects**

Hazlitt and he together gave utterance to the new appreciative and impressionistic sort of criticism. Hazlitt went farther and insisted on the individual's independence of the crowd and the superior delights of the great out-of-doors:

"Give me the clear blue sky over my head, and the green turf beneath my feet, a winding road before me, and a three hours' march to dinner—and then to thinking! It is hard if I cannot start some game on these lone heaths. I laugh, I run, I leap, I sing for joy. From the point of yonder rolling cloud, I plunge into my past being, and revel there, as the sun-burnt Indian plunges headlong into the wave that wafts him to his native shore." [1]

Leigh Hunt, with his cockney affiliations, kept more affection for the town than for the country, but contemplated it in minute detail with a poetic appreciation of its memories and delights akin to Walter Scott's reverence for the border country. De Quincey and

[1] "On Going a Journey."

Coleridge dreamed in their essays as in all their other writings; one wandered where his abundant fancies took him, and the other led his public groping through the mazes of his speculation.

There is much of profit and delight in the writings of all this group, but Charles Lamb in particular has found his way to the hearts of English-speaking people everywhere. Poor, plodding, stammering, much-afflicted Elia, with his infinite affection and infinite jest in the very shadow of a madhouse, he may have failed in drama and may be a poet of one poem, but he is a prince among personal essayists. His personal experience and impressions are not merely transmitted to his readers. They are infused and colored with the enthusiasm of his emotions and the kaleidoscopic lights of his fancy until we recognize the commonplace material out of which they are made only to marvel that the commonplace can be given such a charm and fascination. We remember who and what Bridget Elia was,—the tragedy that darkened her life and the frequent lapses of mind that saddened her relations with her brother,— we compare this with the reminiscences in such an essay as " Old China," and we begin to understand the power of Lamb's art.

*Personality in Lamb*

Much of the secret of Lamb's charm lies in his whimsicality. He possessed to a high degree the faculty of the old "metaphysical poets" whom he loved, the knack of catching a flash of resemblance between things far remote. A blackened chimney-sweep parts his lips in a smile, and Lamb is struck by the contrast to the "white and shining ossifications" thus displayed. "It is," he thinks, "as when

*His Whimsicality*

a sable cloud
Turns forth her silver lining on the night."

The roasting pig is just done to a turn on the spit—" To see the extreme sensibility of that tender age, he hath wept out his pretty eyes—radiant jellies—shooting stars———." His method of construction, which usually proceeds by association of ideas, does so willfully, and fairly flaunts its illogical sequence in your face. "And now," he remarks at the end of "Old China," after pages of reminiscent conversation between himself and Bridget, " do just look at that merry little Chinese waiter holding an umbrella, big enough for a bed-tester, over the head of that pretty insipid half-Madonnaish chit of a lady in that very blue summer house." His tantalizing way of dealing with real people is the height of whimsicality, and reaches its climax in " Christ's Hospital Five and Thirty Years Ago," where Elia takes issue with the statements his old school-fellow, Charles Lamb, had made in a previous essay.

Lamb's style is in keeping with the operations of his thought. His essays are packed full of scraps of quotations, many of them from Elizabethan authors of whom he had almost exclusive knowledge in his time. His sentences constantly take unexpected turns or run off into parentheses, and many of them never really end at all. But sentences in conversation may do just such things. His favorite mark of punctuation is a dash; and next to that, perhaps, comes the exclamation point, for he is much given to emotional outbursts. His vocabulary is full of surprises. He had a rich store of expressions from his old authors, and enjoyed introducing them unexpectedly to startle and perhaps to puzzle the reader. He had his tricks and we recognize them all too well.

**His Style**

But our own regard for him is not because of such vagaries, but in spite of them.

In addition to this closely-associated group of more or less romantic essayists—Hazlitt, Lamb, Hunt, and De Quincey—there are a few others who belong to this revival of the familiar essay in the early part of the nineteenth century. Dickens and Thackeray, we may recall, wrote delightfully in this form. Washington Irving's *Sketch Book* is primarily a book of personal essays, though it begins as a series of travel sketches, and contains a number of short stories in a very slight essay framework. The Victorian period of literature, however, is notable for the maturity of the longer and more formal type of expository essay, in which content is of first importance, clearness and polish of style are secondary, and personality appears chiefly in the opinions presented or the distinctive features of style. The familiar conversational tone is gone, and carefully knit organization has replaced the pleasant ramblings far afield and back again.

The Victorian Essay

Essays of this more formal sort had been appearing since the development of English prose style, but the new life that came to English "reviews" and other magazines with the establishment of the *Edinburgh Review* in 1803 greatly encouraged such compositions. They were printed as book-reviews, but in reality were treatises on the same subject or in some way connected with the same subject treated in the book whose publication served to justify their own appearance. Thus Macaulay's *Essay on Milton*, with its familiar discussion of the Puritans and comparison of Milton's art with that of Dante, was apparently prompted by a current edition of the Latin

The Reviews

*Treatise of Christian Doctrine.* As time went on, and the reading public formed an unmistakable liking for such popularizing of knowledge, these expository essays began to lose even their semblance of book-reviews, though there is an obvious advantage in approaching a semi-technical discussion through the "lead" of some current book or event.

In the vast field of the Victorian expository essay are represented the usual subjects of popular interest,—politics, religion, history, biography, and literary criticism; likewise, a long and familiar list of distinguished literary men,—Macaulay, John Wilson, Carlyle, Matthew Arnold, Ruskin, Huxley, Pater, and John Stuart Mill. It·is impossible to estimate the service of these journalistic scholars in widening the boundaries of English thought and raising the standards of English culture. Their work was not entirely insular. It found worthy models across the Channel, both in Germany and in France; and it was widely circulated and deeply appreciated among American readers. Carlyle was recognized more promptly in New England than at home, Arnold made an American lecture tour, and Emerson and Lowell in return made a distinct impression upon English thought.

**Victorian Essayists**

In recent years the number of reviews and kindred periodicals has continued to increase, and there is apparently an unlimited supply of this scholarly literature to fill their pages. Modern specialization in thought has affected the character of this supply to some extent, limiting the field of each particular essayist and rendering the entire output somewhat more academic. An essayist in literary criticism,

**Critical Essayists of Today**

for example, is likely to occupy a post at some university, and probably discusses no other subject, unless it be the closely connected one of biography. There has been no lack of capable representatives, however, in this or other fields, as is indicated by such names as John and Henry Morley, Frederic Harrison, Leslie Stephen, Edmund Gosse, A. C. Bradley, and Sir Sidney Lee in Great Britain, and in America George E. Woodberry, Thomas Lounsbury, and Brander Matthews.

Along with this continuance of interest in the more formal essay, there has come a marked revival of essay-writing in the familiar, personal manner.

Recent Personal Essayists— Stevenson

The fact that this is almost exactly coincident with the present renaissance of poetry may tend to emphasize the analogy pointed out earlier between personal essay and lyric. At any rate more people are writing bright, pithy, thoroughly readable familiar essays today than in any previous generation, except perhaps that of the romantic poets. The activity began perhaps with Robert Louis Stevenson, whose wide interest in people, susceptibility to impressions, and genial optimism equipped him in an unusual degree to serve the world in this way. His essays, written at irregular intervals and with no very consistent purpose, are most of them accessible in the collection *Virginibus Puerisque* (1881), in *Underwoods* (1887), and in *Memories and Portraits* (1887). His travel papers, *An Inland Voyage* and *Travels with a Donkey*, may be well regarded as only extended personal essays, and exercise the same charm upon us. Any attempt at the analysis of this charm is likely to arrive at nothing better than the one word " personality," and that the personality of Stevenson. As truly as did Lamb and Hazlitt, who were his models, he reveals himself to his readers,—the subtlety of his feeling, the delicacy and whimsicality of his imagination, the buoyancy of his spirit,—and this with a grasp of colloquial phrasing in all its possibilities that few men have acquired.

Criticism of contemporaries in literature is subject to constant modification; there is much uncertainty in merely compiling a list of representative names. Certainly there can be no quarrel with the following: Augustine Birrell, Austin Dobson, A. C. Benson, E. V. Lucas, G. K. Chesterton, John Galsworthy, Hilaire Belloc. If anyone complains that no one of these is an American, it is possible to add with good grace John Burroughs, whose familiar papers about nature easily admit him to the ranks; Charles Dudley Warner and Donald Grant Mitchell, of a somewhat older school; and of the present day Stephen Leacock, the Canadian college professor, and Simeon Strunsky and James Huneker, who are doing so much to find the art and beauty in the sordid details of New York City.

**Contemporaries**

Among the English group, certain modern tendencies are represented clearly enough to be apparent to even the casual reader. They all keep hold rather reverently upon the traditions of Lamb, Hazlitt, and Hunt, particularly Lucas, who has gained fresh inspiration as Lamb's editor and biographer, and Dobson, who has apparently re-created the eighteenth century in his own imagination. They appear, however, to be men of richer emotional possibilities, and to have taken greater pains to convey to their readers all the finer shades of feeling that have entered into their experience. The relation of initial impulse to the mood and reflection it produces is

**Present Tendencies**

often so unique and individual that the essay may properly be classed as impressionistic. The imagination is given the freest possible play, and while the writers rarely attempt the whimsicality of Lamb, they embroider and enrich their utterance with suggestion and implication and allusion until it challenges and gratifies the most alert and appreciative reader. Graceful subtlety has thus become the ideal of the personal essayist, just as an ability to read between the lines, a sensitiveness to harmony and over-tones, is a requisite in his audience. Beauty has entered into the essay as never before. Nature essays revel in the beauty of glade and hill; reactionary urbanites, apostles of Leigh Hunt, find beauty in the crowded ways of some metropolis; all are on the alert to catch a glimpse of it, and to portray it again, heightened and idealized until it glows with warmth and color. The old fondness for satire has not been lost; the old assumption of familiar conversation has not disappeared. But the personal essay is refined and refined again until it is a piece of genuine artistry.

### Technique of the Personal Essay

The difficulty of the personal essay lies in its very familiarity and rambling construction. It is the difficulty of lifting such things above the hopelessly commonplace, of infusing into them a personality that is clearly worth the knowing, an impression or an idea that sparkles with novelty or originality, a grace of expression such as belongs to an artist in words. The problem of the personal essay for the critic lies not on the mechanical side, but on that of appreciation of its inner values.

**Difficulty of the Type**

As already indicated, the conception of such an essay is akin to that of a lyric poem. Something—an incident, a sentence in a book, a bit of conversation—awakens a train of thought or flashes into the author's mind a point of view capable of extended analysis. In almost every case this merely intellectual operation involves the exercise of feeling and imagination, sometimes in advance of the thought, sometimes attendant upon it. Lamb's " Old China " is supposed to grow out of a conversation with Bridget over the odd figures on a china plate, and her longing for the good old times when they could rarely afford to buy such things. A well-known essay of Hazlitt describes the discussion that followed a question by B—— as to what character from the past one would most wish to have seen. Both Lamb and Hazlitt approach the essays thus initiated with something of a lyric mood,—tender reminiscence in the one case not unlike that in "Old Familiar Faces"; suggestions of reverence and love mingled with personal satire in the other. Of course, as is true in poetry, these external impulses may be largely imaginary without weakening the effect, provided the author's creative power is convincing enough.

*Emotional Impulse*

The prose essay, in its development, continues to resemble the lyric in that it employs some combination of these three essential elements: portrayal of the initial impulse, with more or less imaginative detail; presentation of an idea or a train of related thoughts aroused by this impulse; emphasis upon the emotional mood awakened. These appear in varying order and proportions, or are so involved with each other as almost to defy analysis. Most of the " Sir Roger " papers,

*Essential Elements*

Goldsmith's presentation of Beau Tibbs, and all essays that are strongly dramatic or of the narrative type, give most of their space to the external situation, coloring this with imagination and emotion. Since Lamb the emotional feature of essays has grown in importance. There are more passages of rhapsodizing, more exclamation points, as well as a more thorough infusion of all details and passages with the mood in which the author views them The intellectual side of the essay has been always with us, and is the element that associates the familiar essay most closely with the formal or expository essay.

Traditionally the line of thought in an essay is critical and satirical, aiming to bring the weakness of certain existing customs or conditions into ridicule by putting them in comparison with the norm or accepted ideal of human conduct. Sometimes this is made more effective by instituting comparison not with accepted standards but with those of some presumably low stage of civilization, and finding existing conditions still absurdly defective. Thus the naïve comments of Goldsmith's Chinese Official are all the more severe a satire on eighteenth-century England. In most cases, particularly in the later stages of essay-writing, the satire is not an open and organized arraignment of society at all, but is brought out by a series of subtle hints or touches of innuendo, so that it is the cumulative effect that counts.

Satire

In its inner construction the personal essay follows one of two methods or falls somewhere in between them. It may be either a logical organism, as the expository essay usually is, and built upon a skeleton outline that develops the thought naturally and concisely; or a rambling series of paragraphs related as the steps in conversation or the units of thought in an unrestrained mind are, by mere association of ideas. We have all had the experience of pausing in the midst of a wandering conversation or stopping to take stock of our musings when supposed to be attending to a sermon or lecture, and trying to trace the mental processes by which we passed from a fairly definite starting point to the most recent subject of interest. Naturally the writer who can most nearly approximate such a process should be most successful in creating the illusion of conversation.

**Methods of Construction**

This is stating the matter a bit strongly, for in actual conversation educated people are not forever dashing off at tangents, and arriving, after a half-hour or so of such exercise, at a point not even visible from their first position. The first interesting topic they hit upon becomes a sort of center for their wanderings, the open place in the forest to which they return again and again to get their bearings anew before they adventure into untried and perhaps denser thickets. This same analogy will serve for the structural plan of the majority of familiar essays. Wherever their speculation turns, the unifying idea is never far away, and is constantly reiterated so that it directs and dominates the whole.

**A Unifying Idea**

### Subjects for Study

1. The social background of the early periodical essays.
2. Treatment of one of the following topics in the *Spectator:* theaters; fashions; clubs and coffee-houses; women; the Orient; foreigners; vice; nature; philosophical theories; literary criticism.
3. Comparison of methods of characterization in: (a) char-

acter-writings; (b) *Spectator* papers; (c) comedies of Goldsmith and Sheridan; (d) eighteenth-century novel.
4. Relation of current letter-writing to the *Spectator* essays; to the early novel.
5. Relation of Lamb's style to that of Laurence Sterne and his imitators.
6. Comparison of Stevenson the essayist and Stevenson the writer of fiction.
7. The device of the "detached observer" in the popular literature of today.
8. Carlyle as a "personal" essayist.
9. Living English essayists.
10. Preparation of a personal essay based on actual experience or environment.

## Collections

*A Century of English Essays.* Chosen by Ernest Rhys and Lloyd Vaughan. Everyman's Library: Dutton & Co. Cloth, 40 cents.

An anthology ranging from Caxton to Stevenson and the writers of our own time. A rich selection with a slight introduction.

*Selected English Essays.* Chosen and arranged by W. Peacock. World's Classics: Oxford University Press. Cloth, 35 cents.

A convenient and comprehensive selection, except for recent writers. No introduction.

*A Book of English Essays, 1600-1900.* Chosen by S. V. Makower and B. H. Blackwell. World's Classics: Oxford University Press. Cloth, 35 cents. Not unlike Mr. Peacock's collection.

*Selected Essays.* Edited by Claude M. Fuess. Riverside Literature Series: Houghton Mifflin Co. Paper, 30 cents; cloth, 40 cents.

*The English Familiar Essay.* Representative Texts, edited by W. F. Bryan and R. S. Crane. Ginn & Co. Cloth, $1.25.

A limited and somewhat conventional selection of essays from Bacon to Stevenson. Excellent historical and critical introduction and good bibliography.

*English Essays.* Ed. by W. C. Bronson. Holt & Co. Cloth, $1.25.

Representing about twenty-five English writers from Bacon to Stevenson. Notes, but no introduction.

## 146 THE TYPICAL FORMS OF ENGLISH LITERATURE

*The Great English Essayists.* Edited by W. J. and C W. Dawson. The Reader's Library: Harper & Bros. Cloth, $1.00.

Essays preceded by a sketch, "The Genesis of the Essay," and grouped as: Classic Essay, Letter Essay, Short-Story Essay, Biographical and Critical Essay, Impassioned Prose, and Familiar Essay.

*English Essays.* Edited by J. H. Lobban. Warwick Library: Scribner's Sons. Cloth, $1.00.

A fairly full collection, chiefly from the eighteenth century, with critical introduction.

*The British Essayists.* Edited by Alexander Chalmers. 45 vols. First edition in 1803; several times reprinted.

*The Gleaner: a Series of Periodical Essays.* Edited by Nathan Drake. 1811.

These two are the original collections of the periodical essays of the eighteenth century. They are out of print, but have not been superseded.

*The Oxford Book of American Essays.* Chosen by Brander Matthews. Oxford University Press, American Branch. Cloth, $1.25.

A satisfying collection of miscellaneous American essays, covering the entire period of our literature.

*Modern Essays.* Selected and edited by Berdan, Schultz, and Joyce. Macmillan Co. Cloth, $1.25.

Thirty-three essays by modern authors in England and America. About half are of the personal or familiar type.

*Critical Discussions*[1]

I

Dr. Nathan Drake, *Essays Biographical, Critical, and Historical,* illustrative of the *Tatler, Spectator,* and *Guardian.* 3 vols. 1805.

Dr. Drake, *Essays Biographical, Critical, and Historical,* illustrative of the *Rambler, Adventurer,* and *Idler.* 2 vols. 1809-10.

William Hazlitt, *On the English Comic Writers.* 1819.

William M. Thackeray, *The English Humorists of the Eighteenth Century.* 1851.

II

Orlo Williams, *The Essay (The Art and Craft of Letters).* New York (Doran & Co.)

[1] See page 36, note.

Hugh Walker, *The English Essay and Essayists* (*Channels of English Literature*). New York (Dutton & Co.), 1915.

C. T. Winchester, *A Group of English Essayists of the Early Nineteenth Century*. New York (Macmillan), 1910.

Laura J. Wylie, "The English Essay," in *Social Studies in English Literature*. Boston and New York (Houghton Mifflin Co.), 1916.

# VI

# THE NOVEL

*History*

Beginnings

THE English novel has been a comparatively late type to develop, but it more than makes up for this fact by its long and complicated lineage and the immense productivity and popularity it has had in the past two centuries. Occasional specimens of what critics later accepted as novels appeared in the midst of Elizabethan activity, and various approximations of the type—most of them foreign borrowings—were produced in the seventeenth century, particularly toward the close of it; but the genuine English novel belongs to the eighteenth century, beginning before the efforts of Richardson and thoroughly establishing itself before the time of Walter Scott. Only the latest of such stories were spoken of as "novels" in their own day. This word came into the language with the short Italian tales (*novelle*) of the sixteenth and seventeenth centuries, and had its application limited to such stories for a long time. "History" was the more usual word for the more comprehensive story, "memoir" was frequently employed, and "romance" served many purposes. Indeed, the student of the novel who is tempted to search a bit among early specimens is likely to be sadly confused by the terminology he finds there.

Since Scott we have not been particular about distinguishing novels from romances, and even when we set apart a story as an "historical novel," it is likely to be about as true to historical fact as *Cléopâtre* or *Le Grand Cyrus*, typical romances of seventeenth-century France. Some simple distinctions, however, will not come amiss at this point in our study. The romance, we have seen, following hard upon the epic, dealt like it with great historical characters, but submerged the idea of them as instruments of fate fulfilling the destiny of nations. Instead it emphasized their martial achievements, their panorama of adventures, above all their overpowering and all-enduring passion of love. The romance had no such unity as the epic, but piled adventure upon adventure or employed one device after another to keep devoted lovers separated, and was often so constructed that whoever chose might take up the pen that fell from an exhausted hand and add a sequel of many hundred pages. The proper medium of the romance was prose. Even the Arthurian cycle, for all its splendid treatment by French poets, reached and captured the people in prose renderings like Malory's *Morte D'Arthur*.

**The Old Romances**

The middle classes of Europe found entertainment for centuries in another kind of fiction. Sometimes it was in verse, more frequently in prose. It was concerned much less with kings and princesses than with the man of the streets, the sharp-tongued housewife, or the shrewd, intriguing priest. There was much of love and lovers in its pages, but this was the love of Darby and Joan, not the "grand passion." In every sense these were stories of the "here and now," with concrete pictures of manners and customs, and a simple but effective manner of expression. The narrative

**Early Popular Fiction**

rambled at times, but in the main the stories had a distinct objective point, moved toward it with some rapidity, and then stopped—in considerably less than the hundred pages a romance would have used in merely getting under way. These were the *novelle* of Italy and Spain, providing "filling" for the polite framework of Boccaccio's *Decameron* or the *Heptameron* of Margaret of Navarre, supplying the English stage from Shakespeare to Ford with plots of thrilling intrigue, and entertaining the middle classes of all of Europe.

Somewhere between the extremes of heroic romance and popular *novella* lies the province of the novel. It prefers real people to an idealized royalty and presents them in a more or less realistic way. It aims at an organic unity of construction, and—with certain exceptions—has the merit of stopping when it is done. Still the plot of a novel is more comprehensive and the actual time involved is longer than in the *novella*. The novel is largely concerned with love,—neither the supreme devotion of romance nor the hard, cynical thing too common in *novelle*. It would be a simple matter if the novel could be explained as a mere fusion of these two older forms of prose fiction. But modifying influences have entered in to make the problem of origins considerably more difficult.

**The Province of the Novel**

In the first forty years of the eighteenth century, the various ingredients of the English novel were in the crucible. Prior to that period there are only five really significant literary productions, and one or two of lesser importance, that require consideration in tracing the growth of this form. The five great documents, all but one lying within the six-

**Sixteenth and Seventeenth Centuries**

THE NOVEL 151

teenth century, are: Thomas More's *Utopia* (1518); John Lyly's *Euphues* (1579); Sir Philip Sidney's *Arcadia*, written before 1585 and made public in 1590; Thomas Nash's *The Unfortunate Traveller, or The Life of Jack Wilton* (1594); and Bunyan's *Pilgrim's Progress* (1678). All of these were reprinted frequently, and the success of *Euphues* and *Arcadia* called out many other books written in imitation or seeking attention by making use of an already popular title.[1] Attention should be directed also to such works as Roger Boyle's *Parthenissa* (1654), representing an English attempt at the heroic romance then popular in France; Aphra Behn's *Oroonoko* (1688), sentimentalizing romance in the direction of opposition to slavery and idealization of the virtuous savage; the so-called "biography" of this same lady (1696), probably manufactured out of whole cloth; and the unique collection of "*Modern Novels*," preserved in the British Museum, and perhaps only a chance binding into twelve volumes of some forty "novels" or kindred works, originally published before 1693. Most of these last, it may be added, were translations from the French.

The account of an "ideal commonwealth" in *Utopia* was the work of a humanist scholar, in Latin, and probably was suggested by similar documents of antiquity, with a framework derived from the numerous mariners' tales of the period. It was didactic in its purpose, and accordingly deficient in plot and characters, as most of its numerous progeny have been.[2] Lyly's two volumes

More and
Lyly

[1] Cf. *Euphues his censure to Philautus*, by Robert Greene, and Thomas Lodge's *Rosalynde, Euphues golden legacie*, the latter the source of Shakespeare's *As You Like It*.
[2] See the collection of *Ideal Commonwealths* edited by Henry Morley and published in one volume by Dutton & Co.

—*Euphues the Anatomy of Wit* and its sequel *Euphues and his England*—have also little in common with the main developments of later fiction. They are rather compendia of rhetorical discussion and polite conversation, of learned commonplaces exquisitely expressed according to a conversational formula that pervaded the English court for more than ten years. There is one really interesting character—Euphues himself—surrounded by a group of conventional "types," and there is a thread of plot if one can get hold of it. But the real interest is in such polished advice as the "cooling carde for Philautus, and all fond lovers," and in long processions of similes from natural history arranged like this:

"The Sunne shineth upon the dounghil, and is not corrupted: the Diamond lyeth in the fire, and is not consumed: the Christall toucheth the Toade and is not poysoned: the birde *Trochilus* lyveth by the mouth of the Crocodile and is not spoyled: a perfect wit is never bewitched with lewdenesse, neither entised with lasciviousnesse."

**The "Arcadia" and Related Romances**

Sidney's *Arcadia* presents the most complicated problem of ancestry. It is of course a prose romance with interludes of verse, but that is not explicit enough. There were chivalric or heroic romances like those of the Round Table, where knights without fear or reproach risked everything on the chance of perilous adventures to bring fresh honors to the ladies of their hearts. There were romances of adventure, a Greek inheritance made popular once more in the long Spanish and French *Amadis de Gaula,* whose chief purpose seemed to be to send lover and lady separately through the most interminable series of thrilling experiences until they were at last, through sheer exhaustion of artifice, once more united. This sort had various possibilities. It stooped to traffic with people who were not born in the purple. It could be expanded or extended at will, and admitted the "tale within the tale," as each new arrival might insist on telling the story of his own marvelous series of adventures. There was also the pastoral romance, cultivated in Italy and Spain, with a setting of peaceful meadows, in which nobility in disguise or masquerade disported itself beside cool fountains and suffered and analyzed the pangs of disprized love Often these tales also incorporated a series of adventures, after the model of the old Greek *Daphnis and Chloe*, and there was usually a cast of supernatural actors—Pan and a satyr and a group of nymphs—and a very mysterious oracle. In all these romances there might appear at any time touches of realism or satire, only as foil at first, but looking toward the realistic and mock romances of a later day.

The English *Arcadia* is something of all these things, and is still the delight and the despair of source-hunters.

**Lines of Relationship**  It is nominally a pastoral, like the Spanish *Diana* of Montemayor, but as in the *Diana* its shepherds give place to knights and ladies, and sheep are kept at a respectful distance. It has the disguises of pastoral, with the conventional confusion of sexes and endless chain of lovers familiar to us in Shakespeare's *As You Like It*. The knights and ladies do not linger in pastoral solitudes, but pass through "hair-breadth scapes" and "moving accidents by flood and field" like the characters in Greek romances or in *Amadis de Gaula*, or like Shakespeare's own swarthy hero of romance, Othello. There is even the vein of comic realism, developed at some length in Sidney's account of his genuinely rustic shepherds.

This historical composite was written in a style fully as mannered as that of *Euphues,* but in a very different way. Graceful circumlocutions took the place of the plain unvarnished words Lyly grouped in antithesis, and nature similes gave way to a form of nature-personification, thus: "the banks of either side seeming armes of the loving earth, that fain would embrace it; and the river a wanton nymph which still would slip from it."

**Style of the "Arcadia"**

Nash's *Jack Wilton* was in part a protest against the vogue of the medieval romances, which persisted in a rude, popularized form. It took rather the form of the realistic rogue novel, already known in Spain for fifty years through the medium of *Lazarillo de Tormes* and about to win new popularity there by means of Aleman's *Guzman de Alfarache.* But Jack Wilton was not the graceless scamp of a vagabond (*picaro*) that has made these Spanish "picaresque" narratives the hard, unsympathetic things they are. He was a young page who, for all his tricks and evil practices, had good impulses and redeeming motives. Nash was not writing a mere catalogue of sharp practices. He was filling a gallery with vigorously drawn character-portraits fit for comedy, pointing morals and indulging in sentiment, involving well-known figures like the Earl of Surrey in delightfully romantic adventures, but above all he was leading the imagination of the English public back toward truth. In construction *Jack Wilton* resembles the picaresque novels, and likewise not a few romances. It is the customary series of adventures, like beads on a string, always capable of extension so long as there are more beads in the box. Sidney, we shall see, strongly influenced the *bourgeois* romancing of Richardson; Nash is the fore-

**"Jack Wilton"**

runner of Fielding, using the accepted methods but calling men back to the realities.

*Pilgrim's Progress*, while entirely allegorical in its purpose, has its chief historical value in the realistic effects it obtains from the use of simple and concrete details presented in a language that is simplicity itself. The public for which it was composed represented fairly well the audience that would read and pass upon English fiction for generations to come, and the success of Bunyan's work helped arouse these people of the middle class to the desirability of bringing the romances down to earth.

"Pilgrim's Progress"

To bring the romance down to earth: that was the mission that lay before the literary craftsmen of the early eighteenth century, and they achieved it promptly and effectively. The heroine Pamela passed from the pastoral shades of Sidney's *Arcadia* to the servants' quarters of an English country place;[1] Cyrus the Great yielded the center of the stage to Tom Jones, "a foundling." In this transposition of things the picaresque novels and the closely associated military memoirs played a large part, and continued to be popular in England throughout the century. A still larger influence, on the negative side, was that of certain avowed realistic or mock-romances, of which the best known is the Spanish *Don Quixote* (1605) which for a century had been spreading its influence over all of Europe. More important than either of these was the growing popularity of the *novelle* and the employment of them for all sorts of literary purposes. Sometimes they were expanded into stories of considerable scope, sometimes inserted as epi-

Influences Toward Realism

[1] It is a fact that the name of Richardson's Pamela was suggested to him by Sidney's *Arcadia*.

sodes in romances and memoirs; more often they were combined ingeniously to form some longer and apparently organic unit of narrative. Structurally many of these were very well contrived, and with dozens of examples of well-knit comedy available to them on the stage, English writers were able to develop rather high standards of technique in their "novels" also.

A very important factor in this whole development is the matter of character portrayal. In the history of the essay, mention was made of the fondness **Portrayal** of the seventeenth century for "char-**of Character** acters" or satirical type-studies, as displayed on the stage in Ben Jonson's comedies, and in the bookshops by volumes or collections of these much-detailed descriptions, the work of Hall, Overbury, or Butler. These "characters" were generic, but there was a corresponding vogue of "character portraits" that were specific and individual. This vogue began with the French romances of the early seventeenth century, in which analysis of characters and emotions was a stock feature. These romances were produced in and for the fashionable coteries, and soon emphasized the pastoral device of portraying real people from these circles as the heroes and heroines of their adventures. Skillfully managed, this procedure at once piqued the curiosity of the entire reading public, and the power of clever portraiture became an essential in every author's equipment. The widow of Colonel Hutchinson, for example, found such portraits necessary to the biography of her husband, and Bishop Burnet scattered them freely through his *History of His Own Time* (1724).

There were also the *romans à clef* and their nearest of kin, the "secret histories," though the latter term was used vaguely for both varieties. These realistic little romances, often packed with scandal or with novella-stuff that passed for scandal, dealt freely in character-portraits that were meant to be identified. The *roman à clef* depicted living contemporaries as denizens of Atalantis or Caromania or some other Utopian fancy; the secret history professed to lay bare the secret lives of deceased monarchs. Between them they managed to transfer all the essentials of the long-winded romances into condensed and readable narratives about very human personages with their feet upon the earth—or in the mire. They kept the psychological interest already to be found in the romances, toned down adventure and dialogue to the possibilities of everyday life, introduced numerous characters from the middle classes into their pages, and made intrigue—from the *novelle* or from actual experience—a somewhat essential feature of romantic narrative. Novelists of the eighteenth century were not to do new things; only to utilize methods already tried and to use them better.

Secret
Histories

Many of the time-honored statements about the beginning of the modern novel must be taken with considerable qualification. We are told to date it from Samuel Richardson, inventor of the type; but every feature of his technique and practically all his situations had been thoroughly tested out before his time. He did not exactly discover the female heart; he only probed it more deeply and delicately. Addison's "Sir Roger" is said to be a first study of character in action, and Goldsmith is credited with weaving such action into plot. They all contributed, as did scores of less-known craftsmen who kept presses busy and filled book-stalls to an extent th--

Rise of the
Modern
Novel

fronted by an authentic bibliography of the fiction of the century.[1] Cultivating the novel toward the highest artistic achievement was as much an obsession of the eighteenth century as cultivating the language to the height of its literary possibilities was in the Elizabethan period. The average student must be content with an outline of larger movements and tendencies.

The earliest of these tendencies may be designated as realism and sentimentalism. The former has been mentioned frequently and needs no definition.

**Realism and Sentimentalism**
As applied to the novel it may mean a more authentic delineation of character or a portrayal of everyday experiences in their most sordid actuality; it may involve a study merely of the minute details of things, or an unwholesome fondness for the unclean and the disagreeable. Sentimentalism implies primarily a self-consciousness in the exercise of the emotions, particularly the shallower ones. In the midst of an emotional experience the subject is capable of analyzing his own conflicting feelings and enjoying them as mental phenomena. Eighteenth-century sentimentalism acquired in its course certain more obvious features. Under the guidance of Laurence Sterne it indulged sensibility to the point of vagary or whimsicality, and deliberately played with the reader's patience. From the start it was eminently *bourgeois,* and while it brought forth heroes from the middle class that it understood thoroughly, it was tempted constantly toward a royalty it knew nothing about. So

[1] Cf. Charlotte E. Morgan, *The Rise of the Novel of Manners,* New York, 1911; A. Esdaile, *A List of English Tales and Prose Romances printed before 1740,* London, 1912. Prof. J. M. Clapp has in preparation a complete bibliography of eighteenth-century fiction.

Richardson progressed from Pamela, through Clarissa, to Sir Charles Grandison. Likewise it could not decide whether to reclaim the villain, as Pamela did Lord B———, or send him to destruction, like Clarissa's Lovelace. The sentimentalists listened eagerly to Rousseau's call "back to nature," and joined the humanitarians in a rather unctuous sympathy for slaves, savages, criminals, dumb animals, and the victims of oppression generally.

In *Jack Wilton*, Nash had struck upon a distinct note of realism, in spite of the romantic adventures he introduced. The first Spanish picaresque **Picaresque** novels made this all the clearer. Right **Narrative** down to our own time these narratives of the picaresque sort have continued, often romantic in conception but always realistic in their details, always claiming our attention by incident and adventure rather than by character portrayal, always constructed like the necklace of beads and capable of infinite extension. It is of no particular concern whether their heroes are sharpers like Lazarillo or modern scientific analysts of crime like Sherlock Holmes and his host of followers.

In the first half of the eighteenth century picaresque novels were acclimated to England by Daniel Defoe and Tobias Smollett. Defoe approached his **Defoe** work through the training of a journalist and pamphleteer, in which he had caught in a peculiar way the power of suggesting naïve and unstudied veracity. By the time he undertook to develop the incident of Alexander Selkirk's shipwreck into *The Surprising Adventures of Robinson Crusoe* (1719), he had mastered the art that conceals art so thoroughly as to carry complete conviction to his readers. The autobiographical method of picaresque novels fell in exactly with his talents, and he published in rapid succession *Captain Singleton* (1720), *Moll Flanders* (1722), *Colonel Jacque* (1722), and *Roxana* (1724). The realism in all of these is neither pointed into satire nor exaggerated through delight in revolting things for their own sake. It is tempered, indeed, by a rather strict Puritan morality, and the arbitrary conclusion that belongs to the type usually takes the shape of a complete reformation in the leading character.

Smollett's realism was of a bolder, more pessimistic sort. All the sordidness and cruelty of one of the most sordid and cruel periods in English **Smollett** civilization find expression in his work, while the hardships and excesses of English seamen, known to Smollett by personal experience, darken his pictures still more. His style is fluent, racy, and picturesque, with a frequent outcropping of grim humor. His satirical purpose is as evident as in the writings of Swift, and he makes frequent use of the methods of personal satire, direct or veiled, so prevalent since the Restoration. His *History and Adventures' of an Atom* (1769), for example, is one of a long series of the "detached observer" sketches, inaugurated by Le Sage's *Diable Boiteux*. Smollett's picaresque novels, in order, are *Roderick Random* (1748), *Peregrine Pickle* (1751), *Ferdinand, Count Fathom* (1753), and *Sir Launcelot Greaves* (1762). *The Expedition of Humphrey Clinker* (1771) is a later and more complicated product, a novel of letters, presenting the events of the story from various angles and making the correspondence itself a form of characterization.

The novels of Richardson, beginning with *Pamela, or Virtue Rewarded* (1740), are generally considered to inaugurate the novel proper, as opposed to the romance.

They are novels in their distinctively middle-class point of view, in their studied and consistent realism,—of character this time, rather than of incident,—and in the organic unity of structure that their author masters after his first experiments with *Pamela*. Yet they are able to retain and utilize a surprisingly large number of the methods and devices already familiar in a long series of romances and *romans à clef*. Both these forms had introduced a large amount of correspondence, and some of the latter were almost entirely letter novels. The elaborate analysis of passion and emotion was a romance tradition as old as the age of chivalry and medieval courts of love. Richardson's long-suffering and well-nigh indestructible heroines are in direct line of descent from the French romances to Mrs. Anne Radcliffe. Maxims and moral lessons had been employed before with considerable freedom. Even the analogy Richardson discovered between his principles of structure and those of formal tragedy had been anticipated a century earlier under the "heroic" vogue in France. To complete the comparison it should be noted that all of the *risqué* situations that startled Richardson's readers can be paralleled in writers like Mrs. Manley and Mrs. Haywood, and that the public went promptly to work to identify Pamela and Clarissa in real life.

Novel and Romance in Richardson

To Henry Fielding, brought up like Defoe on journalistic pamphlets and picaresque narrative, a self-conscious sentimental moralist was a natural subject for ridicule. The comedy of life appealed to him rather, and a realism that went outside of a lady's boudoir and looked the laughing, sinning, and occasionally repentant old world squarely in the face. If romances, as

Fielding's Reaction

the critics said, were a kind of prose epic, akin to the tragedy in royal dignity, his ambition was to write a "comic epic," and many of his suggestions came from the successfully staged comedies of his own and previous generations. The extravagant sentimentality of Richardson occurred to him as a fit subject for burlesque, and he promptly began the story of *Joseph Andrews*, Pamela's similarly tempted and equally immune brother. The result is partly burlesque, partly picaresque, but partly too a genuine and sympathetic portrayal of English life. For in the process of creation Fielding lost interest in his original purpose and developed his art to a completeness and finality that made his *Tom Jones* (1749) a masterpiece of fiction that has not yet been surpassed.[1] Here for the first time interest and skill in character portrayal reached a parity with interest in adventure, so that a crowd of thoroughly individualized and widely representative Englishmen move busily and naturally about the scene. There is a frank presentation of ugly detail, sometimes with evident satisfaction, but the moral basis of the narrative is sound and wholesome. Finally there is a new conception of unity, manifest in the interdependence of incident and character, and in the complete grasp of all material which enables the author to bring his long and complex account steadily and inevitably to its logical conclusion.

Fielding's last novel, *Amelia*, is more realistic still in its employment of descriptive detail. But this time the realism is directed to certain distinct purposes, and in the

[1] During the summer of 1915, out of about thirty leading novelists of England and America asked to indicate for the *New York Times* their choice of the six greatest novels in the English language, nearly half placed *Tom Jones* at or near the head of the list.

achievement of these, surprising as it may appear, Fielding becomes almost a sentimentalist. He anticipates many a later "doctrinaire" novel in his denunciation of dueling, gambling, masquerades, and particularly English criminal law and prison discipline, but in several of these matters he is also echoing Richardson. The characterization, particularly in his leading figures, is of his best, but unity is weakened by a much-forced conclusion.

"Amelia"

In all these respects *Amelia* bears close analogy to *The Vicar of Wakefield*, Goldsmith's well-known novel, which appeared fifteen years later (1766). The Vicar, his family, and their associates are delightful pieces of portraiture, but the plot is slow and poorly motived. In the course of their experiences there are some rather severe strictures on English customs, particularly as to law-courts and prisons. There is much sentimental tenderness, and an almost idyllic treatment of humble village life which set a new standard for such things throughout Europe.

"The Vicar of Wakefield"

The extreme sentimentalist of the mid-century was Laurence Sterne. To him sentimentalism meant sensibility—the author's own susceptibility to emotional impressions and whims. His *Sentimental Journey* is perhaps the most personal travel sketch ever written, but affords little knowledge of the country traversed. *Tristram Shandy* (1759-67), for all its whimsicality and mechanical trickery, contains some of the most effective character-studies in our literature, and sparkles with a rare humor that is warm and genuine because of the human feeling it contains. Of plot and movement there is little enough, except in the manner Sterne him-

Sterne's Sentimentalism

self has called "progression in digression." The titular hero, whose birth is in prospect when the book opens, does not breathe or cry till near the end of Volume III. But in the meantime the reader has become intimately acquainted with some very interesting people and acquired much equally interesting information. Sterne's popularity aroused a host of imitators, of whom Henry Mackenzie was most successfully sentimental in his *Man of Feeling* (1771).

In the second half of the century, the novel falls into more distinct and constructive categories. Picaresque narrative continued to appear, and the sentimental tone had a way of permeating almost everything. The field was fairly divided, however, among the "doctrinaire" novels, or stories with a purpose, chiefly concerned with social or educational reforms; the "Gothic" novels, developing steadily toward historical fiction; and the novels of manners, replacing the comedies of manners of the Restoration period.

**Later Distinctions**

Richardson's example and the several strong convictions of English sentimentalists were probably enough to produce a series of humanitarian novels, directed against gambling, dueling, and slavery. But the writings of Rousseau in France, exalting a return to nature and a natural system of education, and inveighing against what was false and artificial in the practices of polite society, provided doctrinaire fiction with a much more positive and virile programme. The best known of the educational stories is Thomas Day's *Sandford and Merton,* begun in 1783, which not only depicts the ideal system of instruction in operation, but instills all of the favorite doctrines of Rousseau except

**Doctrinaire Novelists— Thomas Day**

his ideal of studied weakness for women. For this Day and various other English revolutionists substituted a hardening process of severe exertion and strenuous exercises. Various novels depicted the sad fate in store for young women brought up among the vanities and deceptions of fashionable boarding-schools. A good example is Mrs. Inchbald's *A Simple Story* (1791).

The Socialistic Group
The strongest of the doctrinaire novels were produced by Mrs. Inchbald, whose *Nature and Art* (1796) should be added to the book just mentioned; William Godwin, author of *Caleb Williams* (1794) and *St. Leon* (1799) and particularly hostile to English legal procedure; Thomas Holcroft, most thoroughgoing of all this socialistic group, as evidenced by his *Anna St. Ives* (1792); and Robert Bage, author of *Hermsprong, or Man as he is not* (1796). Their method of procedure was much the same in all cases,—to relate the misfortunes of some "child of nature" in the clutches of social and legal procedure. Professor Cross has summarized it in this way: "A tyrant or villain was selected from the upper class, who, hedged about by law and custom, wreaks a motiveless hatred on the sensitive and cultured hero, who, though born free, is not born to wealth and a title. The gentleman after a career of crime may or may not come to a disgraceful end. The hero, after years of drudgery and abject labor,—either is crushed, or by a revolution of fortune gains comparative ease."[1]

In all this there is ample opportunity for treatment of character and for the knitting of incident to incident in an inevitable progression. As a matter of fact, the authors were usually too deeply concerned with the lessons they had to impart to strive after any high excellence in

[1] *The Development of the English Novel*, p. 91.

technique. Of the entire output *Caleb Williams* is perhaps the most impressive piece of structure and best deserving of permanent recognition. The doctrinaire novel, as a whole, is significant not for its technical excellence or lack of it, but for its relation to the general enlivening of human thought and liberation of the imaginative powers that lay at the heart of the Romantic awakening and found its best expression in lyric verse. There was little chance for versatility in characterization when each hero was only the author's ideal self, and each plot but the time-honored conflict of the flower and the leaf or the owl and the nightingale,—practical common sense against unrestrained and ambitious youth.

**Features of Technique**

It is well understood that the Romantic Movement was in great part a renaissance of things medieval, at least so far as the late eighteenth century understood and interpreted these. One result of this was a decided leaning toward the old romances in which imagination had supplanted fact. Another was the prevalence of a notion that the thought and experience of the Middle Ages was largely permeated by the melancholy and the horrible. This notion arose no doubt from the fact that a vogue of gloomy contemplation, a sort of tradition from "Il Penseroso," preceded and ushered in this medieval reaction; although from the time of Addison the "Gothic" in imagination and art had implied in English minds the vast, the gloomy, and the semi-barbarous.[1] At any rate the medieval novel came into England in the decade of the sixties as the "Gothic" novel, and rapidly acquired a fixed list of properties, including a ruined and haunted castle or abbey, with secret panels and hidden passages, a hermit, a friar or two no

**Medievalism**

[1] Cf. *Spectator* No. 63.

better than they ought to be, an owl, and a moon frequently obscured by billowy clouds. Into this setting were transferred the stock hero and heroine of romance and a pastoral tangle of concealed identities, and the plot was ready to unfold.

Credit for inaugurating the English Gothic novel is properly given to Horace Walpole, whose *Castle of Otranto* appeared in 1764; although a strictly historical narrative, *Longsword, Earl of Salisbury, an Historical Romance,* had been published two years earlier, minus the Gothic stage properties. Walpole, a wealthy and cultured man of the world, had become a collector of medieval antiquities and established himself in a pseudo-Gothic castle on his estate of Strawberry Hill. Here, so goes his own account, he fell asleep one night amid his relics, and dreamed out the narrative he recorded in his pages. Appropriately enough it is the story of a haunted castle, whose owner has perished in the crusades, and left a single heir who is roaming about the premises in some humble capacity and is unknown to the usurper. The specter is a complete suit of giant armor, and there is an especially long secret passage, terminating in a distant chapel. But Walpole's sense of the ludicrous failed him somehow, or else escaped his contemporaries, for there are various details that break the imaginative spell, particularly some very modern and colloquial serving-people.

"The Castle of Otranto"

Usually critics associate with this creation of Walpole's dreams the Oriental novel, *Vathek,* written in French by the Englishman, William Beckford, and published in English translation in 1786. It has certain features in common with *The Castle of Otranto.* Beckford was also a wealthy dilettante, who built and furnished a mansion in

168 THE TYPICAL FORMS OF ENGLISH LITERATURE

accord with his favorite hobby,—in his case Orientalism. Both men give free rein to their imaginations and are extremely fond of the terrible and the grotesque. Beckford's is a worthy contribution to romantic art, since the remote in space is just as vague and suggestive as the remote in time. But *Vathek* is not a Gothic novel, and has no particular kinship with medievalism or medieval romances. It descends directly from a cultivation of Oriental tales and legends that began in France with a translation of the *Arabian Nights* at the very beginning of the century. The French found this Oriental material serviceable to point moral lessons, but particularly so in the direction of witty and rather daring satire. Beckford, largely under French influence and writing in French, is primarily carrying on this tradition, retaining both the wit and the moral teaching. He may have found his imagination quickened by English " Gothicism," but his Oriental models were fantastic enough.

"Vathek" and Orientalism

The genuine Gothic activity, which came to include lyric and drama as well as prose fiction, thrived better for a time on German soil than on English. The result is that its next English exponent, Matthew Gregory Lewis, partook of the extravagances of both countries. He tried all the literary forms affected by Gothicism, but made his reputation and a new title—" Monk Lewis "—by his novel *Ambrosio, or the Monk* (1795). The story is built about the downfall of an ecclesiastic, and abounds in supernatural visitants and reeking physical horrors. It is a welcome relief to turn to his contemporary, Mrs. Radcliffe, whose novels are set in gloomy but well-aired old castles in the midst of wild, mountainous

Gothic Novels

landscapes, and whose grisly terrors in moonless midnights are always carefully explained away at the end of the book. It may be partly on account of a sense of burlesque, but several of these Radcliffe novels—*The Romance of the Forest, The Mysteries of Udolpho, The Italian*—are very good reading even today. They revert considerably to the old romances. Their landscapes are very much alike, wherever placed, and this is not surprising, since the author had never seen them. It is surprising, though, that for their day they are comparatively real. The heroes and heroines—and particularly the villains—change little from story to story, and are the usual conventionalized types. But there is much more "sensibility," especially in the heroines. Tears flow freely throughout the pages of Mrs. Radcliffe, and on very slight provocation, but there are always explanations and smiles at the end.

America furnished a successful manipulator of Gothic devices in the person of Charles Brockden Brown, author of *Wieland* (1798), *Edgar Huntley* (1799), and *Arthur Mervyn* (1799-1800).

The Historical Novel

The poet Shelley was not ashamed to try his hand at this form of fiction, and Mrs. Shelley contributed, in *Frankenstein*, one of the most thrilling stories ever written. It is surprising, however, that so few Gothic novels took advantage of the possibilities of a genuine historical background. *Longsword* alone attempted this with any success before 1800, but immediately after that date came Jane Porter, whose *Thaddeus of Warsaw* (1803) and *Scottish Chiefs* (1809) have remained classics until our own time. These novels began to catch the secret of imaginative experiences set against a background of historical fact, and appropriately ushered in the period of the Waverley Novels and Sir Walter Scott. In him we meet the genuine and accurate antiquary, who is able also to grasp large dramatic effects and marshal great masses of men across his pages. His method of procedure, which has been in practice among authors ever since, consists in developing a plot rather closely connected with some great historical personages as leading characters. This gives him all the advantage of historical detail without confining him to painful verification of fact at every point. In the same way he has the art of suggesting "local color" without producing dry handbooks of antiquities.

His plots are vast, complicated creations, suggesting heroic romances, or better still the great historical dramas of Shakespeare. In a thoroughly Shakespearian way he combines under-plots of middle-class people and experiences with his main plots devoted to aristocracy and noble blood. The rapidity with which he worked and the vast extent of his output account easily enough for the absence of compression and revision in his material and his style. His effects are not produced by persistent pruning away of non-essential things. They are cumulative rather, and richly picturesque. In much the same way Scott's characters stand out before us, visualized in our minds through a series of striking impressions. Heroes and heroines are apt to be colorless and conventional, as in the old romances. But characters that are unusual, that have plenty of picturesque and imaginative suggestion, he does admirably and always makes convincing.

**The Waverley Novels**

Most of the novels of the eighteenth century were to some degree novels of manners; that is, a considerable share of their interest lay in depicting the customs of society, with more or less of satirical reaction. Toward the end of the century, however, the treatment of manners as an end in itself was undertaken by certain women, whose closer acquaintance with the feminine point of view, and superior skill in noting and expressing delicate gradations of thought and feeling, made this style of writing almost an art of itself. The first success of this kind was the novel *Evelina*, in 1778, by the young and then utterly unknown author, Fanny Burney. She followed this four years later with *Cecilia*, a similar treatment of the same London frivolities, as seen by innocent young maidens from the provinces. Maria Edgeworth continued the cultivation of the type with her *Belinda* (1801) and her series of *Fashionable Tales*, published 1809-12. In her Irish stories, such as *Castle Rackrent*, she extended her methods to embrace Irish manners as well. The whole development culminates in the work of Jane Austen, who wrote when it was high time to satirize not merely fashionable society, but sentimentalism and the Gothic craze in addition. *Sense and Sensibility* and *Northanger Abbey* attend to these latter obligations. Her entire product belongs to the second decade of the century, and includes also *Pride and Prejudice*, *Mansfield Park*, and *Emma*.

Technically the novel of manners should approximate the standards of well-constructed comedy, and in the work of Miss Austen this is emphatically the case. Characters, however much individualized, are still essentially types, representing what Ben Jonson called "humours"; that is, dominating characteristics somewhat exaggerated as in caricature. These reveal themselves dramatically, in action and in conversation, and often by a process of very subtle suggestion. The plots are subordinate to characterization, but grow out of it, and develop a process of intrigue, carefully built about some central idea. In Miss Austen's best known novels this central motive is a conflict of characters, represented in her titles,—" Sense and Sensibility "; " Pride and Prejudice." There is a pervasive humor, a very real sympathy with the weaknesses portrayed, and always a gracefully managed satire, kept in due restraint, but never for a moment lost from view.

By 1820 Jane Austen's work was done and Walter Scott's was well under way (*Waverley* was published in 1814). The period from this date until the emergence of Dickens and Thackeray is one of wide and comprehensive apostleship, with every successful form adequately represented. Imitations of Scott were most abundant, his influence extending in a few years to Victor Hugo and Dumas in France, to Freytag and Ebers in Germany, and to Manzoni in Italy. The historical novel in England was cultivated by William Harrison Ainsworth, Bulwer-Lytton, and Charles Kingsley, and in America the " *Leatherstocking Tales* " of James Fenimore Cooper owed no small obligation to Scott. Novels of terror were perpetuated in Maturin's *Melmoth the Wanderer* and Emily Bronte's *Wuthering Heights,* and the burlesque of them, instituted in *Northanger Abbey,* was emphasized by the writings of Thomas Love Peacock. Pierce Egan's series of sketches, *Life in London,* gave a new vogue to comic realism, at the same time that old-fashioned novels of sentiment were flooding the cheap circulating libraries. The novel of manners was extending its field to the provinces and including village and

**An Eclectic Period**

country life, and even taking friendly interest in poverty-stricken city slums.

Individual novelists were becoming much more eclectic in subject and in manner of treatment, so that it becomes in numerous cases almost impossible to classify their work under the old and simple categories. Bulwer-Lytton perhaps best represents this sort of versatility. *Pelham* is an extravagant study of manners, in the footsteps of Jane Austen. There is a considerable series of historical novels and dramas, written while these were most in fashion, and including *The Last Days of Pompeii* and *The Last of the Barons*. Two stories, *Paul Clifford* and *Eugene Aram*, are sentimental studies of crime, while *Zanoni* is pure Gothic in its inspiration. Toward the end of his career Bulwer turned to eccentric but realistic novels of village life, of which *The Caxtons* and *My Novel* are the best examples.

**Bulwer-Lytton**

Out of this confused creative activity there arose, about the middle of the century, Charles Dickens and William Makepeace Thackeray, in many respects the Richardson and Fielding of the Victorian era. Dickens was again the sentimental realist, to whom didactic purpose was a matter of great significance. Thackeray began in protest against this sentimentalism, and reverting to Fielding as his model, sought to parallel actual truth in his plots and characters. But he too was richly endowed with human sympathy and a sense of dramatic effects, so that before his work was done he was introducing sentimental situations hardly distinguishable from those in *Amelia* or in *Old Curiosity Shop*. The novels of Dickens may be variously classified. He began, in *Pickwick Papers*, with the same type of comic realism

**Dickens, Realist and Sentimentalist**

cultivated by Pierce Egan, and thereafter rarely departed from the streets and court rooms and hostelries of England, where flowed the great stream of common humanity. Two purposes dominated the long biographical narratives he spun out of such material: one, the humanitarian zeal to better the conditions of living and to right human wrong; the other, the humorous and satirical desire to point out the follies and weaknesses of the classes he knew so intimately. To the first of these, as we have seen, always adheres a very considerable element of the sentimental; the second is certain to produce some exaggeration and distortion, the portrayal of type-characters as in caricature.

Hence we have a Uriah Heep who is humbleness incarnate, a Scrooge who is all miser, a Micawber who fairly breathes improvidence. We know they are not true to life, any more than is the absent-minded professor, or the vaudeville foreigner of today. Yet just in the same way their very obviousness gets a hold upon us, and the something more than half truth there is in them seems to stick. Naturally the skill of the caricaturist is displayed best upon deviations from the normal types, and Dickens has no particular success with his heroines or with any characters that fall into conventional lines. Likewise he is too much employed with his characters and the picturesque episodes into which they can be directed, to be deeply concerned over well-knit, constantly progressive plots always under complete control. The old biographical or epic plot might, under a master-hand, become a splendidly complex structural unit, but its natural tendency is to ramble.

**Characters and Plots**

Thackeray was not a consistent workman, either in construction or in characterization. He was capable of

an epic unity equal to that of his model Fielding, but he did not always attain to it. His characters also varied
from deep and intimate studies of per-
Thackeray sonality to the usual exaggerations of caricature. In one sense, however, his exaggerations were not usual. He was a reactionary against conventional type characters, as he professed to be, but he tore down those old stock figures only to set up new and more accurately-conceived types in their places. A large part of his writing represents the novel of manners, with a pervasive satire of hypocrisy and sham, but he anticipates in this the modern realist, with an immense repertoire of carefully differentiated and intimately studied personages.

Thackeray was in the forefront of a wide reaction to realism, this time largely subjective and psychological.
It involved such authors as George Bor-
A New row, with his unique portrayal of gypsy
Realism life; Charles Reade, ransacking history and biography for a wide range of subjects; Anthony Trollope, at his best in his fictions of an imaginary but realistic Barsetshire; Charlotte Bronte, penetrating the primitive emotions of her native Yorkshire; finally, George Eliot and George Meredith, Thomas Hardy and Mrs. Humphry Ward. All of these last are distinctly modern, and their common key-word is truth,—inner truth, scientifically interpreted. Against a background of village and moorland that is conceived accurately and in spiritual harmony with the action, they show us living people stripped to the very soul, wrestling with the great problems and temptations of our own day, and paying the tragic penalty of rash decision or sinking as the blind and helpless victims of fate—or that more dreadful modern arbiter, *heredity*. All turn by preference

from the highest ranks of society; conduct there is under restraint and not a direct expression of the inner life, as Hardy explains. Hard, unvarying types and their accompanying exaggerations are broken down, and we are face to face with individuals, except as we are conscious that theirs are eternal and universal passions.

Along with a deeper and more comprehensive character-study comes a more thorough grasp of structure.

**Larger Unity of Structure**  The great novel has always made large use of its privilege of a biographic or epic method by which it can portray the entire life-history of a character, in the manner of the great tragedies of Shakespeare. George Eliot's novels are in great part just such tragedies, with a strain of the peculiar "fate-tragedy" developed by Germany in the eighteenth century. But the decision that inaugurates the tragic development is not mere chance; it is the natural manifestation of character, and clearly to be expected. Tito in *Romola* was not a confirmed ingrate when he gave up the project of ransoming his foster-father; but he was at least predisposed to selfish irresponsibility. The consequences of decision are organic and irresistible, whether they proceed logically to catastrophe as in *Adam Bede* or pass through a well-motived process of regeneration as in *Silas Marner*. Meredith, coming later than George Eliot, appears to have a more modern and less somber outlook upon life, and permits his characters to find themselves once more by some severe refining process. Hardy, just as he is the greatest artist in landscapes, makes most out of the influences of environment and inheritance in character-shaping. Stylistically these writers have wide differences; George Eliot and Mrs. Ward being simple and direct, Meredith highly mannered, and Hardy replete with imagery and poetic effects.

No interest in realism, objective or subjective, seems ever to be strong enough or wide enough to eradicate romance. Realists like Charles Reade and George Eliot and particularly Hardy are frequently attracted to the romantic point of view. And there are always distinctly romantic novelists, however much submerged in a deep current of realism. In the comfortably materialistic Victorian period, the English public was reading Wilkie Collins and William Black and H. Rider Haggard, and wisely set its approval upon one classic of genuine romantic art, Richard Blackmore's *Lorna Doone*. Then came Robert Louis Stevenson, the imaginative boy who refused to grow up, and not only revived the old romance of adventure as a labor of love, but dared to defend it as a worthy form of prose art. All the old tricks and devices came readily to his hand save one,—the much-enduring and supremely adorable heroine. Indeed it would not be exaggeration to pronounce the donkey "Modestine" his best feminine character. His is largely a man's—or rather, a boy's—romance, but within this somewhat restricted field there is no dearth of thrill and horror, of piracy and single combat, and of the interminable fascination of the tale within the tale. His style too is almost the perfection of the story-teller's art. It is easy, colloquial, and flexible, with an indescribable flavor derived from rare and picturesque phrases and subtle cadences. Critics have called him mannered; but we long for more of such mannerism.

*The Romance of Stevenson*

Perhaps the most notable development of nineteenth-century fiction is the method of approach that is characterized as "impressionism." This is strictly neither romance nor realism; it may employ the material of either. But the truly romantic rambles over uncharted seas and realism is often lost in the mass of its own authentic detail, while impressionism is primarily selection,—imaginative selection, even inspired selection. The psychological realists have striven constantly to achieve this effect, the novel of manners is always concerned with it, but at its best impressionism is not bound to see a character or plot through to its conclusion; indeed, it can hardly be sustained at all through the length of a biographical novel. With impressionism came shorter stories,—in fact the "Short-story," as some critics prefer to write it. In this virtually new form, in which happily our own country has been able to point out the way to England, Hawthorne and Poe established for all time the artistic value of a prose narrative whose chief source of charm is lyric; that is to say, is found in the flash of imaginative vision or the emotional mood produced by the sympathetic and individualized presentation of a few carefully selected facts of life. In the novel proper the chief exponent of impressionism is Henry James, also American by birth, whose individualism of style, as well as of point of view, has operated entirely too much in limiting the circle of his readers.

**Impressionism and the Short Story**

Our own century is entirely too new for adequate analysis or critical estimate. Today, as always in the past two hundred years, the novel is a form that seems to encourage enormous production of inferior work, and one is likely to be hopelessly confused, and accordingly pessimistic, in the midst of this constant output. A few general statements only may be made with safety in regard to present tendencies. In addition the

**The Present Century**

student may be advised to wait at least a year or two before venturing upon new novels, rather than to follow the current lists of " best sellers."

Romance is still with us, and that too of the good old-fashioned kind. Less than twenty years ago we were in the midst of a vigorous revival of it,
**Romanticists** replete with swarthy villains and handsome heroes struggling for domination of Zenda or Hentzau or some less remote dream-nation. At least one of the authors, Maurice Hewlett, caught the ring of true romance with surprising skill. Of late, novelists have turned once more to seeking their romance in things primarily realistic,—an art at least as old as *Jack Wilton* and the sea-tales of Smollett. Kipling has found it in the experiences of British government officials and territorial soldiers, particularly in India. He has found it too where H. G. Wells has gone seeking it with even more success,—in the achievements and possibilities of present-day science and commercialism, in ocean liner and aeroplane and patent-medicine exploitation. Joseph Conrad, for his romance, has gone straight to the sea, where it always has been found, and John Galsworthy has sought wisely among the social abuses and misunderstandings of the present scheme of things. Both these men are thoroughgoing impressionists, carrying the principle of imaginative selection much farther than the various Americans who are working upon similar material.

This romantic employment of realistic detail has not interfered with the steady progress of realism for its own sake. The revival of romance was
**Realists** immediately followed by a reactionary liking for " muck-raking " fiction, which was only the old novel of manners and the socialistic type of sordid realism made more obvious and spectacular.

On the surer ground of thoroughly assimilated and accurately portrayed fact has appeared Arnold Bennett, literary sponsor of the "Five Towns," and even more recently such men as Gilbert Cannan, D. H. Lawrence, Hugh Walpole, and Compton Mackenzie. They are all thoroughly steeped in knowledge of the people and the conditions they depict,—"saturated," as Henry James puts it. But in this very saturation lies a serious temptation to which all have yielded, the tendency—still quoting Mr. James—toward "squeezing out to the utmost the plump and more or less juicy orange of a particular acquainted state," with little selection or interpretation and much waste of good material. Much the same criticism may be brought against William De Morgan, recently heralded in his advanced years as a second Dickens. However, he provides interpretation if not selection, reverting to the old device of interpolating the author's own views of things throughout the progress of his stories.

America, in recent years, has produced many novelists, but few of generally recognized greatness. We have welcomed in translation the masterpieces **Americans** of almost every nation, and in various instances have stamped our approval on foreign authors still unrecognized at home. A few names may be listed of those worthy to be compared with these cosmopolitan artists, having won like them the appreciation of critics here and abroad. William Dean Howells, with his clean and wholesome realism, has long held chief place among our prose artists. Mrs. Wharton is rather generally regarded as one of the best among our novelists of manners. Robert Herrick is notable for his refinement of characterization and finality of structure. Mark Twain is rapidly taking his place not merely as chief representative of American humor, but as an exponent of our energy, optimism, and hatred of sham. There may be others equally deserving. Perhaps, even, the "great American novel," that philosopher's stone of the publishers' announcements, may by rare good fortune be discovered in our own generation.

## Technique of the Novel

So much has been written of the art of fiction, some of it by professed critics and more by the long line of communicative novelists from Fielding to Henry James and Arnold Bennett, that the essential principles of novel-writing are common property. Historically, as has been seen, the novel is not a thing apart, but is constantly to be considered in its relations to other forms, particularly the romance. Thus with Congreve one may hold that the novel is to the romance as comedy is to tragedy, or with Fielding may declare that the novel is really a comic epic in prose. Certainly in our own day men no longer write prose romances, but do venture upon romantic novels; and the methods of drama have been accepted more and more by novelists until we make a common practice of dramatizing novels and "novelizing" successful plays,—often with lamentable results.

A Related Form

Plays, to be sure, are written presumably to be rendered in action before an assembled audience, while novels are to be read by individuals with time at their disposal. Between the two there is a great gulf fixed. Second only in importance is the distinction growing out of the introduction of the author's personality in a novel when it is practically excluded from dramatic art. This personality is an extremely variable quantity. In the tale of highly

Novel and Drama

182  THE TYPICAL FORMS OF ENGLISH LITERATURE

romantic adventure it has little place; in the biographical portrayal of moral conflict it is constantly in evidence. Realistic fiction steeped in unorganized fact to the point of saturation does not call it into play; impressionistic selection and interpretation of fact makes it as indispensable as in lyric poetry. To make his personality count, the novelist does not need to interrupt his story and chat pleasantly with the " gentle reader " for a chapter or two, as they loved to do in the eighteenth century. Only on rare occasions do we get a sense of autobiography, and thus of personal acquaintance, from a narrative recounted in the first person. We look rather for the author's presence pervading every part of his work, directing our senses and emotions, helping us to grasp the message, yet never actually intruding itself upon our sight.

Like the epic and the drama, the novel must be considered under the familiar heads of plot, characters, and setting. No one of these can well be omitted from any extended narrative; any one of them may predominate. All three are products of the author's imaginative faculties,—the reorganization of odds and ends of his reminiscences, the episodes, people, and scenes derived from actual experience or the substance of his reading. The new alignment of these details during the creative process is not of course the laborious task this would seem to indicate, but rather an intuitive, instantaneous thing, as if the conceptions sprang full-grown from the creative mind. Sometimes literary gossips prattle about the " originals " from whom one novelist or another has modeled his characters. It is more likely that the author has so far familiarized himself with Hoosier villages, or New England fisher-folk, or Southern plantations that his people are composite portraits, truer to the essential

**Artistic Creation**

life of these communities than any mere individuals could be.

The greatest novels are essentially character studies; for the novelist, unlike the dramatist, can take his public past the mere externals of speech and gesture into the very soul of his hero, and reveal every minute phase of the struggle occurring there. The dramatist's resources of action and dialogue are his also, and many recent novelists prefer them to the slower methods of their more analytic brethren. But these more dramatic craftsmen may and do employ in addition various methods of indirect characterization, likewise familiar on the stage. Two people in a story discuss a third one and his possible motives, or a whole community shows its dislike or fear or admiration of a neighbor. Often in novels as in plays there is some minor character in a sort of chorus rôle, whose utterances interrupt the struggles of his fellows, and who may indeed be the personal spokesman of the views and sympathies of the author.

*Methods of Characterization*

In novels as in plays characters vary all the way from extreme simplicity to extreme complexity. The more complex studies are likely to be more carefully worked out and more accurate, though they are not of necessity more attractive or more convincing. Simple characters fall more readily into stock types and suffer from the exaggerations common in types; while complex characters tend to preserve their individuality. These simple characters, drawn in broad lines, are satisfying enough for the minor personages in a story, or even for the more important ones, when character is supposed to remain a fixed thing throughout the vicissitudes of the

*Varieties of Characters*

story. But where, as is so often the case, leading characters develop under their experiences, being refined or debased by the struggles they undergo, we have the well-sustained studies of distinct individuals. In any event characters must be doubly consistent: consistent in their first conception with our accepted notions of human nature, and once conceived consistent ever after with themselves.

Almost as vital as the art of character-portrayal is that of character-grouping. Characters in novels do not stand alone and are not to be considered alone. **Character-** Important traits stand out far more **Grouping** clearly by contrast with other characters where they are deficient or entirely absent. Characteristics impress us more when they are apparent in various people in different strata of society. Frequently a general unity of effect is obtained by presenting a considerable group of people all dominated by some common trait or tendency, though each one, true to his distinct personality, displays this in his own peculiar way. Thus there may appear in one story a series of related studies in greed, or ambition, or passion, displayed in diverse experiences in widely separated walks of life, yet combining in one harmonious impression upon the reader's imagination.

Together with the relation of character to character, author and critic alike must constantly consider the relations of character to plot. It is true that **Relation of** a given group of characters may be sent **Character** through an immense variety of adven- **and Plot** tures, just as a given course of experiences is conceivably open to many different men and women. Such shuffling processes, however, may involve many misfits, in which the only form of interest is curiosity as to how grotesque the effect may be. A character once conceived has only a limited round of experiences through which it may appropriately be guided, and these are such as tend particularly to test its weaknesses or develop its essential strength. Novels primarily of action, like the ever-recurring stories of picaresque adventure, habitually ignore these artistic necessities of character treatment, and are reasonably justified in doing so. But there is little excuse for forcing carefully studied personalities into situations that add nothing to our understanding of the characters, and that are extremely unlikely to have occurred to them. There is no sounder principle in fiction than that of "economy of invention," and it is best observed in this harmonious relating of character and action.

Action or plot in novels is to many readers the first, and even the only consideration. The simplest imagination relishes mere story-telling, and so long as something continues to happen, seems to be pleasantly employed. The reader of more cultivated tastes never ceases to value action in stories, but insists that this action shall be regulated and organized into unity. The picaresque tale, so often referred to, is content with a succession of adventures, like beads on a string, alternately piquing and gratifying curiosity but leading to no particular conclusion. A better knit organization, in which plot may still dominate character-interest, erects certain apparent obstacles and then carries the characters triumphantly beyond them. Strangely enough, in what are recognized as essentially "character-novels" there is the greatest finality of plot construction. These are the stories involving character-development: some-

*Unity of Action*

times extended to cover approximately a lifetime, at others limited to the period of time in which the hero or heroine passes through crucial life-experiences and emerges transformed into a new being. Many such novels may be analyzed into the five-part scheme so familiar to students of tragedy. Rising out of the level course of everyday events, they move from the first clash of forces steadily upward to the climax or turning-point, at which the hero appears to have progressed as far as the gradually conquering force can carry him. Already hints of a decline have probably appeared, and the balance of forces is promptly shifted and the hero precipitated toward a catastrophe that he justly deserves because of error or at least indiscretion. Not all such stories end in complete gloom, however; frequently there is a combination of physical or material disaster with a spiritual regeneration in character that could hardly have been reached without suffering and loss.

In order to secure unity in plot-structure, the greatest attention must be given to the relation of parts. Action must be made to hinge upon action by the **Cause and** operation of cause and effect. For every **Effect** decision that is made, every step that is taken, an adequate motive must be provided, in line with what we already have in mind of the characters involved and the action that has preceded. In the same way the several under-plots usually introduced and concerned with subordinate characters must have definite relation with the main course of action, and indeed some real and vital bearing upon it. In this fashion only can we reach that sense of irresistible, inevitable progress toward an end that sets the plot of a great novel apart from the meanderings of structural weakness. Mere accident may set the train of events in motion; but the steady progress of these events is not to be checked or thwarted by chance.

Setting alone of the several large factors in the novelist's art almost never becomes an end in itself. There are novels of character and novels of plot, but as yet not novels of setting. With the present concern for accuracy of detail in realism, we may soon have them, for entire veracity of fact may easily become the chief end of thoroughgoing realistic art. Kept in proper subordination, setting has always an important function, whether treated realistically or romantically. As knowledge has increased concerning places and times remote and people and conditions at our very doors, it has brought added difficulty to the task of providing accurate backgrounds that shall at the same time give artistic harmony to the entire work of fiction. Realistic saturation faces the dangers of confusion and dullness. Comparatively few descriptive touches are enough, if they really illuminate. The possibilities of natural scenery to reflect emotions were worked out shortly after Rousseau; it remains for the present time to find for us the same artistic pleasure in congested city streets and throbbing factories.

**Setting**

One never-failing requirement of novel as of drama is probability. It applies to characterization, plot, and setting, and holds for scientific realism or the wildest permissible flights of the imagination. Initial assumptions once being granted, everything must follow in such fashion as not to offend the intelligent reader's sense of probability. In such matters, obviously, truth is stranger than fiction. Life is full of accidents and surprises which, introduced into novels, would arouse a storm of protest from the very readers who are sticklers for truth. Good fiction

**Probability**

moves in the world of poetic truth or higher probability, a well-ordered region where events are anticipated some time before they happen, where men and women act as people of their sort might be expected to, and yet where the weird, the supernatural, and the extravagant are welcomed cordially so long as they proceed according to accepted programme.

*Subjects for Study*

1. Plot-comparison: Thackeray's *The Newcomes* and George Eliot's *Romola*.
2. Study of the employment of background: Scott's *Ivanhoe* and Hardy's *Return of the Native*.
3. Study of characterization: Goldsmith's *Vicar of Wakefield*, Dickens's *David Copperfield*, Arnold Bennett's *Clayhanger*.
4. Comparison of Thackeray's *Vanity Fair* with its dramatization, *Becky Sharp*.
5. Comparison of William J. Locke's *The Beloved Vagabond* with its photo-dramatization.
6. History and fiction, as combined in Reade's *The Cloister and the Hearth* and in Maurice Hewlett's *Richard Yea-and-Nay*.
7. Picaresque fiction of today.
8. Novel and romance: Mrs. Ward's *Marriage of William Ashe* and Stevenson's *Treasure Island*.

*Collections*[1]

*The Great English Novelists.* Edited by W. J. and C. W. Dawson. 2 vols. The Reader's Library: Harper & Bros. Cloth, $2.00.

*The English Novel before the Nineteenth Century.* Excerpts from representative types, selected by Annette B. Hopkins and Helen S. Hughes. Ginn & Co. Cloth, $1.60.

[1] Numerous collections of complete English novels were published about 1800, of which Mrs. Barbauld's *British Novelists* in fifty volumes (1810) was the most extensive These are not listed here because important works are equally accessible in separate editions.

THE NOVEL 189

*Critical Discussions*[1]

I

Bishop D. Huet, *The Origin of the Romances*. French original in 1670. English translation in 1715.
Richard Hurd, *Letters on Chivalry and Romance*. 1762.
Clara Reeve, *The Progress of Romance*. 1785.
John C. Dunlop, *The History of Fiction*. 1814.
David Masson, *British Novelists and their Styles*. 1859.

II

Walter Besant and Henry James, *The Art of Fiction*. Boston, 1884.
Richard Burton, *Masters of the English Novel*. New York (Holt & Co.), 1909.
W. L. Cross, *The Development of the English Novel*. New York (Macmillan), 1899.
Arundell Esdaile, *A List of English Tales and Prose Romances printed before 1740*. London (Bibliographical Society), 1914.
Clayton Hamilton, *Materials and Methods of Fiction*. New York (Baker & Taylor), 1908.
Carl Holliday, *English Fiction*. New York (Century Co.), 1912.
Charles F. Horne, *The Technique of the Novel*. New York (Harper & Bros.), 1908.
Henry James, *The Art of Fiction*. In *Partial Portraits*. New York (Macmillan), 1899.
Henry James, *Notes on Novelists*. New York (Scribner), 1914.
J. J. Jusserand, *The English Novel in the Time of Shakespeare*. English translation by Elizabeth Lee. London and New York (Putnam), 1890.
Sidney Lanier, *The English Novel*. New York (Scribner).
Charlotte E. Morgan, *The Rise of the Novel of Manners*. A study of English prose fiction between 1660 and 1740. New York (Columbia University Press), 1911.
Bliss Perry, *A Study of Prose Fiction*. Boston and New York (Houghton Mifflin Co.), 1903.
W. L. Phelps, *The Advance of the English Novel*. New York (Dodd, Mead & Co.), 1916.
Walter Raleigh, *The English Novel*. New York (Scribner), 1903.
George E. Saintsbury, *The English Novel* (*Channels of English Literature*). New York (Dutton & Co.), 1913.

W. E. Simonds, *An Introduction to the Study of English Fiction.* Boston and New York (Heath & Co.), 1913.

F. H. Stoddard, *The Evolution of the English Novel.* New York (Macmillan), 1900.

F. M. Warren, *A History of the Novel Previous to the Seventeenth Century.* New York (Holt & Co.), 1895.

S. L. Whitcomb, *The Study of a Novel.* New York (Heath & Co.), 1905.

# VII

# THE SHORT STORY

## History

IT has been seen that the short story, in the specific sense in which that term is now understood, is a phase of nineteenth-century impressionism in fiction. Out of the rapidly moving current of life-experiences the author's imagination seizes upon an impressive situation or a striking contrast that affects him keenly. The imaginative thrill he experiences is more to him than the facts that aroused it or the dependence of these facts upon each other. But he chooses to impart his impression to others not by the customary means of lyric verse, but by presentation of the facts themselves, selected, shaped, and organized into a story. As in a lyric unit this mood or impression is single, and the story to convey it must be short, and reduced to its absolute essentials.

*Impressionism*

A minimum of incident, perfect unity of organization, an emphasis on imaginative or emotional impression, each of these had been achieved alone many times in the history of fiction before the early nineteenth century. Tales in which one unit of intrigue was carried rapidly and vividly forward to success or an unexpected failure were common enough among the *fabliaux* of the Middle Ages, and found inimitable expression in certain of Chaucer's *Canterbury Tales*,—those of the Reeve and the Miller,

Earlier Short Stories

for example. The prose *novelle* that succeeded these were often only a little less direct in their method. England, under the influence of these *novelle* from Italy and Spain, produced between 1660 and 1830 various brief stories with well-contrived plots, but not notable for economy of detail, or for a distinct grip upon the reader's imagination.

Stories contrived to create certain impressions had been of at least two kinds: the didactic tale often found in the periodical essays and primarily circulated to drive home a moral, and the tale of sentiment and horror first popular in Germany, but shortly cultivated in England in the wake of Kotzebue's plays and the romantic novels of Mrs. Ann Radcliffe (1790-1800):

**Moral and Emotional Tales**

But the well-told tales seldom aroused the emotions to a lasting impression; and the emotional tales, even when they had a unifying idea, were usually rambling and slow. The numerous writers for the periodicals had a sense of restraint and succeeded well in adapting material to their purpose, but their purpose was not to produce a lasting imaginative or emotional impression.

It remained for America to combine the excellences of these several story-types into practically a new product, the popular "short story" of today. Opinion varies as to which particular author is the actual inventor. Washington Irving, amid his periodical sketches (*The Sketch Book* and *The Tales of a Traveller*), produced stories like "Rip Van Winkle" and "The Legend of Sleepy Hollow," where there is a distinctly emotional purpose, and a structure well balanced and restrained, but not yet reduced to the precision and dramatic climax of later writers. Everybody knows "Rip Van Winkle." Consideration of how later authors would present the ma-

**Washington Irving**

terial of this story will do more than anything else to indicate what the short story was still to develop.[1]

This admirable tale of folk-lore and mildly humorous characterization has mood and atmosphere a-plenty. It is always well in hand, no detail of the somewhat lavish descriptions is wasted, and the account moves in a regular but leisurely fashion to its conclusion. In other words, it is just a superior sort of essayist's tale, with a larger emphasis on imaginative impression. According to present standards Irving's version would seem to lack singleness of purpose; there is too much character-study for a good tale of superstition, and too much interest in the supernatural for a good character-study. The proposition that there may be high art in an exquisite blending of the two deserves careful thought, but would be accepted with difficulty by modern critics. The story, we now say, needs a strong dramatic climax to which everything else is subordinated, and this is found in the striking contrast of the ragged, bewildered Rip and the crude, boastful prosperity about the village tavern. In this situation would lie the one "big scene." The short story has developed away from the idyllic personal essay in the direction of the drama, just as today the drama is being shortened to meet the magazine story.

"Rip Van Winkle" and Modern Methods

In seeking the inventor of the modern short story, a much clearer case may be made for Hawthorne or Poe. Both of them began their distinctive work in the short story about 1830, ten years after the appearance of Irving's *Sketch Book*. Significantly both found recog-

Hawthorne and Poe

[1] Cf. Prof. C. S. Baldwin's consideration of this question in the Introduction to his *American Short Stories*.

nition in this field through minor periodicals, Hawthorne by the publication of "The Gentle Boy" in the *Boston Token,* Poe by winning a prize from *The Saturday Visitor* (Baltimore) with "The MS. Found in a Bottle." Both men dealt freely in the gloomy and the supernatural, imaginatively interpreted, and both alike provided keys unlocking the secrets of their workshops to all who care to enter. Hawthorne's art can be understood best through an acquaintance with his *American Note-Books,* where we find the narrative impulses and ideas he jotted down from day to day. Poe put much of his theory of the short story into a criticism of Hawthorne's tales, printed in *Graham's Magazine* for May, 1842.

A single paragraph, from this article of Poe's, will indicate what he found to be essential in his own art and that of his fellow-craftsman:

"A skillful literary artist has constructed a tale. If wise, he has not fashioned his thoughts to accommodate his incidents; but having conceived, with deliberate care, a certain unique or single effect to be wrought out, he then invents such incidents,—he then combines such events as may best aid him in establishing this preconceived effect. If his very initial sentence tend not to the outbringing of this effect, then he has failed in his first step. In the whole composition there should be no word written, of which the tendency, direct or indirect, is not to the one preëstablished design. And by such means, with such care and skill, a picture is at length painted which leaves in the mind of him who contemplates it with a kindred art, a sense of the fullest satisfaction. The idea of the tale has been presented unblemished, because undisturbed; and this is an end unattainable by the novel."

**Poe's Idea of the Type**

The creative process here described is probably more

THE SHORT STORY 195

mechanical and self-conscious than Hawthorne conceived of, but Poe emphasizes exactly the phases of it that meet us constantly in Hawthorne's *Note-*
Situations *Books*,—namely, situations and effects.
and Effects Thus Hawthorne notes such conceptions as these: "To have ice in one's blood"; "A phantom of the old royal governors,—on the night of the evacuation of Boston by the British"; "The print in blood of a naked foot to be traced through the streets of a town"; "A person to catch fire-flies, and try to kindle his household fire with them,—it would be symbolical of something."

The symbolizing of something, suggested in this last quotation from Hawthorne, so long as it was held in check, gave idea as well as emotion to the
Allegory final impression left by the stories, and was the supreme achievement of Hawthorne and Poe alike. In both these men, however, it had a tendency to get beyond its bounds. In Hawthorne the result is often philosophizing sketches that are scarcely stories at all, but rather essays of the eighteenth-century type. In Poe there is a corresponding fondness for the remote and fantastic, sometimes even characterized as "fable" or "parable." Hawthorne is often weak in building up or sustaining a plot, but Poe carries his principle of studied invention so far that the very artistry of his plots seems artificial.

Both writers, on the other hand, have certain means of arriving at the effect of realism. Hawthorne, however unusual his situations, puts into
Methods of them characters that he has studied
Realism deeply and in detail, so that we recognize them as human, like ourselves. Poe's people, when individualized at all, are likely to

be mere replicas of his own moods, and sadly lacking in Hawthorne's variety. Poe's realism, indeed, lies largely in his style. This at times is as ornate and artificial as his plots and the settings in which these are enacted. But at his best he has the accumulation of what seems to be unconscious detail after the manner of Defoe, coupled with the picturesqueness of description achieved later by Stevenson. This is seen in all his best stories, particularly "The Gold Bug" and "The Cask of Amontillado," and is of peculiar service in his tales of mystery and crime.

Poe's activity extended exactly to the middle of the century, and Hawthorne lived until 1864. By the latter date the stories of both of them had become fixed in many American minds as models of a new structure in fiction. Naturally various American writers diligently set about imitating these models. Fitz-James O'Brien, a young Irish journalist on the staff of *Harper's Monthly,* found in Poe a kindred spirit. He wrote abundantly in the manner of Poe's short-story technique, and showed a marked preference for subjects that were grotesquely imaginative or uncanny. But he gave to his stories a greater realism, by drawing them apparently out of the commonplace conditions of everyday life. Thus the memorable mystery of his "What Was It?" is developed not in a land of the imagination or in a dream-palace with bizarre decorations, but in an old-fashioned New York boarding house on Twenty-sixth Street between Seventh and Eighth Avenues. O'Brien had not yet attained Poe's brevity and directness, when he was killed, at the age of thirty-four, in the Civil War. He is another of those literary men about whom one can only wonder what they might have done with a few years more in which to develop their art.

<small>Immediate Imitators— O'Brien</small>

A more developed and a more complex art is that of Bret Harte, another journalist, who first won recognition in 1868 by the publication of "The Luck of Roaring Camp" in the *Overland Monthly*. He had in the experiences of the California prospectors a rich vein of material, as yet undeveloped, and he appreciated fully the possibilities in its unique characters and picturesque experiences. It was the ideal combination for narrative,—abundance of detail to be presented with great show of realism, but located so remotely from general experience that it inevitably strikes the imagination as romance. To his task Harte brought a sense of vivid, somewhat exaggerated characterization acquired from the novels of Dickens, and a skill in receiving and imparting unique impressions after the manner of Poe. Again, as in the case of O'Brien, this was an instance of applying the new impressionism of the short story to affairs of daily life, but the life was that of a specific portion of the country, and rather highly colored at that.

Bret Harte was not far wrong, when he explained, in 1899,[1] that the success of his stories was due to the fact that they were the first to present a distinct phase of American life, sympathetically and with truth of detail. He might have added that this was a phase of life particularly rich in motion and color, that his sympathy found expression in the finest technique yet developed for such fiction, and that the truthfulness of his detail was strained considerably to make people and things striking and memorable. As Professor Canby puts it, the man who would look for Yuba Bill at Sandy Bar,

**Bret Harte**

**His Local Color**

[1] In an article, "The Rise of the Short Story," in *The Cornhill Magazine*, July, 1899.

would search for Pickwick in London, and Peggotty on Yarmouth Beach. At any rate, the unique interest of one section of the country or another soon claimed the attention of various authors who undertook to phrase their impressions of this localized panorama of life according to the methods of Poe and Harte, and as they succeeded there came into popularity the familiar American short story of local color.

One other author, cultivating one other variety of short story, came into prominence by 1870, as an essential factor in this general movement toward life **Henry James** around us as the material of the writer's selective impressions. This was Henry James, who has remained until our own day,[1] in short story and in novel, chief sponsor for the impressionistic treatment of realistic and uncolored detail. This detail of his is not external, however, like so much of the picturesqueness of Bret Harte and the later local-colorists. It is rather the detail of the psychologist, the detail of mental experience and intellectual contrast, and a sort of detail too that James interprets with extreme thoroughness and the last touch of subtlety. In his striving after the exact and entire expression of the situations that have impressed him, he has evolved a corresponding subtlety of phrasing, with the result that his short stories and his novels are extremely difficult for the mere casual reader.

With all his apparent difficulty of approach, Henry James is by no means to be set aside and reserved for the elect. He has been a potent influence in **His Influence** American letters for nearly half a century, turning the eyes of authors inward to the real essentials of personality and life experience, holding in check the realists who would lose us in a maze

[1] Henry James died February 29, 1916.

of unordered truth, counteracting that other tendency of realism to revel in filth for filth's sake. Better than these things for the student of the short story, he has been a master-craftsman in this form of literary art, with delicate perceptions, unerring touch, and a richness of utterance that is a constant source of satisfaction to those who love fine phrasing. The situations that have caught his eye are exquisite things,—the penniless representatives of the " real thing " glad to serve as artist's models and even to do menial tasks for low-born rivals in this humble occupation; the strong-willed daughter who plays the part of " chaperon " for the mother whom society has rejected. Equally satisfying are the methods by which he has presented these situations, from just the proper angles, so as to impress his readers with the mood that should accompany them.

Up to this point the account of the short story has been entirely in terms of America. At first France alone of European countries exhibited a comparable development in the art of fiction, and in more recent years it has been the largest foreign influence upon the American short story. Closely corresponding to the achievements of Poe and Hawthorne were those of their French contemporaries, Mérimée and—in a limited portion of his work—Balzac. France like America was still dominated largely by romantic imagination and was just learning to trim close in its modes of expression. This romantic dreaming and exquisite finish were fused most thoroughly in the stories of Gautier, who profited not a little by acquaintance with the work of Poe.

The Short Story in France

Shortly after the middle of the century, France, following the lead of Russia, became strongly addicted to naturalism in her fiction,—that is, the minute and scientific presentation of life in all its realism, with an apparent detachment of the author and his sympathies from the circumstances described. While this objective treatment made less direct appeal to the emotions, it had possibilities of great imaginative unity and encouraged the portrayal of small units and detached threads of experience. Under such conditions the French short story reached the height of its effectiveness and became a model both for Europe and America. At the hands of such men as Daudet and Maupassant, one vital situation after another is deftly caught out of the passionate languor of southern France, or the hard and sordid selfishness of the North, or the veneered immorality of the capital, and held up to view pitilessly, cynically, but always—from the mechanical point of view—exquisitely. Thus Maupassant's well-known story, "The Necklace," depends for its strength partly on the situation of utter falseness and pretense upon which it is developed, partly on the merciless way in which it lays bare the poor little ambitious heart of Mme. Loisel, and more than all on the supreme skill with which every detail is made to play its part in the rapid and unerring creation of the impression. "Ah, the good *pot-au-feu!*" exclaims M. Loisel, as he settles down to the humble noonday meal; and we have no further doubt about *his* social aspirations.

**French Naturalism**

England was won over very slowly to the ideal of the modern short story. Not until Robert Louis Stevenson, who came into prominence in 1877-78, did she find a man who consistently produced stories of this type worthy to rank with the notable achievements of America, Russia, and France. English writers of other forms, usually novelists, had occasionally mingled vivid, single

**Beginnings in England**

impression with economy of form and succeeded at it; for example, Sir Walter Scott, in "Wandering Willie's Tale," as early as 1824, Charles Dickens in "The Signal Man" (1866), Mrs. Gaskell in "Cousin Phillis" (1864), and Dr. John Brown in "Rab and His Friends" (1858). But for one reason or another this success was not followed up, and the technique involved was not thoroughly mastered. Stevenson indeed was less Briton than cosmopolitan, with his Scottish tenderness, his exotic imagination, and his French sense of form. At any rate he mastered the secret of the short story: "You may take a certain atmosphere, and get action and persons to express and realize it."[1]

Stevenson, a master spinner of yarns, gave a new sparkle and zest of romance to the short story in English, and kept it from becoming somewhat bloodless in its impersonal impressions of realistic details and its trim economy of expression. The impressions of Stevenson are unified and vivid, but they are derived from romantic material, as in "The Sire de Malétroit's Door," or rich in imaginative detail, like "Markheim." The language, too, while apt and effective, is enriched and picturesque to an unusual degree. Certain of his stories, particularly "Markheim" and "Dr. Jekyll and Mr. Hyde," suggest the mystic probings into character so common in the tales of Hawthorne.

Robert Louis Stevenson

Strangely enough the other great English writer of short stories is also eminently cosmopolitan, for all his vigorous patriotism. Rudyard Kipling's short stories are as a rule located in remote British colonies, and among the territorial armies, where detail may be minutely realistic, but is still rich in romantic suggestion to the un-

[1] Balfour's *Life of Robert Louis Stevenson*, Vol. II, p. 169.

traveled reader. Thus he has supplanted Bret Harte as the acknowledged master of local color in the short story in English, having at the same time a wide acquaintance with a life unknown but fascinating to the average man, the trained eye of the journalist to see at once to the center of interest in his raw material, and the skill in language necessary for one who would always put the right word in the right place.

**Rudyard Kipling**

It may be argued, indeed, that his journalistic craftsmanship is too obtrusive. Local color like his, that always puts an emphasis on things that are vivid or full of rich tints, is very prone to exaggerate. People and events in Kipling's India are probably no nearer life than Bret Harte's Argonauts or various later American creations that might be mentioned. But so long as they are sufficiently detailed and we are not called upon to verify them, we are likely to care very little about exaggerations. This constant emphasis on "big situations" and "good stories," from the journalist's point of view, is itself open to criticism. But the more subdued sort of thing, the realism of daily life, has had a sufficient share of exponents since Henry James pointed out the way. Moreover Kipling himself has done more modest things, some of them, like "They," among his very finest work. Other debatable tendencies may be mentioned,—his somewhat flippant treatment of themes, his fondness for stories with a surprise at the end, his vocabulary of picturesque phrases that are just a bit startling,—but one power his training has given him on which there can be no debate. His skill in organizing his richness of detail into organic units, moving inevitably to conclusions and leaving no doubtful impressions behind them, represents the highest

**His Art**

THE SHORT STORY 203

art of the short story,—not rejecting details but utilizing them.

Rudyard Kipling has shown such a large productivity in the short story that the limits of this chapter permit only a bare listing of the collections into which
His Work  separate stories from the magazines have been gathered. The first of these was *Plain Tales from the Hills* (1888), made up largely of stories first published like his "Departmental Ditties" in the *Civil and Military Gazette,* of Lahore, India. The success of this volume immediately encouraged further reprints, among them *Soldiers Three,* relating additional adventures of his three famous heroes already introduced in *Plain Tales.* A much stronger collection of stories is his *Life's Handicap* (1891), in which are famous titles like "The Courting of Dinah Shadd," "The Man Who Was," "Without Benefit of Clergy," and "At the End of the Passage." Later collections of note have been *Many Inventions* (1893), *The Jungle Book* (1894), *The Second Jungle Book* (1895), *The Day's Work* (1898).

While England was finding a worthy place in the history of the short story, American writers were by no means idle. One group, including
Later  Thomas Bailey Aldrich, Frank R. Stockton, and H. C. Bunner, developed a distinctly American type of story, told with all the brevity and deftness of the French. The material itself was slight, little more than an anecdote, and there was sly humor throughout, usually leading to a turn of surprise at the end. Everybody knows—or does not know—the conclusion of Stockton's "The Lady or the Tiger?" The local-colorists of this period became continually more numerous and prolific, so that by 1900 little of America remained virgin soil. What Bret Harte had

done for the gold-seekers of California, George W. Cable did for Louisiana in "Creole Days," Thomas Nelson Page for Virginia, Sarah Orne Jewett and Mary E. Wilkins-Freeman for New England, Hamlin Garland for the Middle West, and later Jack London for the Alaskan goldfields. William Sidney Porter (O. Henry) sought and found local color in various localities, particularly Texas and New York City. In technique and mannerisms he followed the lead of Kipling, at the same time having much in common with the authors of anecdotal stories just mentioned.

At the present time the magazines of both England and America are free to choose out of an abundance of good manuscripts submitted for inspection. A large list might be prepared of conspicuous authors in both countries whose work is always in demand and of a consistently high standard. Still every year brings into notice various stories of the highest merit by writers previously unheard of. This fact, together with the recent flood of manuals on short-story technique and the numerous catch-penny plans advertised to aid beginners in preparing and marketing their manuscripts, has set hundreds of unprepared and unqualified persons to work upon stories. There are so many magazines and syndicate schemes in existence that many stories get into print that should never see the light of day. The reader will hardly be conservative enough to limit himself to well-known names, such as Jacobs, Quiller-Couch, Conrad, and Hewlett from England, and Zona Gale, Mary Heaton Vorse, and Mrs. Gerould in our own country. But before he goes far afield he would do well to equip himself with a thorough acquaintance with the tried and accepted models of short-story writing.

**Present Activity**

## Technique of the Short Story

The technique of the short story may be considered most conveniently in its relations to that of the novel. Such an attempt will in no sense oppose the contention, stated emphatically in every manual of short-story writing, that the short story is not a condensed novel and cannot be expanded into a novel, that its point of view, its principles of structure, and its artistic impression are all peculiarly its own. When all this is granted, the fact remains that novel and short story are at least kindred forms of prose fiction, making use of the same elements of narrative under the same traditional principles of art. The short story has affiliations also with lyric poetry, and with the one-act play now growing so rapidly in popular favor. But there are numerous pieces of good fiction, such as Henry James has written from time to time, that challenge the ingenuity of critics to determine whether they are brief impressionistic novels or long short stories.

*Relation to Other Forms of Literature*

In actual fact, it is probably as difficult to generalize on the mental processes by which an author works toward a finished short story as on those that go to the completion of a great novel. The assumption is, however, that for the short story they are analogous to those of a lyric poet, with a fairly definite initial impulse, a vivid imaginative impression capable of being communicated, and an intellectual power to see the end in the beginning. Just as the lyric is personal the short story is personal, selecting out of the kaleidoscope of events the few related ones that have caught the author's fancy, and undertaking to produce with them an imaginative

*Personality and Impression*

experience for us that is akin to the author's own. The circumstances chosen may be unusual to the bounds of probability, or they may be common as the dust beneath our feet, only seen in a new light. They may be presented with all the resources of the writer's emotion or in the hard, cynical manner of Maupassant and his imitators. It is for us to lend ourselves to the author's purpose and see these things with his eyes.

Like the novel the short story is compounded of the elements of plot, character, and setting. As usual one of these must predominate, but in the short story this fact often carries with it the practical exclusion of all subordinate interests. Not that a good plot-story can be constructed without characters or good characters portrayed without incidents. But time is so limited and excision so marked in these stories that plot may be reduced to a single point of decision or characters become puppets in order that some other end may be served. An author's first impression usually comes to him from a situation,—a new grouping of circumstances, a haunting personality challenging analysis, a bit of background giving new color to people and events. But essential to the impression itself is some one of these story-elements, crowding the others into the background, and suggesting the method to be employed in the final treatment of the material. Stevenson understood this threefold manner of procedure and illustrated each phase of it in his work. "The Sire de Malétroit's Door," from its first conception till the last word is spoken by its puppet characters, is a story of plot. "Will of the Mill" is a character study with just enough plot to keep it from being a sketch. "The Merry Men" is Stevenson's own example of a story of atmosphere. "There," he says, "I

began with a feeling of one of those islands on the west coast of Scotland, and I gradually developed the story to express the sentiment with which that coast affected me."
As a rule plot and character are both portrayed in dramatic fashion. Action is organized into scenes,—or if possible into a single scene. These scenes represent the vital steps in the procedure and are themselves planned for climactic effects. Characters are at the best not complex and can undergo little development. Hence they are able to reveal themselves in dialogue and require no analysis or explanation at the writer's hands. The time involved in the story is condensed as much as possible. When a long stretch of time is unavoidable, as in Maupassant's "The Necklace" or Kipling's "Baa, Baa, Black Sheep," this is suggested quietly and adroitly, so as not to destroy unity of impression. All these conditions throw an undue emphasis upon that which is striking or unusual, even to the point of being fantastic. Characters are in constant danger of becoming caricatures, just as the situations may force probabilities to the very verge of patience.

**Unity in Plot and Character**

It is much easier to have short stories dominated by their setting, and thus to keep an "atmosphere," than it is to get this effect with novels. Not often does nature enter into a novel so thoroughly as Egdon Heath penetrates Thomas Hardy's *Return of the Native*. Short stories of atmosphere abound, particularly in the numerous varieties of "local color" that have parted among them the motley garments of America. There is no need to remark that this local color, like the dialect that frequently accompanies it, may impart spirit and artistic beauty to the narrative, or may be overdrawn

**Stories of Atmosphere**

till it becomes crude and obtrusive. Like many another fine phase of art, it is easy to do moderately well—or badly.

Under the constant pressure of economy of phrasing and singleness of effect, style and diction have taken on new importance for the writer of short stories. Dickens and Scott could afford to be prodigal—and accordingly careless —in the words and sentences they poured into their novels. The ideal short story, however, should be as perfect an organism as the sonnet, admitting no word that has not been weighed and considered and found to be the one word for the place, performing its small but vital part in enhancing the impression of the whole. Yet this perfection of phrasing should never call attention to itself or become more than a means to an end. The perfectly groomed gentleman is vastly superior to the tailor's model. French short stories, at the hands of Gautier, Daudet, and Maupassant, fixed the standard in this respect. Kipling at his best has measured up to this. But Kipling at other times has fallen into a mannered sort of smartness, in which he has been followed all too frequently by O. Henry and the host of other Americans who have coveted O. Henry's meteoric career of success.

*Style and Diction*

*Subjects for Study*

1. Reconstruction of Addison's Sir Roger de Coverley material as a short story.
2. The bible story of Ruth as a short story.
3. Comparison of Defoe's "Apparition of Mrs. Veal" and Poe's "House of Usher" as presentations of the supernatural.
4. Criticism of Poe's "Philosophy of Composition" based on personal experience.
5. Reconstruction of a current newspaper story as a short story.

## THE SHORT STORY

6. The short story involved in Rossetti's painting, "Found."
7. The short story in Scott's "Lochinvar," Hood's "The Bridge of Sighs," or Keats's "La belle Dame sans Merci."
8. Reconstruction of the one-act play, *War Brides,* as a short story. (*The Century,* February, 1915.)
9. Stylistic comparison: Kipling, Conrad, Maupassant.
10. Suggestion, plan, and completion of a short story of incident; of character.

### Collections

*Selected Short Stories.* Introduction by Hugh Walker. World's Classics: Oxford University Press. Cloth, 35 cents.
A cheap and convenient miscellaneous collection.

*A Book of Short Stories.* Selected and edited by Stuart P. Sherman. English Readings: Holt & Co. Cloth, 35 cents.
A limited but very useful selection, with helpful introduction.

*The Short-Story.* Specimens illustrating its development. Edited by Brander Matthews. American Book Co. Cloth, $1.00.
Twenty-four representative English and foreign selections, with introduction reduced from editor's earlier treatise.

*The Book of the Short Story.* Edited by Alexander Jessup and Henry S. Canby. Appleton & Co. Cloth, $1.10.
Specimens of tales and short stories representing the entire history of the form. Introduction by Professor Canby and extensive reading lists.

*Modern Short Stories.* Edited by Margaret Ashmun. The Macmillan Co., $1.25.
Twenty-one famous modern stories, English and foreign. The introduction is commendable and there is a considerable list of additional stories.

*Modern Masterpieces of Short Prose Fiction.* Edited by Alice V. Waite and Edith M. Taylor. Appleton & Co. Cloth, $1.50.
Fewer stories, but of considerable variety.

*The Great English Short-Story Writers.* Edited by W. J. and C. W. Dawson. Harper & Bros. 2 vols., each $1.00.
About thirty representative stories, those in the first volume by earlier writers, in the second by contemporaries. Good introduction.

*American Short Stories.* Selected and edited, with an Introductory Essay on the Short Story, by Charles S. Baldwin. Wampum Library: Longmans, Green & Co. $1.40.

## 210 THE TYPICAL FORMS OF ENGLISH LITERATURE

### Critical Discussions

Evelyn M. Albright, *The Short Story: Its Principles and Structure*. New York (Macmillan), 1907.

C. R. Barrett, *Short-Story Writing*. New York (Baker & Taylor), 1900.

Henry S. Canby, *The Short Story in English*. New York (Holt & Co.), 1909.

Henry S. Canby, *A Study of the Short Story*. (Condensation of the above for class use ) New York (Holt & Co ), 1913.

Sherwin Cody, *How to Write Fiction*. Especially the art of short-story writing. London (Bellairs & Co.), 1895.

E. A. Cross, *The Short Story*. Chicago (McClurg & Co ), 1914.

J. Berg Esenwein, *Writing the Short Story*. A practical handbook. New York (Hinds, Noble & Eldredge), 1908.

Carl H. Grabo, *The Art of the Short Story*. New York (Scribner), 1913.

Hale and Dawson, *The Elements of the Short Story*. Study plans. New York (Holt & Co.), 1915.

Brander Matthews, *The Philosophy of the Short Story*. New York (Longmans, Green & Co ), 1901.

R. W. Neal, *Short Stories in the Making*. New York (Oxford University Press, American Branch), 1914.

Notestein and Dunn, *The Modern Short Story*. New York (Barnes Co.), 1914

W. B. Pitkin, *The Art and the Business of Short-Story Writing*. New York (Macmillan), 1912.

# VIII

## THE DRAMA

### History

Beginnings of Tragedy

AFTER more than twenty centuries the tragedy and comedy of the ancient Greeks are still accepted as the supreme achievement in these forms of art. Aristotle's great critical document, the *Poetics,* based directly upon the practice of these classic dramatists, remains the foundation stone of all critical interpretation of modern plays. Yet these Greek dramas have at no time had an appreciable direct influence on English stage plays, and have been practically unknown to many of the most effective playwrights. This is not merely because they were poetic plays; all the great dramas of Elizabeth's day were poetic. But they began as essentially lyric compositions with the accompaniment of music and choric dancing; and the dialogue that developed in the succession of Æschylus, Sophocles, and Euripides came into being later to present more graphically the circumstances celebrated by the chanting throng. Æschylus, as Aristotle explains, increased the actors from one to two and gave prominence to their dialogue; Sophocles added a third actor and introduced painted scenery.

Tragedy among the Greeks concerned itself largely with holy things. Immortals and supermen were thus brought before the eyes of the populace. That their majesty might not be forgotten, the platform on which they stalked on elevated sandals was separated from the amphitheater by the dancing-place of the chorus, with a sacrificial altar in the midst of it; and the faces visible above their flowing robes were not of flesh and blood, but the unchanging outlines of carved and distorted masks. If one compares with this remoteness the pageant-wagons of English bible-plays and the rough intimacy of performances on the Elizabethan stage, with apprentices on three sides and dandies on the very boards, it will appear that the English people not only preferred to see things acted out, but they wanted the performance as tangible and realistic as possible. The Greek comedy of Aristophanes had indeed much of the action and reality England has always craved, but even in this form it has always been convenient for English drama to find models closer at hand.

**Greek Remoteness of Effect**

As observed elsewhere, modern Europe during the Renaissance had a strange fashion of searching through classical literature backward, and often stopped contented with late Latin models instead of early Greek. This was true of the drama. Scholarly men, in England as on the continent, seeking after classical standards for their comedies, found some to their satisfaction in the Latin work of Plautus and Terence, two hundred years later than the Greek plays of Aristophanes. By this choice they lost little in stage effectiveness, so far as concerns comedy, but the compromise they made in tragedy was more costly. Here for some reason they fixed upon the series of tragedies usually ascribed to the orator and philosopher Seneca, favorite and later victim of the Emperor Nero. Though based on Greek myths and modeled considerably on the work of the Greek

**Latin Models for England**

masters, these plays were plainly not intended for the stage, but to serve as forensic exercises in the schools of oratory then popular. Even Aristotle's *Poetics* came late to the knowledge of the Renaissance as a manual of dramatic art, and had to contest popularity with the *Ars Poetica* composed by the poet Horace as a letter to his friends the Pisos.

When dramatic composition in England first developed an artistic consciousness, it did so under the influence of men of learning, and the programme these men proposed was,—"Seneca for tragedy, Plautus and Terence for comedy, Horace for critical theory." Hence at the threshold of this account, there is more reason to define the art of Seneca and Plautus than that of their Greek predecessors. Seneca's plots, like those of Greek tragedy, are based on the legendary history of gods and mighty heroes, with a marked fondness for horrible crimes and appropriate retribution. In two plays at least —*Thyestes* and *Octavia*—a spirit is recalled from the Shades to participate in the action. Horror and bloodshed is carefully removed from the stage, however, and formally described or reported by messenger. In fact, genuine action gives way almost entirely to long set speeches and eloquent moralizing, the former by the dignified characters, the latter by the equally solemn chorus. The plot is carefully trimmed of all extraneous matter, and the five acts in which it is always presented do not develop successive stages of the entire action, as in Shakespeare's great tragedies, but are concerned with various phases of the situation that marks the crest or climax of the dramatic movement. There is indeed an extended exposition of earlier events, related or presented as soliloquy, but the action proper represents a cross-section of the entire plot at its crucial moment, rather than an extended narrative of the whole.

Various technical details of the Senecan tragedies have had considerable influence upon modern playwrights. Most important of these probably is the arrangement in five acts of a variable number of scenes, a scheme almost held sacred by the Elizabethans. Somewhat less significant was English imitation in matters of characterization and style. The chorus, while still employed by Seneca, was withdrawn from participation in the action and given an explanatory and moralizing function merely. The separate characters were balanced against each other in a stiff and formal grouping. There was little subtlety of characterization and no chance for development. All speeches were in high-style, the one concession from the constant oratory being the Greek device of "stichomythia," an artificial sort of dialogue in alternate lines. Antithesis was frequently employed, hyperbole abounded, and every character was inclined to speak "*sententiae*," or moral aphorisms, upon the slightest pretext. Any or all of these features were likely to appear at any time in Elizabethan tragedy.

**Influences from Seneca**

Latin comedies, as written by Plautus and Terence, were what may be called "comedies of manners," and have served as ultimate models for all such comedies down to our own day. That is, their primary purpose was to present with a mild spirit of ridicule, elements of weakness or extravagance in the society of their day; to satirize, in other words, obvious deviations from the accepted standards of right living. Characters and situations, while true enough to life to be accepted as probable, had their typical features in-

**Latin Comedy of Manners**

tensified to the exclusion of other qualities. Thus misers became practically greed personified, fops were incarnate foppishness, and hungry servants were all stomach. Frequently the names they bore implied as much. Plots were well-constructed fabrics of intrigue, almost fascinating enough to justify themselves apart from their satirical connections. These plots, however, were made to grow naturally out of the peculiarities of the characters, generally under the manipulations of some clever and unscrupulous trickster, a scapegrace servant or a professional parasite. The entire treatment was unemotional, unsympathetic. If a doting old father suffered from placing too much confidence in a contriving son, or a self-righteous youth trusted his own powers too far and fell, there was no pity for the victim. Justice and not mercy dominates the comic stage.

Little if any knowledge of this Latin drama penetrated to the distant island of Britain, where Rome set up her military outposts in the last century before Christ. Indeed, this island was to see the withdrawal of these outposts, and bear the impress of invading forces of Saxons, Danes, and even Normans before it witnessed a single dramatic performance at all worthy of the name. Then the drama appeared in a new guise, crude and childishly serious, an outgrowth of the worship of the medieval Christian Church. The models of classical antiquity were to remain neglected in England for some four hundred years more.

First English Drama not Classical

From a few uncertain records of the twelfth and thirteenth centuries, we gather that in England, as on the continent, simple plays began to be developed from the events connected with the two chief anniversaries in the Christian calendar—Easter and Christmas. Gradually the dialogue for these dramatizations passed from the actual Latin of the Vulgate Bible and the service book to the spoken English of the day. Scenes were staged first in churches, then in churchyards, later on platforms along the street and on the village-green, and in some instances on wagons drawn from corner to corner along the village thoroughfare. Actors were ecclesiastics, so long as the performances were on church property. Afterward these men were supplanted by tradesmen and peasants of the vicinity, who in time, no doubt, came to take a genuine professional interest in their annual assignments, as in recent years the simple folk of Oberammergau have in their Passion Play.

**Early Religious Drama**

As skill increased the subject-matter was extended from its original centers of interest to cover practically all the effective episodes of the four gospels, a few from the old testament, and a number of saints' legends. By 1400 various communities, such as Chester, York, and Coventry, had organized the material of these Miracles or Mystery Plays, as they were called, into connected cycles, performed regularly on the festival day of Corpus Christi (the sixtieth day after Easter) and occupying the entire period from daybreak to nightfall. The trade-guilds, then prominent in municipal affairs, shared responsibility for various parts,—sometimes with nice appropriateness, as when the shipwrights staged the Building of the Ark, and the vintners the Marriage at Cana.

**Mystery Plays**

The stage was a rough platform, open on all sides, but curtained beneath to provide a dressing-room; or else, as was certainly the case at Chester and York, there was a series of wheeled stages or "pageants," drawn through the town and stopping one after another for a performance at each crowded street corner. Stage-settings were according to the principle of what is called "simultaneous staging," the crude suggestions of the several scenes required for one episode being in place at once. Because of the frequent intercourse with heaven and hell, much use was made of an upper platform from which descended angels with gilt hair and out of which the Almighty himself might speak; also of a gaping pair of dragon's jaws (Hell Mouth) emitting black smoke and occasional sprightly little devils. For one episode, such as the Wakefield "Second Shepherds' Play," the scene was supposed to shift rapidly from the shepherds' camp to Mac's cottage, back to the camp-fire and again to the cottage, and then upon the fields outside descended the Angel of the Lord—from the upper platform—proclaiming "Gloria in excelsis!" Upon occasion a messenger in character might elbow his way through the throng of spectators, or Herod "rage in the pageant and in the street also."

*Methods of Staging*

The text of the plays was an expanded paraphrase of the scriptures, in a long series of dramatic situations marked by vigorous action and frank realism. Every step of importance was included, every event visualized. Speeches were in the current vernacular, arranged loosely in a rapid, easy-going verse. Things essentially serious or sacred, such as the Sacrifice of Isaac or the attitude of Christ through the experiences of Passion Week, were managed with becoming reverence and restraint, and often expressed in language of rare beauty. The English public, however, loved low comedy and horse-play, and had already become familiar with it in May-games and other buffoonery. Farce of this sort

*Text of the Plays*

passed easily into the Miracle Plays, and pleased the populace without offending the fastidious, for it was confined to incidental happenings and minor characters. Thus the comic experiences of the shepherds with the thievery of their neighbor Mac merely mark time before the appearance of the angel; Noah's shrewish wife and her " gossips " afford a harmless diversion before the horror of the deluge, and even Joseph, the elderly husband of Mary, serves by his rough and ignorant protests to emphasize the miracle of the virgin birth. These comic characters, too, are stock English types, and add considerably to the realism of the whole.

Miracle Plays, particularly in cycles, continued to be performed until the time of Shakespeare. Before 1500, however, they began to divide the field with the Moralities, which in turn soon developed in the direction of the Interludes. These Moralities were first performed by amateurs on temporary stages, but eventually passed into the hands of strolling players who acted in inn-yards and banqueting-halls. At first they were closely connected with a favorite device of writers in the Middle Ages, the abstract controversy or " debate." There had long been elaborate discussions between the Flower and the Leaf, the Owl and the Nightingale, the Body and the Soul. Early Moralities were dramatized struggles between selected Virtues and Vices for the Soul of Man. They lacked the charm of detailed characterization and at first subordinated action to eloquence. But they had the art of arranging certain selected events from a human life in a logical order to produce an effect of climax and create a single impression.

These early abstractions came gradually to have more of realism and individuality. The colorless figure of

Mankind himself, when he refused to take distinct shape, was occasionally dropped out altogether. A single Vice was developed beyond the rest in wit and resourcefulness until he lost abstract meaning, and was simply "The Vice," with some chance name like Ambidexter or Titivillus, and played a part like that of the intriguing slave or parasite in Roman comedy. Here again there was an opening for horseplay and buffoonery, and the chance was not lost. Another importation from the continent, the French farce, helped to point the way. The result was the rather vaguely defined Interlude, usually developing a slight intrigue plot with little restraint and much amusing dialogue and lively stage "business." Serious moralities did not die out under this opposition, but turned to more concrete realism, sometimes to actual historical facts.

**Course of Their Development**

In the middle of the sixteenth century, when the term "interlude" was being used indiscriminately for various dramatic forms, serious or comic and of whatever length, the influence of Latin models first began to be felt in England. It entered by way of the schools, the universities, and the Inns of Court, places where amateur dramatic performances of a more scholarly sort were a frequent form of entertainment. From such sources came *Ralph Roister Doister*, a comedy by Nicholas Udall, head master of Eton; and soon after, *Gammer Gurton's Needle*, performed at Christ's College, Cambridge. About the same time appeared the distinctly Senecan tragedy, *Gorboduc*, or *The Tragedy of Ferrex and Porrex*, written by Sackville and Norton for presentation at Whitehall by the Gentlemen of the Inner Temple. Of the two comedies, *Ralph Roister Doister* is considerably nearer the

**First Latin Influences**

work of Plautus. It has a well-knit plot of intrigue, even though the gull is exceedingly gullible and the slap-stick is worked rather vigorously. Characters are very obvious types, indicated broadly enough in the names they bear. Merrygreek is a direct descendant from the Greek slaves or parasites whose scheming kept the plots of Roman comedy in constant motion. Yet he inherits likewise from the Vice of English Moralities. Roister Doister himself is the braggart soldier of all the ages, only slightly localized. Suggestive names extend even to household servants, like Tibet Talkapace and the old nurse Madge Mumblecrust. There is little satire outside the treatment of the title character, but there is much realistic portrayal of well-to-do English life.

*Gammer Gurton's Needle* is more frankly realistic, more representative of the interlude, more English. Diccon, the Bedlam beggar, was no classic importation. He and his kind were familiar on every English highway, but he is none the less successful as arch intriguer in the mischievous plot. Characters generally are of a lower social order,—too low in fact to admit many possibilities of cleverness or complexity. The plot, however, moves steadily forward, connects its riotous incidents naturally, and produces a totally unexpected dénouement that modern farce-makers may well envy.

"Gammer Gurton's Needle"

Both these comedies act well today, but the value of *Gorboduc* is almost entirely historical. It attempts to localize the dramatic methods of Seneca amid a vigorous, action-loving English public. Its story is British, but very remotely British, like Shakespeare's *King Lear* or *Cymbeline*. The tragic material is arranged with considerable

"Gorboduc"

unity of structure, but the action is presented step by step in its development instead of being caught, after the classical manner, at the crest of its dramatic interest. Characters are few and princely, and are grouped with mechanical precision. They speak at great length, report crime rather than perform it, and at rare intervals lighten their conversation to the extent of various lines of "stichomythic" line-for-line rejoinder. As if to atone for lack of action, each act is preceded by a "dumb-show," to suggest in pantomime what is taking place. This device is not found in Seneca, but had already been used in Italy. Everywhere there is moralizing, the reflective speeches of the chorus—" four ancient and sage men of Britain "—being particularly replete with it.

Through the fifty years that followed *Gorboduc*, Senecan tragedy, adapted in one way or another to native English taste, was constantly knocking at the doors of the Elizabethan stage. It continued to appear, little changed in form, in the frequent amateur performances of the Universities and Inns of Court. It was cultivated for a time in society under patronage of the sister of Sir Philip Sidney. It found most appropriate exemplification in the Roman plays of Ben Jonson early in the seventeenth century. But except for one limited class, the Senecan "tragedies of revenge" yet to be treated, it never really found a welcome in the English theater. Certain things it did accomplish, however. It held continually before playwrights the ideal of unity of structure and effect, a thing hard enough to maintain amid the multiplicity of events and personages that came to crowd the Elizabethan stage. As distinct mechanical aids to this unity it provided the division into five acts and a strong tendency to group characters for

**Further Imitation of Seneca**

parallel and contrast. It established for tragedy a tradition of exalted personages and eloquent speeches, particularly in the case of the central figure who suffers retribution for his guilt or error. Finally, from Seneca came the impulse toward the tragedy of revenge out of which Shakespeare evolved his *Hamlet*.

Elizabethan drama seems to have found itself about the year 1590, at a time when numerous eager young literary men were hard at work seeking to develop the highest possibilities of their native tongue. Shakespeare had just begun his career in London, where he had fallen in with the group of talented but improvident playwrights that included Peele, Greene, Kyd, and Marlowe. Upon this group rested the responsibility of choosing between two very different methods of dramatic construction: one, that of the Miracles, which transcribed in detail from historical narrative; the other, the Senecan method, selecting the climactic point of an action, discarding the rest, and focusing interest upon a tragic hero. Their decision, as revealed in their practice, was in the nature of a compromise, and gave rise to four rather distinct varieties of serious plays. For convenience, these may be called (1) the panoramic chronicle history, (2) the organic chronicle history, (3) the hero-tragedy, and (4) the tragedy of revenge.

**The Decision of England**

The first of these may be said to transfer to secular history, as recorded by Stowe or Holinshed, the treatment that the Miracles had applied to bible story. There is the same multiplicity of scenes, each vigorously dramatic in itself. Patriotism enters in to replace piety, but comic relief is still liberally provided. Such tragedy as appears is of the simple medieval type,—

**Plays from Chronicle History**

THE DRAMA 223

the experience of one of high estate brought low by a turn of Fortune's wheel. The several parts of *Henry VI.*, on which Shakespeare collaborated with Marlowe and the rest, afford a good example of this panoramic sort of history, and Shakespeare continued the type for himself in the two parts of *Henry IV.* and in *Henry V.* The organic history play developed its form from the hero-tragedies of Marlowe and found its model in that author's *Edward II.* Shakespeare followed this plan for *Richard III.* and *Richard II.* The treatment is identical with that of the hero-tragedy, except that lyric passages seem to take the place of comic scenes and characters. Indeed certain of Shakespeare's greatest tragedies, such as *Macbeth* and *King Lear,* are in reality based on British chronicle history.

From the work of Marlowe, Shakespeare and all the great Elizabethans learned the art of the character-tragedy, with interest centered in the spiritual
**Christopher** struggles of the hero. Marlowe first ap-
**Marlowe** proached his task under sway of his splendid romantic imagination, crowding the stage with a wealth of picturesque detail such as that suggested in the tradition of Tamburlaine, the Scythian shepherd lad that well-nigh conquered the world. But Tamburlaine's career was not all spectacular achievement. The very extravagance of his ambitions brought due punishment and ultimate disaster,—the Nemesis of classical tragedy. Marlowe left the character of Tamburlaine as he found it,—simple as a child's,—and managed the decline of his hero's fortunes with much less skill than he displayed in the rising action. Later tragedies, *Doctor Faustus* and *The Jew of Malta,* make more of the psychology of their ambitious heroes, but all Marlowe's plots show in their decline a tendency to get away from him and

lose coherence. His best organization, indeed, is in *Edward II.*, his chronicle history play.

Shakespeare, studying Marlowe's success, found that the problem of tragedy for Elizabethans had been largely solved. Tragic material might be the same for the English stage as for the Greek or Roman. The new secret lay in portraying *in action* the whole course of the tragic experience from the first indiscretion to the last penalty, and allowing the character of the hero to deteriorate before the eyes of the audience. With a supreme vitalizing and realizing imagination, Shakespeare went to work upon any kind of material that afforded a good tragic experience,—earlier plays, ancient British legends, and Roman biography as recorded by Plutarch. Across the rude Elizabethan stages there walked at his command tragic figures that have immortalized his name and his generation: Romeo and Juliet, Brutus, Macbeth, Othello, Lear, Antony, and Coriolanus. They are not so hampered by realism of antiquarian detail that we of today must approach them through a maze of explanation. Each one of them is first of all a fairly convincing human being. Like his great creator,

Shakespeare's Methods

"He is not of an age, but of all time."

And while we thrill with horror at his fate, we pity the essentially human frailty that has brought such fate. Playwrights since Shakespeare have done their work differently, but they have done it no better.

*Hamlet*, the best known of Shakespeare's tragedies, is somewhat different from the others, and may be placed in a class by itself. Two at least of the tragedies of Seneca emphasized the avenging of crime, with ghostly personages returned from the Shades to supervise the process of revenge. From these plays Thomas Kyd took the revenge motive. As early as 1587 he wrote **Significance** *The Spanish Tragedy*, still extant, and **of "Hamlet"** has had ascribed to him a dramatized first part of the same story, under the title *Jeronimo*, as well as an early "Hamlet" play, both lost. Some years later, at the zenith of Shakespeare's career, interest in such plots was revived. Chapman and Marston tried their hands at them. Ben Jonson revised *The Spanish Tragedy*, and Shakespeare himself produced his *Hamlet*, the supreme achievement in this form.

Being immediately derived from Seneca, the revenge tragedy seems to have retained much more of the Senecan manner than other tragedies did. Crime **Development** and ghosts it had as a matter of course, **of Revenge** with every encouragement to carry these **Tragedy** to extravagance. It seized with great gusto upon the long ranting speeches of its models, as well as their constant stately moralizing. But it tickled the Elizabethan palate by realizing in action all the extravagant horrors that in the Latin would only have been reported in formal declamation. Certain quite incidental devices were picked up by the way, such as real or feigned madness, a play within the play, and the broad comedy inseparable from English dramatic action. Spectacular features must have had a large share in its popularity, for structurally the revenge tragedy is an imperfect or negative sort of product, the second half or decline of an entire tragic experience. Thus Shakespeare's *Hamlet* represents the decline of the larger tragedy of the ambitious usurping king, and young Hamlet is the reluctant leader of the forces of retribution. Many such plots were actually constructed and produced in two parts, like *Jeronimo* and *The Spanish Tragedy*. Others chose one of two courses. They deepened the characterization of the avenger and gave him a weakness or indecision deserving of tragic punishment, or made him a villain seeking vengeance for trivial or only imaginary crimes. This latter method was adopted after Shakespeare by playwrights like Webster and Tourneur.

English comedy on the popular stage at first drew very slightly from the methods of Plautus and Terence. In the schools Latin comedies in classic form continued to be written and acted, together with various imitations in English after the fashion of *Ralph Roister Doister*. Actual stage practice, however, was affected more by influences from pastoral plays on the continent and by popular pastoral and heroic romances at home. The English comedies of John Lyly, while highly influential upon later efforts, were a sort of hybrid form, bred of the Plautan tradition and the Italian pastoral drama, and their allegorical allusions and courtly audiences throw them into more immediate relation with the English masque than with professional drama. They did encourage in other playwrights the employment of an easy, clever, but somewhat mannered, prose dialogue in comic writing.

**Lyly's Comedies**

Naturally enough, Elizabethan comedy showed a marked fondness for the material of current fiction. Even today the successful novel is likely to reach the stage, or at least the picture-films. English fiction of that day was largely imported, and represented the confusion, and to some extent the fusion, of two very distinct forms. One of these was the romance,—pastoral or heroic,—with its high-born person-

**Romance and Novella in Comedy**

ages, extravagant sentiment and adventure, long rambling plots, and artificial settings. The other was the *novella*, a sort of exalted *fabliau*, involving lower orders of society, realistic experiences and setting, and a crisp, unsympathetic intrigue plot. In both, the characters were little individualized, and the events, however serious for the moment, led inevitably to a happy ending.

In English versions these two extreme types met and became involved in every possible fashion. *Novella* tales were interspersed in romances or were strung together like beads to form a rambling realistic romance of the picaresque variety. Romances were shortened to *novella* form or *novelle* took on the setting and situations of romance. In such variety this Elizabethan fiction served the purposes of the dramatists, who went several steps farther in the process of combining and telescoping various tales for one plot. Here again the activities of Shakespeare are typical, except that he led all his contemporaries in the matter of giving reality and enrichment to events and characters. A long line of his comedies, from *Midsummer Night's Dream* and *Merchant of Venice* to *Winter's Tale*, move in a holiday world, make light of improbabilities, and temper apparent tragedy with the assurance that

**Comedies of Shakespeare**

"The man shall have his mare again, and all shall be well."

To illustrate these points one need only recall the casket test at "beauteous Belmont," the fauna and flora of Arden, the constant tangles of identity and even sex in all the plays, and the surprising reversals of situation in *Much Ado* and *Winter's Tale*. There is occasional ridicule of manners or of character types, and considerable rejoicing at the discomfiture of people like Malvolio, victimized through intrigue. But the treatment is primarily friendly rather than satirical. Shakespeare laughs with his people instead of at them.

Shakespeare, like all Englishmen of culture, had a saving sense of the ridiculous that made it impossible for him to go all the way seriously with the extravagant romances. Such reverent appreciation, however, lingered on in the English populace of his day, and kept the romances in demand, in chap-book versions, for many years after society scorned them. For this reason it is not surprising that most extreme specimens of romance plays came from the pens of writers sprung from the London middle classes, who were equally fond of portraying the life of these middle classes, with realism of detail, but with a poet's sympathy. This apparent paradox may be noted first in the work of the poet Greene, author of *Alphonsus of Aragon* and probably of *George-a-Greene, the Pindar of Wakefield,* and combining rural simplicity with romantic magic in *Friar Bacon and Friar Bungay.* Similar tendencies are combined in the work of Thomas Dekker and Thomas Heywood. Dekker's fame rests on two plays, *Old Fortunatus* and *The Shoemaker's Holiday.* In one, representatives of the populace figure in romantic magic; in the other humble craftsmen are idealized into everlasting attractiveness. Heywood's *Four Prentices of London* displays such romantic absurdities as to have called out a more famous burlesque, *The Knight of the Burning Pestle.* His *Woman Killed with Kindness* is one of the greatest domestic dramas in the English language.

**Realism and Romance**

There is every reason to believe that the opening

years of the seventeenth century saw the tastes and interests of the middle classes fastening themselves upon the English stage. There were many plays, it is true, with foreign sources and settings. But there was room as well for a host of plays distinctly English, and almost photographic in their detail. Some of them, like *The Shoemaker's Holiday,* idealized their pictures. Others portrayed things as they were, without attempting coloring of any kind. Still others emphasized the foibles and weakness of English life, being mildly satirical comedies of manners like those of Middleton and Fletcher, or taking the severe and cynical tone of Ben Jonson's " humour comedies." Among the uncolored pieces of English realism appear various minor sorts of drama, including journalistic crime plays—recounting episodes from the career of some one just deceased—and plots of intrigue and adventure direct from the busy life of London. The comedy of manners, in its several degrees, requires more extended study.

{Comedies of English Life}

In the London comedies of Middleton, the lowly characters not only fell into types or classes, but each of these had its pet weakness or absurdity emphasized to enhance the comic effect, and at the same time to ridicule such failings. The plots, while still evolved out of clever intrigue, became subordinate to a larger desire to satirize these various phases of urban life. John Fletcher's comedies of manners presented fascinating pictures of the city, but he had little interest in satire and was fondest of courtly society. Even more than in his tragi-comedies the characters were sprightly and adventurous, the action was brisk and entertaining, and the plot packed with disguises and sudden and ill-motived turns. He was always

{Middleton and Fletcher}

fond of romantic themes and made a place for them even in his comedies of manners, so that the line between these plays of manners and his tragi-comedies is often hard to draw.

Ben Jonson was in no sense related to this activity, but developed plans of his own that paralleled it closely.

**Jonson's Humour Comedy**
As in all his literary ventures, the inspiration was classical. The comedies of Plautus and Terence, through him, first came to have a vital influence on the English stage. They provided models for just such moral scourgings as he was determined to inflict upon English society. It was his part to adapt these to local conditions. He found a name for his new drama in the current physiological belief in the four "humours," one of which was supposed to prevail in each individual and determine his peculiarities. He began with *Every Man in his Humour* (1598), a play of intrigue, with an Italian setting and with various type characters satirically interpreted. Later he rewrote the play, making scene and characters English. This localizing treatment, indeed, was characteristic of the second stage of his work. At the same time he developed unity, partly by making his plot appropriate to the weakness of his characters, partly by portraying in each character a distinct phase of some larger, dominating "humour" or peculiarity. The bitterness of Jonson's satire increased also as time went on and various unfortunate experiences came into his life to darken it. The series of his great comedies—*Volpone, the Fox* (1606), *Epicœne, the Silent Woman* (1609), *The Alchemist* (1610), and *Bartholomew Fair* (1614)—may not be pleasant reading, but they are strong plays and powerful indictments of his time.

"Humour" and "humours" were extremely popular

THE DRAMA 231

words in London about the year 1600,[1] and the "humour" character, as conceived by Jonson, passed into many plays of various sorts. Chapman made use of it as early as Jonson, in *A Humorous Day's Mirth* (1598); and Shakespeare does much the same thing with certain characters in *Henry V.* and *Twelfth Night.* The influence of the humour comedy continued to the closing of the theaters (1642) and was prominent once more after the Restoration.

*"Humours"*

Jonson, being a thoroughgoing classicist, was as much concerned with adapting Senecan tragedy to the English stage as with localizing the comedy of Plautus and Terence. He contributed to the tragedy of revenge by rewriting Kyd's *Spanish Tragedy.* But he did not stop there. Taking plots from Roman history, as Shakespeare had a way of doing, he constructed his two severely impressive hero-tragedies, *Sejanus, his Fall* and *Catiline, his Conspiracy.* In these plays there is no attempt to keep the "unities" of time and place. The chorus is omitted from one of them as unessential. Four things, however, Jonson professed to strive after, and even the most casual reader will grant that he attained them. In his own words these are: "truth of argument," implying accuracy of details; "dignity of persons"; "gravity and height of elocution"; and "fullness and frequency of sentences," the last involving constant moralizing upon all events of the dramas.

Jonson's Tragedies

About this time, following close upon Shakespeare's *Hamlet,* the tragedy of revenge developed certain new traits, quite irreconcilable with the original models from

[1] Note Nym's frequent expression, "That's the humour of it," in Shakespeare's *Henry V.*

Seneca. Shakespeare had developed the psychology of the contemplative, hesitant avenger, and touched lightly on physical horrors. The tragedies of Webster and Tourneur in particular revealed a new mastery of the horrible, physically presented but still gripping the imagination. Sympathetic interest was shifted once more, away from the avenger to his victim, whose crime was often trivial enough as compared with the vengeance heaped upon it. Webster's Duchess of Malfi suffered unspeakably for having married in secret a perfectly respectable man who was beneath her in station. The avenger is no longer a philosopher, but a malcontent and a villain, or at least employs such a character as the instrument of his wrath. Bosola was just such a tool in the hands of the Duchess's incensed brothers. The very increase of crime and horror seems to have inspired imagination and eloquence, for these plays of Webster and Tourneur flash into white heats of romantic passion, rise to heights of splendid characterization,—such as Webster's vampire-woman, Vittoria Corombona,—and abound in striking utterances great in their way as Marlowe's mighty lines.

*The New Tragedy of Revenge*

The reign of James I. saw another dramatic form established on the English stage, the tragi-comedy. Tragedy of revenge, starting from the classical repression of Seneca, finally achieved romantic daring in plot, character, and expression. The tragi-comedy was romantic from the first, and like the romances that largely inspired it, knew no bounds for its emotional extravagances. It was never fully acclimated to English life, but was popular with all who liked courtly magnificence and thrived under patronage of the English cavaliers.

*Tragi-Comedies*

The form began under the influence of Italian pastoral plays like Guarini's *Pastor Fido*, was sustained by the example of successful Spanish dramas of the so-called "cloak and sword" variety of romantic intrigue, and closely paralleled a fondness for prose-romances that pervaded France and England to the middle of the century.

John Fletcher was responsible for the success of this form in England, as he was for that of the comedy of manners. Alone and in collaboration with Beaumont and Massinger in particular, he produced such typical plays as *Philaster, The Maid's Tragedy, A King and No King,* and *The Lovers' Progress,* each tragic in possibilities, but provided as he pleased with a happy or unhappy ending.

**Fletcher's Technique**

The material was the usual stuff of the heroic romances, except that its personages moved in a riper and less innocent courtly environment. The playwright, however, seemed to be striving constantly after novelty and striking effect, at the expense of unity of structure and impression. Each play was a series of "big" situations, many of them built about crimes and passions of the most obnoxious sort. Characters ran to types and underwent surprising transformations. Startling contrasts were in evidence, such as the device of introducing characters and scenes of idyllic simplicity as foils to the more intense life of the court,—the episodes of Euphrasia, for example, in *Philaster*. The language was courtly vernacular, and the verse a particularly easy and harmonious line. Form and substance shared in the fault of irregularity, being often pleasantly commonplace, and at occasional moments rising to genuine heights.

The possibilities of English tragi-comedy, paralleled as it was by an intense interest in heroic prose romances and by the emergence of a highly refined type of courtly society, would seem to have been almost unlimited. It did indeed receive large cultivation, and no **Tragi-Comedy** doubt affected the tone of all tragedies **and Romantic** written in the language before the Resto-**Tragedy** ration. Shakespeare apparently accepted the new form readily, and contributed to it *Cymbeline, Winter's Tale,* and *The Tempest.* All of these are distinctly comedies in spirit and outcome. Fletcher himself carried the romantic spirit of his tragi-comedies into two unmistakable tragedies, *Valentinian* and *Bonduca,* and produced a third, *The Bloody Brother,* in collaboration with Massinger. Ford and Shirley, who dominated the drama just before the closing of the theaters, continued to employ in tragic themes the familiar devices of tragi-comedy,—the bold and striking situations, the typical characters often undergoing unexpected transformations, courtly politeness, sensuality, and easy, irregular dramatic verse.

The first half of the seventeenth century must be credited with the perfection of the English masque, a hybrid form of art appealing to several **Beginnings** senses and making its appeal through **of the** spectacle, dancing, music, and finally **Masque** dramatic action. It arose in large measure from costumed and masked dances introduced at social festivities, as Romeo and his friends visited the assembly at the house of the Capulets. Gradually these came to be introduced by some prelude or other, which at times took dramatic form. Another related tradition was that of the pastoral play, never adopted by the regular stage in England, but confined to schools, amateur performances at court, and the repertoires of the children's companies of actors. In these plays the shepherds and their calling were idealized into an artificiality appropriate to the no-man's-land of Arcadia that furnished the scene. The effect was lyric rather than dramatic, with numerous songs all along the way. There was always a suspicion that local personages were represented in the characters, and often the whole play was a political allegory. By virtue of having somewhat private performance these plays were more lavishly costumed and were more ambitious in the matter of scenery. In Italy, indeed, these pastoral plays were mounted with perspective scenery and stage mechanism in a way that far anticipated English practice.

Just after the death of Elizabeth, courtly society with the consent of the king set its approval on more elaborate and formal masked dances or "masques" as they came to be called. The dramatic preludes to the dance itself were developed more and more until finally they were the significant thing and the dance a mere appendage. This dramatic development accorded with the methods of pastoral plays, was sentimental and allegorical, and made large use of music and of expensive scenery. At times there was even a sort of preliminary scene or "curtain-raiser" called the antimasque, which preceded the dramatic action of the masque proper and provided a realistic foil to it. Some of the best talent in England was employed upon these masques, including Ben Jonson, Shirley, and even Milton himself for the dramatic features, Thomas Campion and Henry Lawes for the music, and Inigo Jones for the scenery and stage devices. Jonson was probably the most prolific of masque-makers, but Milton's work is most widely known through his *Comus*. As a form the masque must be regarded not only as important in itself, but as an important preparation for opera.

**The Interregnum 1642-1660**
From 1642 until nearly 1660, the year of the Stuart Restoration, the theaters of England were legally closed, and because of the Civil War would have had little support if permitted to open. The last years of Cromwell's protectorate brought some relief to playwrights and actors, and almost immediately upon the arrival of Charles II. two dramatic companies were instituted and two theaters were opened by royal letters patent. There is some diversity of opinion as to the effect of this interregnum on the dramatic product that followed. Perhaps the safest statement is that foreign influences, encouraged by the return of royalty from the continent, had considerable bearing upon the subsequent dramatic product, but these influences only confirmed tendencies already clearly under way before 1642. The roots of all forms of Restoration drama are firmly imbedded in Elizabethan soil.

**New Stage Conditions**
In stage practice there are marked differences between the two periods, though even here the last years of Elizabethan activity were preparing for change. Movable and painted scenes arranged in perspective take the place of the somewhat barren Elizabethan platform with curtained recess and balcony in the rear. There was a large interest in stage machinery and extensive properties, so that many plays drew crowds by virtue of spectacle and clever stage-craft. Costumes were planned with regard to at least a conventional kind of appropriateness, but as yet with little regard for historical accuracy. Women definitely took their place among the stage-performers. Their appearance must have increased

dramatic realism, but for a time at least it had anything but a purifying effect. Many of the parts, and particularly the Epilogues then popular, were ill adapted to a woman's lips.

A considerable part of the plays that followed close upon the Restoration were revivals from the first half of the century. Various plays of Shakespeare, some by Jonson, and specimens of Fletcher's tragi-comedies and comedies of manners were most in evidence. The managers and their assistants felt free to adapt and revise these plays at their pleasure. The results, especially for Shakespeare, are rather startling to modern students. *Lear* and *Othello* with happy endings, *Midsummer Night's Dream* as an operatic spectacle, *The Tempest* as an opera, and *Antony and Cleopatra* transformed into *All for Love, or a World Well Lost*,—such is the treatment accorded to Shakespeare, and its significance is not far to seek. There were two main activities in the dramatic development of England in this period. One, the satirical comedy of manners, could draw nothing from Shakespeare. It did find inspiration, however, in the various revivals from Jonson and Fletcher. The other activity emphasized the extravagantly heroic and sentimental type of play, descended from Fletcher's tragi-comedy and constantly inspired by the prose romances of France. Shakespeare's romantic comedies were not extreme enough to satisfy this taste, but his serious plays could be sentimentalized in accord with it.

*Elizabethan Plays Revived*

The " heroic plays " of the Restoration period constituted a distinct and unique type, for which the poet Dryden was sponsor and chief exponent. They were " heroic " as the French romances of that century were heroic. That is, they celebrated colossal exploits and extravagant emotional experiences of **Heroic Plays** some powerful and magnanimous hero. The adventures recorded had a slight basis of historical fact, just as the characters were presumably historical figures. But these Romans and Spaniards and Orientals were of necessity mirrors of courtesy, masters of oratory, and lovers *par excellence*. Structurally the plays were hybrids. They dealt with all the action of Elizabethan historical tragedy, but undertook to fit it into a semblance of the classic unities. They were painfully serious, but insisted frequently on happy endings for their heroes. They aimed at exalted passions and attained only to bombast and the effect of burlesque. In a way they were the last stand of native English romance against French restraint and eighteenth-century sentiment. Even at that they were a forlorn hope.

In a much narrower sense, the heroic plays were those written in heroic couplet, the rhymed pentameter popularized in England some time before the **Dryden's** Restoration for every other kind of **Contribution** poetry but the dramatic, and destined to remain supreme for nearly a century after. Certainly this couplet form was employed by Dryden for all his notable plays in this serious and exalted manner, including *The Indian Emperor* (1665), *Tyrannic Love, or the Royal Martyr* (1669), *Almanzor and Almahide, or the Conquest of Granada* (1669-70), and *Aureng-Zebe* (1675). Heroic couplet was satirized among other things by the still famous burlesque upon heroic plays, *The Rehearsal*, written by the Duke of Buckingham and others, and produced in 1671. Students of today will find it almost impossible to approach the heroic plays in the spirit of their authors. But the gay mockery

THE DRAMA 239

of extravagance and rant that pervades *The Rehearsal* is as everlasting as Dogberry's ignorance or Bully Bottom's self-complacence. It is not true that this satire drove heroic plays from the stage. There can be little doubt, however, that Dryden felt it very keenly.

After the heroic plays, tragedy reverted for a time to the Elizabethan form and spirit, blank verse taking the
place of the rhymed couplet. Lee and
Restoration    Otway, both of whom began their careers
Tragedies      with rhymed plays, discarded rhyme in
their more mature work and caught a note of real pathos and genuine tragic poetry for which the heroic plays seemed to strive in vain. Lee was irregular in his genius. Otway developed artistic restraint, and in *The Orphan* (1680) and *Venice Preserved* (1682) reached heights sacred to the great Elizabethans. Nicholas Rowe also patterned his work somewhat upon Shakespeare, particularly after his edition of that poet's dramas in 1709. His best known plays, *The Fair Penitent* (1703) and *Jane Shore* (1714), are both based on themes already treated by Elizabethan playwrights. These plays enjoyed wide popularity in their day and lingered long upon the stage. One character in *The Fair Penitent*, the " gallant, gay Lothario," has become a byword in society.

In Rowe's work, however, it is an easy matter to note
the brief reaction to Elizabethan method
Sentiment     and spirit giving way once more before
and           the advance of sentiment and classical
Regularity    regularity. Rowe's plays were heavily
weighted with moralizing, his chief characters were women, his subject-matter was usually

"A melancholy tale of private woes."

Under the influence of Racine and the critics, he rigidly excluded comic scenes, reduced the number of characters, and set up formal regularity of structure as an ideal. Similar developments were taking place all about him. Even before the appearance of *Jane Shore,* Colley Cibber and Steele had inaugurated the sentimental drama of middle-class life, and *The Distrest Mother* of Ambrose Philips, together with Addison's *Cato,* had at last established classical tragedy in the English language.

By far the most brilliant dramatic achievement of the later seventeenth century was in Restoration comedy. It was simply a new phase of comedy of **Restoration** manners, employing the resources of an **Comedy** unusually sparkling wit upon the intrigue and amorous exploits of society about the court and the metropolis. There is much exaggeration in the treatment, as is true of all such comedy. Situations are constantly overdrawn, and characters fall into conventional types,—either the " humours " of Jonsonian tradition or the professional or class portraits of the character-books. It is to be hoped that the frivolous and licentious ideals expressed are also considerably heightened, but various of the "sentiments" uttered over and over again are all too well sustained by the evidence of other documents.[1] Such stock notions as the contempt for truth and virtue, the depreciation of the country and country life, the snobbish attitude of the aristocracy toward the tradesman class, the mockery of marriage vows, probably dominated entirely the narrowed and artificial circles of gallant society in which playwrights persisted in locating their plots.

Worse than all these features is the constant delight of

[1] The diaries of Samuel Pepys and John Evelyn, and the *Memoirs of the Comte de Gramont,* by Anthony Hamilton.

authors, and obviously of audiences also, in situations of studied indecency, placed with evident purpose at the very heart of the dramatic action. The boudoir scene, which has had a part in so many plays of questionable tone in recent years, was used frequently in the most daring fashion. Playwrights beginning with Dryden insisted strongly upon the value of the moral lessons they imparted,—again suggesting practices familiar in our own day. But in reality the unforgivable crime to the authors of Restoration comedy appears to be dull and heavy-witted innocence. This trait, it might be added, seems to have been confined to husbands.

**Its Immorality**

For reasons like these, the plays of this period remain unread today. The skill of their technical contrivance, the flash and sparkle of their dialogue, the cleverness of numerous character-creations is a closed book, and the period is known chiefly through the names of the authors. George Etherege and William Wycherley are among the first of these, the grace and facility of the former contrasting with the cynical coarseness of such plays as the latter's *The Plain Dealer* and *The Country Wife*. William Congreve, whose pen was not confined to dramatic writing, stands out as the chief representative of wit in these comedies. The sparkle of his clever dialogue interferes often with movement and naturalness, but his style in general is of very high order, and his fame rests worthily on such plays as *Love for Love* and *The Way of the World*. The rather heavy wit of the Flemish Vanbrugh and the Irish freshness and resourcefulness of Farquhar round out the list.

**The Playwrights**

Much is said by critics of the indebtedness of these comedies to French plays, particularly those of Molière.

The account of detailed obligations to this master of comic construction can be carried, it appears, as far as anyone is disposed to extend it. These **Obligations** Englishmen plundered him freely and **of Molière** made him suffer in the process. They coarsened everything they touched in the process of adapting it. Subtlety was thrown aside, action was increased, and immorality was greatly magnified. His skillful plots they found inadequate until they had complicated them by episodes and situations drawn from others of his plays. The result is bold and rapid, but is a far cry from Molière. Nevertheless, when all has been said, the authors of Restoration comedy were clever, high-spirited men of the world,[1] who produced a distinct and by no means negligible addition to the total of English stage-literature.

So free was this comedy in thought and language that the greater portion of the eighteenth century was piously engaged in reaction to the other extreme. **A Moral** The sentimental drama of middle-class **Reaction** life, which halted in its tenderness between the alternatives of punishing villains to the uttermost or forgiving and regenerating them, was indeed not entirely a protest against Restoration doctrines. It came naturally enough with the emergence once more of middle-class interests and ideals, and the growth of certain deistical theories as to the essential virtues of man. Some vigorous protests against immorality on the stage, particularly Jeremy Collier's *Short View of the Immorality and Profaneness of the English Stage* (1698), have often been held accountable for the

[1] Restoration comedy also marks the appearance of the professional literary woman, in the person of Aphra Behn, Mrs. Centlivre, and others.

THE DRAMA 243

fall of one type and the rise of another; but they are as much symptoms as causes. That sort of protest had been appearing at intervals for a hundred years and is still popular.

At any rate morality and sentiment came into the drama together. Certain writers of the Restoration period who offended most against decency in their plays were accustomed to insist upon their moral purpose in so doing. Colley Cibber, at the opening of the eighteenth century, produced plays much in the Restoration manner, except that he diluted earlier immorality, had it forgiven on the stage, and made a feature of his own moral intentions in the process. Steele went a step further. He made the morality of his moral personages a self-conscious thing and kept them talking of it. Emotional experiences became similarly self-conscious, and were analyzed with all the detail of the old romances. "Laughter's a distorted passion," Steele declared in an epilogue. So his happy endings were made up largely of forgiveness and regeneration—and more moralizing. But this sentimentalizing was in the air. *The Lying Lover* (1703) may have been "damn'd for its Piety," but *The Conscious Lovers*, twenty years later, could not be put down.

The New Sentimental Comedy

The sentimental play was to achieve still greater things. Comedy under sentimental sway had mingled tears with its laughter and turned its prose toward blank verse again. Tragedy becoming sentimental stooped to the affairs of tradesmen and appropriately made them speak in prose. George Lillo's *The London Merchant, or the History of George Barnwell* (1731) is one of the significant plays of the century. The weakling who is its

"The London Merchant"

victim-hero played upon the sympathies of all of Europe, and at the same time the deeply moved audiences and readers had the benefit of abundant moral instruction and came to realize the tragic possibilities even of middle-class life. Besides, the tragic downfall of young Barnwell through the wiles of the courtesan Millwood is vividly and effectively managed, despite the fact that his successive crimes are very slightly motivated.

Exaggerated characters, slight motivation, abundant moralizing, and a maidenly delicacy and restraint are chief characteristics of the comedies conspicuous during the next stage of sentimental drama. They were the work of Hugh Kelly and Richard Cumberland, contemporaries and literary rivals of Goldsmith and Sheridan. Kelly, whose *False Delicacy* reached the stage only six days before *The Good Natured Man* (1768), appreciated to some degree the extravagances of the sentimental cult portrayed in his genteel lovers, as his title and portions of the treatment indicate. Cumberland was entirely devoted to the cause. *The West Indian* (1771) and numerous plays of slighter success continued to carry somewhat impossible heroes and heroines through harsh experiences to surprisingly happy conclusions, scattering moral aphorisms as they went. They had, too, a devoted audience, which resented the satire of Goldsmith and Sheridan, and the more open attack in Samuel Foote's burlesque, *The Handsome Housemaid, or Piety in Pattens* (1773).

**Kelly and Cumberland**

Formal tragedy on the eighteenth-century stage varied between the romantic fervor of Elizabethan days and the severe regularity of Racine. There was indeed rather a dearth of tragic writers in the period, so that the productions of Shakespeare in particular were constantly being performed. As critical editions multiplied these plays were largely restored to their original form and found to be as pleasing as the Restoration revisions. Among new authors appeared such men as Edward Young and James Thomson, both of whom did heavy rhetorical tragedies in addition to the poems that have given them fame. Aaron Hill, more French in his leanings than either of these, was attracted by the example of Voltaire, himself a strict classicist, and adapted several of his plays to the English stage. Adaptation of Voltaire continued through the century as his popularity in England waxed and waned. At the middle of the century three famous classical tragedies appeared almost together,—Dr. Johnson's *Irene*, William Whitehead's *The Roman Father*, and John Home's *Douglas*. Shortly after came William Mason's Greek tragedy *Caractacus*. But all these plays, however successful, aroused vigorous opposition that amused itself by continual burlesque of numerous palpable extravagances. The irony of the situation is that only the burlesques are known today. Among these are Gay's *What-d'ye-call-it?*, Fielding's *Tom Thumb*, Henry Carey's *Chrononhotonthologos*, and Sheridan's *The Critic*.

**Tragedy, Classical and Elizabethan**

The story of English drama in the eighteenth century would be incomplete without some mention of opera. Before 1642 it was unknown in England, but was anticipated in many essential features by the numerous masques and pastoral tragi-comedies. During the enforced exile of the Stuarts foreign example had its effect, and it is not surprising—though the immediate purpose was to tempt Cromwell

**Early English Opera**

—that Davenant opened the first playhouse of the new era with "a Representation by the Art of Prospective Scenes, And the Story sung in Recitative Musick." Perspective scenery, as well as recitative, had already become associated with operatic drama abroad. Once under way, opera in England developed in three fairly distinct stages. The first of these appeared about 1670-90, contemporary with the beginning of opera proper in France and to some degree influenced from there. It was marked in England chiefly by the musical compositions of Matthew Locke and Henry Purcell. A second stage, immediately after 1700, was that of Italian opera, inaugurated by *Arsinoë*, in 1705. The translations and the worse mixtures of English and Italian in which these compositions were sung by mixed companies of native and imported singers aroused harsh criticism among literary men. Still the fashion persisted until English composers, like Handel, arose to reveal the possibilities of a strictly native product. Addison's activities, as author of an English opera—*Rosamond*, 1707—and critic of the Italian importations,[1] bear directly upon this development.

At length opposition to Italian opera resulted in the discovery of a new type, the ballad opera. The discoverer was John Gay, and the novelty was *The Beggar's Opera*, presented in 1728. Gay had training in the art of satire and burlesque, which he utilized to good effect in this play. There is the framework, usual in burlesque plays, supplied by dialogue between the Player and the Beggar who is represented as author. The deliberate choice of scenes and characters that were "low," together with constant parallels between these

**Ballad Opera**

[1] *Spectator*, Nos. 5, 13, 18, and 29.

and high society, served the double purpose of satirizing society and making sport of the ideals in sentimental plays. The practice of these plays is also ridiculed, as in the celebrated "double ending," urged by the Player to "comply with the Taste of the Town." The Italian operas come in for their share of ridicule, while perhaps the largest factor in the unparalleled popularity of the opera was the series of mocking political allusions people were disposed to find in it. After all, though, it was good, rollicking, tuneful entertainment. The songs, sprinkled rather freely through it, were set to familiar ballad airs that everybody knew, like "Good morrow, Gossip Joan," or "Green Sleeves," or "Lumps of Pudding." The dialogue was realistically clever prose. The actress who played Polly Peachum was so pretty that she married an earl. What more could be desired? Ballad operas were still in vogue at the end of the century, encouraged by the more recent success of Sheridan's *The Duenna* (1775).

The advent of Goldsmith and Sheridan was in general a step toward wholesome realism on the English stage. Both men found it very hard to avoid the practices of "genteel" sentimentalism even while they were making sport of these, and Sheridan before his death lent his authority to the new fashion of imitating the German Kotzebue, who was more sentimental and melodramatic than any Englishman had yet dared to be. Under the circumstances plays like *She Stoops to Conquer* (1773), *The Rivals* (1775), and *The School for Scandal* (1777) may be regarded as a reaction to the wit and gayety of the best Restoration comedy, purged and purified until we have distinct originality rather than mere imitation. Horace Walpole called

*The School for Scandal* "a marvellous resurrection of the stage." That this promising initiative was not followed may be variously accounted for. The new romantic and sentimental drama introduced from Germany was a large factor in the result.

It is fairly easy to point out technical weaknesses in these plays. Situations and characters in *She Stoops to Conquer* are exaggerated to the point of farce. Young Marlow could hardly have been the bashful suitor in the drawing-room and the gay dog below stairs, nor could he have been tricked so long into believing himself at an inn. All the people in *The Rivals* are broad caricatures, tagged by appropriate names—Lydia Languish, Mrs. Malaprop, Lucius O'Trigger—in the good old-fashioned way. *The School for Scandal* is unnaturally rich in clever speeches and draws too much upon the favorite devices of the Restoration period. But it is undeniable that these plays *live*. They still give pleasure on the stage among all the diverse products of the last generation. They are and always will be fine plays to "romp through." They have the perennial charm of Shakespeare, in that under such exaggeration as appears there are the genuine comic traits of everyday humanity, so presented that we laugh with the people rather than at them.

**Realism in Comedy**

The vogue of Kotzebue on the English stage belongs to the eighteenth century. His plays represent the blend of sentimentalized socialism and romantic stage-setting first made popular in Germany by youthful products like Schiller's *Robbers* and Goethe's *Götz von Berlichingen*. Kotzebue possessed all the intuitions of a modern stage-manager in regard to spectacular effects

**The Plays of Kotzebue**

THE DRAMA 249

and telling situations. With him poetic idealism gave way to false sentiment and cheap staginess. English critics stormed; *The Rovers*, by Canning and Frere, deliciously burlesqued the type in the *Anti-Jacobin;* but the play-going public, that genteel middle-class public that has supported melodrama from *The London Merchant* to its submersion in picture-plays, heartily approved of Kotzebue's dramas, particularly *The Stranger* (*Menschenhass und Reue* in the original), *The Child of Love*, and *The Spaniards in Peru*. "Monk" Lewis, already concerned with exaggerated balladry and romance from German sources, did his part in the general translation of these plays into English, and then added to the type from his own pen *The Castle Spectre, Adelgitha*, and others, thus carrying the fashion well into the nineteenth century.

The nineteenth century is emphatically not a period of activity in the drama. Its product may be summed up rather completely in words from Professor Herford: "plays which are not literature, and literary exercises which are not in the fullest sense plays."[1] Of great, or even memorable contributions to the repertoire of the stage there were very few. A play or two by Sheridan Knowles, Robertson's *Caste*, and Bulwer-Lytton's *Lady of Lyons* and *Cardinal Richelieu* are practically all that time has preserved from the faded play-bills of the first three-quarters of the century. At the same time it was a period of wide experiment and notable achievement in the poetic and purely literary drama, the drama of the closet rather than the playhouse. Just prior to 1800 this movement began, in the attempts of Wordsworth, Coleridge, and Joanna Baillie.

Romantic
Literary
Drama

[1] Used of the drama in the age of Wordsworth, in his *Age of Wordsworth*, p. 135.

The early experiment of Coleridge was revised by him and produced as *Remorse*, in 1813, and followed with *Zapolya* shortly after. Shelley's *The Cenci* (1819) was printed but not performed. Two of Shelley's disciples did distinctive things in lyrical drama: Thomas L. Beddoes with his *Death's Jest Book*, and Charles J. Wells with *Joseph and his Brethren*.

In the final decade of the nineteenth century there was a complete reversal in the fortunes of English drama.

**Recent Dramatic Activity**
New influences were brought to bear upon it, new ambitions and ideas seemed to awaken, and the results, appearing continuously until today, promise to revolutionize many of our oldest and best-established conceptions of this form of art. The work of foreign playwrights—French, German, Belgian, and particularly Scandinavian—has had much to do with this activity. America's contribution has been painfully slight. How far England would have succeeded alone it is difficult to say; the work of Arthur W. Pinero was well under way by 1890 when England began to be actually acquainted with the plays of Ibsen. The Ibsen influence, however, when once established, was really the most considerable factor in the movement until very recent years.

The plays of Ibsen have been strictly in accord with the methods and conclusions of modern science. Technically they represent the highest type of

**The Example of Ibsen** mechanical efficiency, reducing stage action as nearly as possible to the crucial moment, making every word, every movement bear directly upon this moment, discarding many well-worn stage conventions such as asides and soliloquies, and achieving clear exposition of what has gone before with supreme naturalness and penetrating characterization. The treatment of his subjects shows the calm aloofness of the trained investigator, and the subjects themselves are exactly those that advanced and liberated thought has forced men to consider, often against their will. For all their strong emotional impressions, these were plays of ideas, and the dramatic conflicts they involved were fundamentally those of independent, individualistic thought with time-honored conventionalities and the hypocrisy so often cloaked by these. Here was the emergence of the "problem play," ready at any moment, as soon as the author takes sides and presses his case, to become the "thesis play." *A Doll's House* turns the light of reason upon the old conception of the wife as her indulgent husband's ignorant toy, just as *The Pillars of Society* reveals the wickedness too often hidden under smug prosperity. *Ghosts* and *Rosmersholm* spell the defeat of individualism, in conflict with the mighty forces of heredity and family tradition.

The problem play, sometimes with an attempt at Ibsen's finality of construction, more often without it, has received worthy treatment on the continent of Europe at the hands of such men as Hauptmann and Sudermann in Germany, Strindberg in Sweden, Hervieu and Brieux in France. In England Pinero and Henry Arthur Jones were for some time the only playwrights that worked in Ibsen's manner. Pinero was particularly concerned with the tragedy of womankind as the "weaker sex" through the acceptance of a double standard of sexual morality. This is the theme of his best-known play, *The Second Mrs. Tanqueray* (1893), and appears with variations throughout his later work. The subjects chosen by Jones are similar, but his point of view is usually that of the conservative side. In technique he

"Problem Plays"

is often tempted, as in *Michael and his Lost Angel,* by the possibilities of a melodramatic "big scene." John Galsworthy has emerged somewhat later than these two men as a dramatist of social problems. His *Strife* and *Justice* are thoroughly knit and trimmed examples of structure that attain to really tragic heights.

Galsworthy's *Justice* is distinctly a thesis play, in which he frankly takes sides and allows his characters to preach to the audience. Another English writer, more widely known than any of these others, not only uses his plays as instruments to give expression to his theories, but defends this practice as representative of the best methods of modern drama—the "drama of ideas." This is George Bernard Shaw, the avowed opponent of all doctrines accepted merely because they have always been so. His plays are frequently lacking in action or any form of mental or spiritual conflict, but are rather a series of scenes made up of sparkling and epigrammatic conversation. The fact that certain of them, such as *Man and Superman,* are irresistible on the stage may be due to this sheer cleverness of dialogue coupled with rather a startling point of view, but is taken by their author as evidence that the modern play is at its best a lively intellectual exercise, with plot and emotional values as minor matters. In this theory he receives the support of Granville Barker, whose plays seem utterly devoid of structure according to old standards. Their dialogue is keen and penetrating in its character-portrayal, however, and certain problems in the thought of the day are presented in them with a completeness that is rarely equaled. One may well turn to *The Madras House* for a most suggestive study of woman's place in society.

Problem plays and dramas of ideas are not the only

results of the dramatic activity of the last generation. Ibsen cultivated more or less the use of symbolism in all

**Allegorical Plays**

his naturalistic dramas, and after him various writers gave such allegorical suggestions a much larger place. Hauptmann did so often; Maeterlinck in Belgium has been particularly noted for his symbolism, culminating in his well-known *Blue Bird;* D'Annunzio represents the same tendency in Italy. Edmond Rostand, the poet-playwright of France, is entirely allegorical in *Chanticler,* and the Irish fairy plays of William Butler Yeats are not far removed from such treatment. In England it is illustrated by such plays as Jerome K. Jerome's *Passing of the Third Floor Back* and Charles Rann Kennedy's *The Servant in the House,* in America by Percy Mackaye's *The Scarecrow.*

There are still playwrights of imagination and mood, without theories to advance or traditions to demolish.

**Plays of Mood and Atmosphere**

Rostand, for example, did an eminently old-fashioned piece of work in *Cyrano de Bergerac,* appealing to sympathy and the childlike delight in color and light and motion. Sir James M. Barrie, while he enjoys making sport of solemn conventionalities sometimes, is at his best in flights of fancy like *Peter Pan* or plays of mood and atmosphere like *Quality Street.* Other popular plays whose chief charm is in their atmosphere are Louis N. Parker's *Pomander Walk,* the Scotch plays of Graham Moffat, and the product of Lady Gregory's Abbey Theater in Ireland. The theater-going public, particularly in this country, has by no means lost faith in plays with the obvious melodramatic thrill, plays with type characters and " big scenes," and the managers are all too willing to cater to this taste. Clyde Fitch represented this interest at its best, and many of our most successful plays in recent years have been of this variety, but the spirit they represent is being appropriated to the photo-play, where action and thrill are apparently the prime requisites.

With the revived interest in play-writing have come some important developments in methods of staging. First the naturalistic plays, with their scientific fidelity to the facts of life, encouraged a corresponding realism in stage settings and properties. Within a great picture frame the stage was to reveal a section of actual life in its natural surroundings. Real books were on real shelves; real food was eaten from real plates; real batter cakes were browned before hungry eyes. More recently the drama, regarded as a somewhat composite art-product, is being subjected in its staging to the principles of modern art and pure design. Properties are as simple and unobtrusive as possible. Scenery does not photograph outside life, but grows out of the theme of the play, its lines and colors and lighting suggesting the mood and spirit that the author has undertaken to convey. Such settings have been found most appropriate with the plays of symbolism, though they are conceivable with all but the most mechanical of realistic plays. They lend themselves in a peculiar way to the revivals of Elizabethan drama, before the English stage was revolutionized by pictorial backgrounds and perspective scenery. As of old, the imagination is given free rein, the eye is gratified as well as the ear, and the play once more becomes a genuine artistic unit.

**Methods of Staging**

## Technique of the Drama

Granville Barker, an exponent of the modern drama of ideas, defines drama by saying: "A play is anything that can be made effective upon the stage of a theater by human agency. And I am not sure that this definition is not too narrow." The general reader may be pardoned for considering the definition a trifle broad. Adaptability to performance on the stage is of course a requisite, but the dramatic value of the piece may be supposed to vary with its inherent effectiveness for such performance. Etymology, tradition, and current usage are one in recognizing the essential factor of drama to be action, real or potential. This may mean conflict of will with will, of personality with personality, or the struggle of an individual against circumstances. It may involve rather the tenseness that comes with moments of decision or crisis. This does not mean physical activity or a crowded stage. Some of the most dramatic moments are passed in silence with few to participate in them. But there are vital forces at work and there is a feeling of suspense in the very air, as in the hush before an electric storm.

*Dramatic Action*

The novel may have a number of these dramatic situations. Many of the strongest novels structurally have the plots of first-class tragedies, and differ from them chiefly in luxuriance of details and analysis of passions and emotions in the characters. Modern short stories are often highly dramatic and could be adapted with little change to performance on the stage. Forms of the drama itself are distinguished chiefly by the way these conflicts and crises are pre-

*Employment of Conflict and Crisis*

sented and the angle from which the audience is asked to view them. If we are to laugh at the struggler rather than sympathize with him, realizing that his unscrupulous schemes have failed or the bubble of his foolish ambition has been pricked, it is comedy. Malvolio in *Twelfth Night* or Young Marlow in *She Stoops to Conquer* is comic, provided we do not feel sorry for him. In melodrama the spectacular events about the crisis become more important than character interest and may even force the characters to do unnatural things. In farce the events are still more emphasized and crowd upon each other in all sorts of improbable and unexpected but amusing ways, while the characters are the most superficial of types.

Aristotle, who defined tragedy as "the imitation of a serious, complete, and significant action," regarded a well-constructed plot as fundamental to good drama. Characters, he said, are like the beautiful colors laid on a canvas, but plot is the underlying chalk outline that keeps the picture true. English practice has consistently recognized the importance of well-constructed plots, but has not always succeeded at them. Because of its short duration and massed effect, the drama has particular need of unity in its plot,—unity in every sense of the term. There is need of unity in the selection of material; of an economy of this material that permits nothing in the entire play that has not its justification as serving to advance the story toward its climax, to illuminate characters as they bear upon this story, or to order the imagination and emotions toward the ultimate impression. Once selected, this material should be so knit together that each step seems to follow in natural sequence, without straining or forcing; not calling attention to itself, but on consideration found to be an essential part of the whole. Witness-

**Unity of Plot**

THE DRAMA 257

ing a play like this—Shakespeare's *Othello* or Ibsen's *The Doll's House*, for instance—is no small intellectual exercise, with all the faculties alert for the slight but significant details that enrich action throughout.

The unified plot does not stand still; it gets somewhere and loses no time about it. Most good plays have a climactic situation, a peak of interest
Movement toward which all preliminary activity
in Drama ascends and from which there is a fairly rapid progress to complete overthrow, or moral regeneration, or the first stages of living happy ever after,—all depending on the character of the play. In most comedies and in farces, where the interest is largely in uncertainty as to "how it will come out," this climactic point is very near the end, for when this is past the audience is satisfied. In tragedy of the Shakespearian type the climax comes near the middle of the play, and there is a serious problem of sustaining interest till the distant but inevitable catastrophe. This is usually managed by introducing a retarding force, making it appear for a time that the hero may escape the fate that is impending. Modern procedure extends the rising action, often confining the decline to the last act, which is still the despair of many otherwise competent playwrights.

The methods of dividing plays into acts and scenes have varied greatly with the conceptions of the nature of interesting dramatic action and of the
Acts and amount of that action to be portrayed
Scenes upon the stage. Notions of a realistic or suggestive staging of plays, and facilities for stage realism have had some effect on these divisions; mere tradition or imitation perhaps more. As already noted, classic drama dealt with a cross-section of the entire action, preferably the day of crisis. The entirely ade-

quate three parts of Greek drama became five acts in Seneca, and this plan served as a model for all the Elizabethans and throughout the eighteenth century in England. But the Elizabethans, with their fondness for action and with the traditions of the religious pageants before them, must needs dramatize not a crucial day but the entire dramatic development, however far afield it carried them. The pageantry of their plays became an end in itself, and strictness of unity was relaxed for the sake of enrichment. Hence the stage was alive with actors, each act was conceived of as an accumulation of scenes, some carefully planned with an eye to their inner unity and progress, others apparently just kept going.

The drama of our own day approaches the action once more in the manner of the Greeks. We have lost in the process the privilege of following a char-
**Recent** acter throughout its development, but we
**Developments** have simplified our problem so that we can know character most intimately while it is under observation. No long stretches of time, no marked changes of stage-settings are involved, and as our study of character becomes more intimate there is need of fewer persons. Plays with one setting throughout and a mere handful of characters are no longer a novelty. Three acts, or at most four, are the rule, and of late there is a decided movement toward the one-act play. The Elizabethan fondness for panoramic presentation is now gratified by film-plays and by the wide-spread cultivation of pageantry. With fewer scenes has come the necessity of organizing each particular scene, not merely as a part of the dramatic whole, but as an organism in itself, with its own problems of exposition, enrichment, and climax.

In characterization the centuries have brought little

## THE DRAMA

advance. Since the days of Shakespeare, no one can think of character as having really a subordinate part in drama, however much Aristotle has been interpreted as saying so. Indeed in all good plays characters must dominate the action rather than be dominated by it. The problem is always what a given character *would* do under certain conditions, not what the plot would have it do. All questions of character are ultimately questions of consistency. To be acceptable the dramatic personage must be consistent with life, with our notions of humanity. Make him conform too far, draw him in too broad outlines, and he becomes a type, the composite portrait of a class, as characters in comedies of manners are always likely to be. Individualize him too far and he loses his consistency with life and becomes an eccentric. Once conceived of, he must remain consistent with himself, and never drop out of character.

**Characterization**

This " motivation " of action in accord with character is an important feature in distinguishing dramatic structure of the better sort. Melodrama and farce may take liberties with it, but tragedy and comedy must appeal to our sense of probability in a somewhat subtle way. As in other forms of fiction, there is a kind of poetic truth, a land of higher probability, presenting not the actual facts of any particular piece of genuine experience, but a series of imaginary developments in which there is less of accident and more of logical cause and effect than men have a right to expect in life. Day by day we encounter surprises and coincidences and strange turns of fortune. Truth, the popular proverb tells us, is stranger than fiction. But many of these occurrences, if put into plays, would be condemned at once as highly im-

**Probability in Drama**

probable and melodramatic. Coincidence is likely to play a considerable part in the best dramatic plots because of the desire to focus interest on some one vital moment. The point, however, at which plots so constructed overdo the matter and become melodramatic is hard to fix. Many of our most successful American plays are essentially melodramas.

Needless to say, drama differs from every other literary type in the medium by which it is to be conveyed to an audience. Perhaps in time, just as the lyric has developed far away from its original rendering in song, drama will come to be merely the presentation of clever or spirited conversation in a certain mechanical form for reading in the study. The present drama of ideas appears to tend that way, and certainly more plays are being read today than ever before. But as yet we think of our plays in action, and thus delegate to the arts of acting and stage-decoration, which are the vehicles that bring them before audiences, a large share of the responsibility for their effectiveness. While the ideals and practices of these two arts have varied greatly from generation to generation, they have usually followed the same course, and whatever they have done has been done with a sincere desire to get out of the manuscript play the best emotional and imaginative values there were in it.

**The Acted Drama**

At present both acting and stage-craft vary between the opposite poles of complete realism and sheer suggestion. A stage-picture minute in photographic detail, backed by an elaborately painted back-drop that can be seen through a practicable window, and framed in a great square of gilded molding, has become familiar enough to the theater-goer, who wonders

**Realism in Stage-Craft**

what new bit of realism each first-night will bring forth. He has heard also of picking actors who physically " look the parts," and of making characters to fit the peculiarities of certain performers. No wonder he protests that this realism of detail has become an end in itself and has distracted his attention from the proper appreciation of the play; moreover, that this detailed mechanical representation of things is not art, any more than the tiny moving reaper and the falling swaths of pasteboard wheat in the panorama of a harvester exhibit.

Artists have felt these conditions keenly and are taking decided measures to counteract them. They propose to approach the problem not from the detailed impressions of actual life, but from a study of the inner motives and essential impressions of the play. Thus staging would become not an objective imitation of something already objective, but an objective rendering of things originally subjective, the moods and impulses the literary artist is trying to convey by means of a play. This calls into service the principles of pure design, the effects of simple lines and spaces, of lighting and of color. Photographic detail in scenery is forsaken, costumes are indefinite as to place or period, properties are few and beautiful. The entire adequacy of this for Shakespeare and for poetic drama in general is soon apparent. For *Bought and Paid For* or *The Lion and the Mouse* or nine-tenths of our Broadway " successes " it would never do. The fact is that the large majority of our recent plays have been based on realism, and even when imaginative have had to do with the poetry of realism. For such as these there must be realism of staging as well, but confined to reasonable limits. The romantic or poetic play will always have an honored place, and this is the

Suggestive Staging

field to which we may look with confidence for the development of true art in presentation.

### Subjects for Study

1. Our best knowledge of the Elizabethan stage and staging.
2. Comparison of Kyd's *Spanish Tragedy* and Shakespeare's *Hamlet*.
3. Technique of the Miracle Plays and of modern pageantry.
4. Technique of Shakespeare's English history cycle and of the modern photo-play.
5. Melodrama, a hardy perennial.
6. Restoration versions of Shakespeare's plays.
7. Comedy study: a play each of Plautus, Ben Jonson, Sheridan, and Clyde Fitch.
8. "Psychology" in Shakespeare and in some representative modern play.
9. Present tendencies in methods of staging.
10. The problem play.
11. Organization of a tragic plot from one of the following: Richardson's *Clarissa Harlowe*, Godwin's *Caleb Williams*, Emily Bronte's *Wuthering Heights*, Thackeray's *Vanity Fair*, Thomas Hardy's *Tess of the D'Urbervilles*.
12. Arrangement of some current short story as a one-act play.

### Collections

*Representative English Dramas from Dryden to Sheridan.* Edited by Frederick Tupper and J. W. Tupper. Oxford University Press, American Branch. Cloth, $1.25.

Not many plays, but those of chief importance. An excellent piece of editing.

*Representative English Plays from the Middle Ages to the End of the Nineteenth Century.* Edited by J. S. P. Tatlock and R. G. Martin. The Century Co. Cloth, $2.50.

*The Chief Elizabethan Dramatists.* Edited by W. A. Neilson.

*The Chief Contemporary Dramatists.* Edited by T. H. Dickinson.

*The Chief European Dramatists.* Edited by Brander Matthews. Series published by Houghton Mifflin Co. Each, cloth, $2.75.

Companion volumes, each comprising about twenty representative plays well printed in good type. All plays are complete.

## THE DRAMA

*Masterpieces of Modern Drama.* English and American.
*Masterpieces of Modern Drama.* Foreign.
Both volumes edited by John A. Pierce. Doubleday, Page & Co. Each, cloth, $2.00.
Not complete plays, but abridgments: important scenes, with the remainder of the story told in narrative.

. . . . . . . .

*A Select Collection of Old English Plays.* Edited by Robert Dodsley. 1744. Republished by W. Carew Hazlitt, 1874. 15 vols.
Bell's *British Theatre.* 34 vols. 1797.
Mrs. Inchbald, *The British Theatre.* 25 vols. 1808.
Mrs. Inchbald, *The Modern Theatre.* 10 vols. 1811.
Mrs. Inchbald, *Supplementary Collection of Farces.* 7 vols. 1815.
Oxberry's *English Drama.* 12 vols. 1818.
*The Mermaid Series.* (Elizabethan and Restoration dramas.) 25 vols. and others in preparation. Charles Scribner's Sons.
*Specimens of the Pre-Shaksperean Drama.* Edited by John M. Manly. 2 vols. Ginn & Co.
*Representative English Comedies.* Edited by Charles M. Gayley. 3 vols. The Macmillan Co.
*Specimens of the Elizabethan Drama from Lyly to Shirley.* (Selected scenes only.) Edited by W. H. Williams. Clarendon Press.

### Critical Discussions

#### I. History of Criticism

Sir Philip Sidney, *The Defense of Poesy.* 1595 (written before 1585).
Ben Jonson, *Timber, or Discoveries upon Men and Matters.* 1641 (written 1620-1635?).
Sir William Davenant, Preface to *Gondibert.* 1650.
John Dryden, *An Essay of Dramatic Poesy.* 1668.
John Dryden, *An Essay of Heroic Plays.* 1672.
John Dryden, *Defence of the Epilogue* (*An Essay on the Dramatic Poetry of the Last Age*). 1672.
John Dryden, Preface to *Troilus and Cressida* (*The Grounds of Criticism in Tragedy*). 1679.
Thomas Rymer, *The Tragedies of the Last Age.* 1678.
Thomas Rymer, *A Short View of Tragedy.* 1693.
John Dennis, *The Impartial Critic.* 1693.

William Congreve, *Concerning Humour in Comedy*. 1695.
Jeremy Collier, *A Short View of the Immorality and Profaneness of the English Stage*. 1698.
Alexander Pope, Preface to his edition of Shakespeare. 1725.
W. R. Chetwood, *The British Theatre*. 1750.
Joseph Warton, Shakespeare papers in the *Adventurer*. 1753.
Samuel Johnson, Preface to his edition of Shakespeare. 1765.
Richard Farmer, *An Essay on the Learning of Shakespeare*. 1767.
Elizabeth Montagu, *On the Writings and Genius of Shakespeare*. 1769.
Charles Lamb, *Specimens of the English Dramatic Poets*. 1809.
William Hazlitt, *Characters of Shakespeare's Plays*. 1817.
William Hazlitt, *Dramatic Literature of the Age of Elizabeth*. 1821.
Mrs. Jameson, *Characteristics of Shakespeare's Women*. 1832.
Samuel Taylor Coleridge, *Notes and Lectures upon Shakespeare*. 1849.

## II. General Works

Ernest Bernbaum, *The Drama of Sensibility (1696-1780)*. Boston (Ginn & Co.), 1915.

C. F. Tucker Brooke, *The Tudor Drama*. Boston and New York (Houghton Mifflin Co.), 1911.

Ferdinand Brunetière, *The Law of the Drama*. English translation by P. M. Hayden; introduction by Henry Arthur Jones. Publications of the Dramatic Museum of Columbia University. New York, 1914.

C. H. Caffin, *The Appreciation of the Drama*. New York (Baker & Taylor), 1908.

Lewis N. Chase, *The English Heroic Play*. New York (Columbia University Press), 1903.

Harriott E. Fansler, *The Evolution of Technic in Elizabethan Tragedy*. Chicago and New York (Row, Peterson & Co.), 1914.

Gustav Freytag, *The Technique of the Drama*. English translation by E. J. MacEwan. Chicago (Scott, Foresman & Co.).

Brander Matthews, *A Study of the Drama*. Boston (Houghton Mifflin Co.), 1910.

George Meredith, *An Essay on Comedy and the Uses of the Comic Spirit*. New York (Scribner), 1905. (Written, 1877.)

Elizabeth Woodbridge Morris, *The Drama: Its Law and Its Technique*. Boston (Allyn & Bacon).

George H. Nettleton, *The Drama of the Restoration and Eighteenth Century*. New York (Macmillan), 1914.

THE DRAMA 265

John Palmer, *The Comedy of Manners*. London (Bell & Sons), 1913.
John Palmer, *Comedy* (*The Art and Craft of Letters*). New York (Doran & Co.).
W. T. Price, *The Technique of the Drama*. New York (Brentano).
W. T. Price, *The Analysis of Play Construction*. New York, 1908.
F. H. Ristine, *English Tragi-comedy*. New York (Columbia University Press), 1910.
C. E. Vaughan, *Types of Tragic Drama*. London (Macmillan), 1908.
A. W. Ward, *A History of English Dramatic Literature to the Death of Queen Anne*. Revised edition. 3 vols. New York (Macmillan), 1899.
Lauclan M. Watt, *Attic and Elizabethan Tragedy*. New York (Dutton & Co.), 1908.

### III. Contemporary Drama

Charlton Andrews, *The Drama To-day*. Philadelphia (Lippincott), 1913.
Charlton Andrews, *Technique of Play-Writing*. Springfield, Mass. (Home Correspondence School), 1915.
William Archer, *Play-Making. A Manual of Craftsmanship*. Boston (Small, Maynard & Co.), 1912.
George P. Baker, *The Technique of the Drama*. Boston and New York (Houghton Mifflin Co ), 1915
Richard Burton, *How to See a Play*. New York (Macmillan), 1914.
Richard Burton, *The New American Drama*. New York (Crowell & Co.), 1913.
Huntly Carter, *The New Spirit in Drama and Art*. New York (Mitchell Kennerley), 1913.
F. W. Chandler, *Aspects of Modern Drama*. New York (Macmillan), 1914
Barrett H. Clark, *The Continental Drama of To-day*. Outlines for its study. New York (Holt & Co.), 1914.
Barrett H. Clark, *The British and American Drama of To-day*. Outlines for their study. New York (Holt & Co.), 1915.
E. Gordon Craig, *Towards a New Theatre*. New York (Dutton & Co.), 1913.
E Gordon Craig, *On the Art of the Theatre*. Chicago (Browne), 1911.

T. H. Dickinson, *The Case of American Drama*. Boston and New York (Houghton Mifflin Co.), 1915.

Ashley Dukes, *Modern Dramatists*. Boston (Small, Maynard & Co.), 1912.

E. E. Hale, Jr., *Dramatists of To-day*. New York (Holt & Co.), 1911.

Clayton Hamilton, *The Theory of the Theatre*. New York (Holt & Co.), 1911.

Clayton Hamilton, *Studies in Stage-Craft*. New York (Holt & Co.), 1914.

Archibald Henderson, *The Changing Drama*. New York (Holt & Co.), 1914.

Alfred Hennequin, *The Art of Playwriting*. Boston and New York (Houghton Mifflin Co.), 1890.

James Huneker, *Iconoclasts: A Book of Dramatists*. New York (Scribner), 1905.

Henry Arthur Jones, *The Renascence of the English Drama*. New York (Macmillan), 1895.

Ludwig Lewisohn, *The Modern Drama*. New York (Huebsch), 1915.

H. K. Moderwell, *The Theatre of To-day*. New York (John Lane Co.), 1914.

George Bernard Shaw, *Dramatic Opinions and Essays*. New York (Brentano), 1907.

# INDEX

## A

Achilles Tatius, 89
acts and scenes, 257-258
*Adam Bede*, 176
Addison, Joseph, 99, 101, 111, 113, 125, 127-131, 133, 157, 240, 246
*Adelgitha*, 249
"Admiral's Ghost, The," 27-28
adventure ballads, 15, 18, 32-34
*Adventurer, The*, 131
*Æneid*, 7, 86-90, 92-95, 101, 105, 107, 109
Æschylus, 211
*Age of Wordsworth, The*, 249 n.
Ainsworth, W. H., 172
airs, 49-50
*Alchemist, The*, 230
Aldrich, Thomas B., 203
Aleman, Mateo, 154
allegory, 95
*All for Love*, 237
*Almanzor and Almahide, or The Conquest of Granada*, 238
*Alphonsus of Aragon*, 228
"Alysoun," 42
*Amadis de Gaula*, 152-153
*Ambrosio, or The Monk*, 168
*Amelia*, 162-163, 173
*American Note-Books*, 194-195
American novels, 180-181
American poets, 60, 64-65, 69, 72-73
American short stories, 178, 192-199, 203-204
*Amoretti*, 46
Anacreontic poetry, 51, 59
"Ancient Mariner, The," 54

Anglo-Saxon lyric, 41-42
"Animal Fair, The," 50
*Anna St. Ives*, 165
*Anthology of Magazine Verse*, 73
*Anti-Jacobin, The*, 249
antimasque, the, 235
*Antony and Cleopatra*, 237
*Arabian Nights*, 168
Arbuthnot, John, 133
*Arcadia, The*, 46, 151-155
Ariosto, 93
Aristophanes, 212
Aristotle, 4, 10, 110, 112, 114, 131, 211, 213, 259
Arnold, Matthew, 61-62, 64, 138
*Arsinoë*, 246
*Ars poetica* (Horace), 87, 110, 213
*Ars poetica* (Vida), 93, 110
art-epic, 86, 94, 99, 102
Arthurian romances, 7, 149, 152
*Arthur Mervyn*, 169
artist, the, 58, 66-67
art-lyric, 51, 57, 63, 69
arts, fine, 1-2
association of ideas, 121-122, 143-144
*Astrophel and Stella*, 46-49, 63
*As You Like It*, 74, 151 n., 153
*Atalanta in Calydon*, 67, 77
"At the End of the Passage," 203
*Aureng-Zebe*, 238
Austen, Jane, 171-173

## B

"Baa, Baa, Black Sheep," 207
"Babylon," 16-17
Bacon, Francis, 4, 123-124, 129

267

Bage, Robert, 165
Baillie, Joanna, 249
ballad ,collectors, 25
ballad definition, 13-14
ballade, 43, 69
ballad history, periods of, 15-16
ballad imitations, 26-28
"Ballad of Reading Gaol, The," 70
ballads, 5, 13-37, 249
ballad scholarship, 16, 26
ballad stanzas, 17, 18
ballad themes, 29, 33
Balzac, Honoré de, 199
Barker, Granville, 252, 255
"Baron of Brackley, The," 19
*Barrack Room Ballads*, 71
Barrie, Sir James M., 253
Bartas, G. S. Sieur du, 96
*Bartholomew Fair*, 230
Beaumont, Francis, 233
Beau Tibbs, 127, 133, 143
beauty, 57
Beckford, William, 167-168
Beddoes, T. L., 250
*Bee, The*, 132
*Beggar's Opera, The*, 23, 246-247
Behn, Mrs. Aphra, 151
*Belinda*, 171
Belloc, Hilaire, 140
Bennett, Arnold, 180-181
Benson, A. C., 140
*Beowulf*, 7, 84-86
"Bewick and Grahame," 22, 33
Birrell, Augustine, 140
Black, William, 177
Blackmore, Richard, 177
Blackmore, Sir Richard, 98-99, 106
Blake, William, 54
blank verse, 102, 107, 114
"Blessed Damozel, The," 66
*Bloody Brother, The*, 234
"Blow, blow, thou winter wind," 74
"Blow, bugle, blow," 63
"Blow, northern wind," 42
*Blue Bird, The*, 253
Boccaccio, Giovanni, 150

Boiardo, 93
Boileau - Despreaux, Nicolas, 103
*Bonduca*, 234
"Bonnie George Campbell," 19, 31
border ballads, 18-20, 32-34
Borrow, George, 175
*Boston Token, The*, 194
Boswell, James, 132
*Bought and Paid For*, 261
bourgeois literature, 158, 161, 240, 243-244
Boyle, Roger, 151
Bradley, A. C., 139
Braithwaite, W. S., 72-73
"Bridge of Sighs, The," 61
"Bridge, The," 65
Brieux, Eugène, 251
*British Essayists, The*, 131-132
broadside ballads, 15, 22-25, 34
Brontë, Charlotte, 175
Brontë, Emily, 172
Brown, Charles Brockden, 169
Brown, Dr. John, 201
Brown, Tom, 128
Browning, Mrs. Elizabeth Barrett, 61-62, 64, 77
Browning, Robert, 61-62, 64, 72
Buckingham, George, Duke of, 238
Bulwer-Lytton, Sir Edward, 172-173, 249
Bunner, H. C., 203
Bunyan, John, 151, 155
Bürger, Gottfried, 26, 55
burlesque, 102-105, 162, 238, 245-246, 249
Burnet, Bishop Gilbert, 156
Burney, Fanny, 171
Burns, Robert, 24, 54, 61
Burroughs, John, 140
Butler, Samuel, 104-105, 156
Byron, Lord, 55-57, 59

C

Cable, Geo. W., 204
*Caleb Williams*, 165-166
Campion, Thomas, 50, 235

INDEX 269

Canby, Prof. Henry S., 197
Cannan, Gilbert, 180
Canning, George, 249
*Canterbury Tales*, 43, 191
"Captain Car," 19
*Captain Singleton*, 160
*Caractacus*, 245
*Cardinal Richelieu*, 249
Carey, Henry, 245
Carlyle, Thomas, 138
"Cask of Amontillado, The," 196
*Caste*, 249
*Castle of Otranto, The*, 167
*Castle Rackrent*, 171
*Castle Spectre, The*, 249
Catholic Reaction, The, 94
*Catiline, his Conspiracy*, 231
*Cato*, 240
Catullus, 51
*Caxtons, The*, 173
*Cecilia*, 171
*Cenci, The*, 250
Cervantes, Miguel de, 104
Chalmers, Alexander, 131-132
Chamisso, Adelbert von, 56
*Chanticler*, 253
Chapman, George, 225, 231
character and plot, 185-186, 215, 259
character grouping, 184, 214, 221-222
character portraits, 156-157
character writings, 128-129, 156
characterization: in simple ballads, 29; in adventure ballads, 34; in epic, 91-92, 112-113; in essays, 133; in novels, 166, 169-171, 174-176, 182-187; in short stories, 193, 197, 201, 206-207; in drama, 214-215, 223-224, 233, 240, 248, 258-259
Chatterton, Thomas, 32
Chaucer, Geoffrey, 6, 29, 43, 191
Chesterton, G. K., 140
Chettle, Henry, 24
"Chevy Chase," 24
Chiabrera, 52
child actors, 234
*Child of Love, The*, 249

Child, Prof. F. J., 26
"Children in the Wood, The," 31-32
chivalric romances, 89, 152
chorus in drama, the, 183, 213-214, 221, 231
"Christ's Hospital Five and Thirty Years Ago," 136
chronicle history plays, 222-224, 238
*Chrononhotonthologos*, 245
Cibber, Colley, 240, 243
Cicero, Marcus Tullius, 117, 130
*Citizen of the World, The*, 132
*Civil and Military Gazette, The*, 203
*Civil Wars of York and Lancaster, The*, 96
*Cléopâtre*, 149
*Clitophon and Leucippe, The Loves of*, 89
closet-drama, 249-250
closing of the theaters, 231, 234, 236
"Coaches, Of," 121-122
Coleridge, Samuel Taylor, 54-55, 57-59, 61, 135, 249-250
collections: the ballad, 35-36; the lyric, 80-82; the essay, 145-146; the novel, 188; the short story, 209; the drama, 262-263
collectors of ballads, 25
Collier, Jeremy, 242
Collins, Wilkie, 177
Collins, William, 53-54
Colman, George, 131
*Colonel Jacque*, 160
comedy of manners, 126-127, 129, 156, 162, 164, 171, 214-215, 229-231, 233, 237, 240-242, 259
communal authorship, 13-15
*Comus*, 235
Congreve, William, 127, 241
*Connoisseur, The*, 131
*Conquest of Granada, The*, 238
Conrad, Joseph, 179, 204
*Conscious Lovers, The*, 243
consistency in characters, 184, 259

contemplative lyrics, 77-78
conventional devices, 48, 87-88, 100-101, 103-104, 107, 109, 250
Cooper, James Fenimore, 172
Cornwall, Barry, 61
coteries, 156
Countess of Pembroke, The, 46, 221
*Country Wife, The*, 241
courts of love, 161
"Courting of Dinah Shadd, The," 203
"Cousin Phillis," 201
Coverley, Sir Roger de, 130, 133, 142, 157
cowboy ballads, 28
Cowley, Abram, 52, 98, 125
Cowper, William, 60
Crashaw, Richard, 52
critical discussions: the ballad, 36-37; the lyric, 82-83; the epic, 115-116; the essay, 146-147; the novel, 189-190; the short story, 210; the drama, 263-266
critical essays, 125, 137-139, 143
critical theory, books on, 10-11
*Critic, The*, 245
Cross, Prof. W. L., 165
"Cruel Brother, The," 31
Cumberland, Richard, 244
cycles of romance, 90, 92
*Cymbeline*, 220, 234
*Cyrano de Bergerac*, 253

D

"Daffodils, The," 52
Daniel, Samuel, 46, 96
D'Annunzio, Gabriele, 253
"Danny Deever," 27-28
Dante, 102, 137
*Daphnis and Chloe*, 89
D'Arblay, Mme., 171
Daudet, Alphonse, 200, 208
Davenant, William, 97-98, 246
"Day is done, The," 65
*Day's Work, The*, 203
Day, Thomas, 164
*De Amicitia*, 117
*Death's Jest Book*, 250

debate, the, 218
*De Brevitate Vitæ*, 117
*Decameron, The*, 150
*Defence of Guinevere, The*, 107
Defoe, Daniel, 159, 161, 196
Dekker, Thomas, 125
*Delia*, 46
Deloney, Thomas, 24
De Morgan, William, 180
Denham, John, 52
*De Officiis*, 117
*Deor's Lament*, 41
*Departmental Ditties*, 203
*De Providentia*, 117
De Quincey, Thomas, 134, 137
*De Senectute*, 117
detached observer, the, 128-129, 143, 160
*De Tranquilitate Animi*, 117
*Devil on Two Sticks, The*, 129, 160
*Diable Boiteux, Le*, 129, 160
dialect, 71
*Diana*, 153
Dickens, Charles, 137, 172-174, 180, 197, 201
didactic poetry, 57, 111
dirge, the, 64
*Discorsi dell' Arte Poetica*, 94
*Distrest Mother, The*, 240
*Divine Comedy, The*, 102
*Divine Weeks and Works*, 96
Dobson, Austin, 69
*Doctor Faustus*, 223
*Dr. Jekyll and Mr. Hyde*, 201
doctrinaire novel, 163-166
*Doll's House, A*, 251, 257
domestic relations, ballads of, 15, 18
*Don Quixote*, 104, 155
Dooley, Mr., 129
Douglas, 245
Douglas, ballad hero, 20
drama, beginning of, 5, 211-212
drama, definition of, 255
drama of ideas, 251-252, 260
drama, subdivisions, 255-256
Drama, The, 211-266
dramatic conflict, 255-256
dramatic elements: in ballads,

31; in lyrics, 75; in essays, 133; in novels, 161, 176, 181-183; in short stories, 193, 207
"Drink to me only with thine eyes," 52
Dryden, John, 53, 97, 101, 111, 125, 129, 237-239, 241
*Duchess of Malfi, The*, 232
*Duenna, The*, 247
Dumas, Alexandre, 172
dumb show, 221
Durfey, Thomas, 25
*Dynasts, The*, 108

E

"Earl Brand," 20
Ebers, Georg M, 172
economy of invention, 185, 194, 201, 208
*Edgar Huntley*, 169
Edgeworth, Maria, 171
*Edinburgh Review*, 137
"Edward," 31
*Edward II.*, 223-224
Egan, Pierce, 172, 174
eighteenth century, the, 53
Elderton, William, 24
*Election Ballads*, 24
"Elegy in a Country Churchyard," 54, 62
*Elia*, 135-136
Eliot, George, 175-177
*Eliza*, 98
Elizabethan literature, 40-41, 46-51, 75, 134, 136, 148, 158, 211, 221
*Elizabethan Lyric, The*, 73
Elizabethan songs, 49-51
Emerson, Ralph Waldo, 60, 138
*Emma*, 171
emotional impulse: of lyrics, 74; of personal essays, 119-120, 142-143; of short stories, 191, 194-195, 205
*English and Scottish Popular Ballads*, 26
*Epicœne, the Silent Woman*, 230
Epic poetry, 7, 84-116, 162, 181-182

epic simile, 87, 93, 110, 114
epigram, 8, 50
epithets, 113-114
Erskine, Prof. John, 73
*Essay on Milton*, 137
Etherege, George, 241
*Ethiopica*, 89
*Eugene Aram*, 173
*Euphues and His England*, 152
*Euphues his Censure to Philautus*, 151 n.
*Euphues, the Anatomy of Wit*, 151-152, 154
Euripides, 211
"Eve of St. John, The," 27
*Evelina*, 171
Evelyn, John, 240 n.
*Evergreen*, 25
*Every Man in his Humour*, 230
*Expedition of Humphrey Clinker, The*, 160
expository essay, 125, 137-139, 143

F

fable as literary type, the, 8
fabliau, 6, 191, 227
*Faerie Queene*, 7, 48 n., 94-96, 109
*Fair Penitent, The*, 239
*False Delicacy*, 244
farce, 217-220, 248, 256-257, 259
Farquhar, George, 241
*Fashionable Tales*, 171
fate-tragedy, 176
*Ferdinand, Count Fathom*, 160
*Ferrex and Porrex*, 219-221
Fielding, Henry, 155, 161-163, 173, 175, 181, 245
fine arts, 1-2
Fitch, Clyde, 253-254
"Flee fro the presse," 43
Fletcher, John, 229-230, 233-234, 237
Fletcher, Phineas, 48 n.
Florio, John, 123-124
"Flower in the crannied wall," 74
Folio Manuscript, Percy's, 25

272  INDEX

folk-epic, 84-85, 105
folk-lore, 15, 193
Foote, Samuel, 244
Ford, John, 150, 234
*Four Prentices of London,* 228
*Frankenstein,* 169
French heroic poetry, 96-97, 102, 113, 161
French lyric, 43-45, 49, 51, 59, 69
French Revolution, the, 55
French romances, 156, 161, 237
French short stories, 199-200, 203, 208
Frere, John H., 249
Freytag, Gustav, 172
*Friar Bacon and Friar Bungay,* 228
fusion of literary types, 9

G

Gale, Zona, 204
Galsworthy, John, 140, 179, 252
*Gammer Gurton's Needle,* 219-220
Garland, Hamlin, 204
Gaskell, Mrs. Elizabeth, 201
"Gather ye rosebuds," 52
Gautier, Théophile, 199, 208
Gay, John, 23, 69, 245-247
genres, literary, 4
"Gentle Boy, The," 194
*George-a-Greene, the Pindar of Wakefield,* 228
German romanticists, 26, 55, 58, 61
Gerould, Mrs. Katharine F., 204
*Ghosts,* 251
Glover, Samuel, 105
Godwin, William, 165
Goethe, Johann Wolfgang, 248
"Gold Bug, The," 196
*Golden Treasury, The,* 80
Goldsmith, Oliver, 127, 129, 132-134, 143, 157, 163, 244, 247-248
*Gondibert,* 97-98
*Good Natured Man, The,* 244
*Gorboduc,* 219-221

Gosse, Edmund, 139
"Gothic" novels, 164, 166-169, 171-173
*Götz von Berlichingen,* 248
*Graham's Magazine,* 194
*Grand Cyrus, Le,* 149, 155
Gray, Thomas, 53-54, 62
Greek drama, 211-221
Greek lyric, 38-39, 51-52, 211
Greek romances, 89, 152-153
Greek theater, 211-212
Greene, Robert, 151 n., 222, 228
Gregory, Lady, 253
*Guardian, The,* 131
Guarini, Giovanni Battista, 233
Gummere, Prof. F. B., 13-14, 40
*Guzman de Alfarache,* 154

H

Haggard, H. Rider, 177
Hall, Joseph, 156
Hamilton, Anthony, 240
*Hamlet,* 222, 224-225, 231
Handel, G. F., 246
*Handsome Housemaid, The,* 244
Hardy, Thomas, 108, 175-177, 207
"Hark, hark, the lark," 50
*Harper's Monthly,* 196
Harrison, Frederic, 139
Harte, Bret, 197-198, 202-203
Hart, Prof. W. M., 29 n.
Hashimura Togo, 129
Hauptmann, Gerhart, 251, 253
Hawkesworth, Dr. John, 131
Hawthorne, Nathaniel, 178, 193-196, 199, 201
Haywood, Mrs. Eliza, 161
Hazlitt, William, 134, 137, 139-140, 142
Heliodorus, 89
Henley, William E., 69
*Henry IV.,* part I, 24; parts I and II, 223
*Henry V.,* 223, 231 and n.
*Henry VI.,* 223
Henry, O., 204, 208
*Heptameron, The,* 150

Herd, David, 26
Herder, Johann Gottfried von, 26
Herford, Prof. C. H., 249
*Hermsprong*, 165
heroic ballads, 21, 33
heroic plays, 97, 237-239
heroic poems, 96-97, 101-102, 111, 113
hero of romance, the, 92, 97, 167
Herrick, Robert (novelist), 180
Herrick, Robert (poet), 51-52
Hervieu, Paul, 251
Hewlett, Maurice, 179, 204
Heywood, Thomas, 228
Hill, Aaron, 245
"Hind Horn," 22
historical novel, the, 149, 169-170, 172-173
*History and Adventures of an Atom*, 160
"history," the, 148
*History of His Own Time*, 156
Hobbes, Thomas, 4
Holcroft, Thomas, 165
Holinshed, Raphael, 222
Holmes, Sherlock, 159
Home, John, 245
Homeric epithets, 113-114
Hood, Thomas, 61, 69
Horace, 51, 87 n., 110, 213
*Hours of Idleness*, 55
Howard, Henry, Earl of Surrey, 45
Howells, W. D., 180
"How sleep the brave," 54
*Hudibras*, 104-105
Hugo, Victor, 172
humanitarianism, 61, 134, 159, 174
humor, 163, 172, 174
*Humorous Day's Mirth, A*, 231
humour comedies, 156, 171, 229-231
*Humphrey Clinker*, 160
Huneker, James, 140
Hunt, James Henry Leigh, 134, 137, 140-141
Hutchinson, Colonel, 156

Huxley, Thomas, 138
hymns, 42

I

Ibsen, Henrik, 250-251, 257
*Ideal Commonwealths*, 151 n.
*Idler, The*, 132
*Idylls of the King*, 105-107
*Iliad*, 84, 86-87, 105
images: in sonnets, 48
imitation, arts of, 1-2
imitation of ballads, 26-28
impressionism, 141, 177-178, 182, 191-195, 197-199, 205
Inchbald, Mrs. Elizabeth, 165
incremental repetition, 16-17, 31
*Indian Emperor, The*, 238
indirect characterization, 183
"*in medias res*," 87 and n., 100, 103, 107, 112
"In Memoriam," 63
interlude, the, 219-220
"Intimations of Immortality," 59
*Irene*, 245
Irish poets, 71
Irving, Washington, 137, 192
*Italian, The*, 169
Italian epics, 92-95, 106-107, 111-112
Italian lyric, 44-45, 49-52, 59
Italian operas, 246-247

J

*Jack Wilton*, 151, 154, 159, 179
Jacobs, W. W., 204
James, Henry, 178, 180-181, 198, 202, 205
Jamieson, Robert, 26
*Jane Shore*, 239-240
Jerome, Jerome K., 253
*Jeronimo*, 225-226
*Jerusalem Delivered*, 94
Jewett, Sarah Orne, 204
*Jew of Malta, The*, 223
"Johnie Armstrong," 20 n., 24
Johnson, Dr. Samuel, 31-32, 79, 102, 131-133, 245

Jones, Henry Arthur, 251
Jones, Inigo, 235
Jonson, Ben, 51-52, 58, 124-125, 156, 171, 221, 225, 229-231, 235, 237
*Joseph and His Brethren*, 250
*Joseph Andrews*, 162
journalistic ballads, 15
journalistic methods, 202
*Jungle Book, The*, 203
*Justice*, 252

### K

Keats, John, 40, 55-57, 59, 61, 69, 75
Kelly, Hugh, 244
Kennedy, Charles Rann, 253
*Kind-Harts Dreame*, 24
*King and No King, A*, 233
*King Arthur*, 98
"King Estmere," 22
*King Lear*, 220, 223, 237
Kingsley, Charles, 172
Kipling, Rudyard, 27-28, 71, 179, 201-204, 207-208
Kitchener, Lord, 63
*Knight of the Burning Pestle, The*, 103, 228
Knowles, Sheridan, 249
Kotzebue, A. F. F. von, 192, 247-249
Kyd, Thomas, 222, 225-226, 231

### L

"La Belle Dame sans Merci," 75
*Lady of Lyons, The*, 249
*Lady or the Tiger?, The*, 203
Lamb, Charles, 134-137, 139-143
lament in ballads, 30-31
Lang, Andrew, 69
Langham, Robert, 24
Latin comedy, 212, 214-215, 219-220, 226
Latin hymns and songs, 42
Latin lyric, 51-52, 69
Latin versification, 46

Lawes, Henry, 235
Lawrence, D H., 180
*Lay of the Last Minstrel, The*, 55, 57
*Lazarillo de Tormes*, 154, 159
Leacock, Stephen, 88 n., 140
*Leatherstocking Tales, The*, 172
Lee, Nathaniel, 239
Lee, Sir Sidney, 139
"Legend of Sleepy Hollow, The," 192
*Leonidas*, 105
Le Sage, Alain René, 129, 160
Lessing, G. E., 40
letters, familiar, 8, 128-129
Lewis, Matthew Gregory, 27, 168, 249
liberalism, 56
*Life in London*, 172
*Life's Handicap*, 203
Lillo, George, 243-244
*Lion and the Mouse, The*, 261
*Lives of the Eminent Greeks and Romans*, 118
local color, 197-198, 202, 207
Locke, Matthew, 246
Lodge, Thomas, 151 n.
Lomax, Prof. J. A., 28
London, Jack, 204
*London Merchant, The*, 243-244, 249
Longfellow, Henry W., 64-65
*Longsword, Earl of Salisbury*, 167, 169
Longus, 89
*Looker-on, The*, 132
*Lorna Doone*, 177
*Lounger, The*, 132
Lounsbury, Prof. T. R., 139
*Love for Love*, 241
*Lovers' Progress, The*, 233
Lowell, James Russell, 138
Lucan, 89
Lucas, E V, 140
Lucian, 128
"Luck of Roaring Camp, The," 197
*Lutrin, Le*, 103
*Lying Lover, The*, 243

## INDEX

Lyly, John, 151-152, 226
*Lyrical Ballads, The*, 54-55
lyric, definitions, 38-41, 73-74
Lyric, The, 5, 38-83, 119-120, 139, 142, 178, 182, 191, 205, 211, 235, 260

### M

Macaulay, Thomas B., 102, 137-138
*Macbeth*, 223
Mackaye, Percy, 253
Mackenzie, Compton, 180
Mackenzie, Henry, 164
*Madras House, The*, 252
madrigals, 49-50
Maeterlinck, Maurice, 253
*Maid's Tragedy, The*, 233
Malory, Thomas, 149
*Man and Superman*, 252
"Man in Black, The," 133
Manley, Mrs. Mary, 161
*Man of Feeling, The*, 164
*Mansfield Park*, 171
*Many Inventions*, 203
Manzoni, Alessandro, 172
Margaret of Navarre, 150
"Markheim," 201
Marlowe, Christopher, 222-224, 232
Marston, John, 225
Masefield, John, 40, 70-71
Mason, William, 245
masques, 226, 234-236, 245
Massinger, Philip, 233-234
Matthews, Prof. Brander, 139
Maturin, C. R., 172
Maupassant, Henri de, 200, 206-208
medievalism, 25-26, 65-67, 107, 119, 134, 164, 166-170
medieval romances, 89.
*Melmoth the Wanderer*, 172
melodrama, 256, 259-260
melody in lyric, 40, 61, 67, 70-71, 78-79
memoirs, 8, 126, 148, 155-156
*Memoirs of the Comte de Gramont*, 240 n.

*Memories and Portraits*, 139
*Menschenhass und Reue*, 249
*Merchant of Venice, The*, 227
Meredith, George, 175-177
Mérimée, Prosper, 199
"Merry Men, The," 206
meters in poetry, 78-79
*Michael and his Lost Angel*, 252
Middleton, Thomas, 229
*Midsummer Night's Dream*, 24, 227, 237
Mill, John Stuart, 138
Milton, John, 7, 58-59, 70, 99-102, 105, 107, 113-114, 137, 235
Minot, Lawrence, 43
*Minstrelsy of the Scottish Border*, 26
Miracle Plays, 212, 215-218, 222, 258
*Mirror, The*, 132
Mitchell, Donald G., 140
mock-heroic verse, 102-105
*Modern Novels*, 151
Moffat, Graham, 253
Molière, J. B. Poquelin, 127, 241-242
*Moll Flanders*, 160
*Monk, The*, 168
Montaigne, Michel de, 118-125, 129-130
Montemayor, George de, 153
Montesquieu, Charles, Baron de, 129
Moore, Edward, 131
Moore, Thomas, 59, 61
*Moral Epistles*, 117, 120
*Moralia*, 118, 120
Morality Plays, 218
moral tales, 126, 192
More, Thomas, 151
Morley, Henry, 139, 151 n.
Morley, John, 139
Morris, William, 65-67, 107-108
*Morte d'Arthur*, 149
Motherwell, William, 26
motion-pictures, 226, 258
"MS. Found in a Bottle, The," 194

*Much Ado About Nothing*, 227
Munday, Anthony, 24
music, 39-40, 48-51, 54, 61, 67, 70, 130, 234-235
"Musical Instrument, A," 64, 77
*My Novel*, 173
*Mysteries of Udolpho, The*, 169
Mystery Plays, 212, 215-218, 222, 258
mysticism, 66

N

Nash, Thomas, 151, 154, 159
nature, 58, 60, 66, 68, 134, 140-141, 159, 164-165, 169, 176, 187
"Necklace, The," 207
negro ballads, 28
news-letters, 128
*New York Times*, 162 n.
*Nibelungenlied, The*, 84
*Northanger Abbey*, 171-172
Norton, Thomas, 219
novel, definition, 150, 181-182
novella, 6, 148, 150, 155, 157, 192, 227
novel of manners, the, 164, 170-175, 179
Novel, The, 7-8, 148-190, 226
Noyes, Alfred, 27-28, 40, 70, 108-110

O

Oberammergau, 216
O'Brien, Fitz-James, 196-197
*Octavia*, 213
"Ode on a Grecian Urn," 59
"Ode on the Death of the Duke of Wellington," 63
ode, the, 39, 52-53, 59
"Ode to a Nightingale," 59
"Ode to Autumn," 59
"Ode to Dejection," 59
"Ode to Liberty," 59
"Ode to the West Wind," 59

*Odyssey*, 84, 86-88, 105, 108
"Old China," 135-136, 142
*Old Curiosity Shop*, 173
"Old Familiar Faces," 142
*Old Fortunatus*, 228
opera, the, 23, 236-237, 245-247
organization: of ballads, 30-31; of lyrics, 73-77; of epic, 91, 99-100, 111-112; of essays, 121-122, 124, 130-131, 143-144; of novels, 170, 185-186; of short stories, 191, 202-203; of drama, 257-258
Orientalism, 126, 167-168
*Orlando Furioso*, 93
*Orlando Innamorato*, 93
*Oroonoko*, 151
*Orphan, The*, 239
*Othello*, 153, 237, 257
Otway, Thomas, 239
outlaw ballads, 18, 28, 32-34
Overbury, Thomas, 156
*Overland Monthly, The*, 197

P

pageant-wagons, 216
Page, Thomas Nelson, 204
painting, 2, 51, 65-67
Palgrave, Francis Turner, 80
*Pamela*, 160
*Paradise Lost*, 7, 99-102, 107
*Paradise Regained*, 99
Parker, Louis N., 253
*Parlement of Foules*, 43
*Parthenissa*, 151
"Parting at Morning," 64
*Passing of the Third Floor Back, The*, 253
Passion Play, The, 216
pastoral drama, 226, 233-235, 245
pastoral romance, 153, 167, 226
*Pastor Fido*, 233
Pater, Walter, 138
patriotism: in epic, 88-89, 95; in drama, 222
*Paul Clifford*, 173
Peacock, T L., 172

INDEX 277

Peele, George, 222
*Pelham*, 173
"Penseroso, Il," 166
Pepys, Samuel, 25, 240 n.
Percy, ballad hero, 20
Percy, Bishop Thomas, 25-26
*Peregrine Pickle*, 160
Personal Essay, The, 117-147, 193
personality: in essays, 119-120, 133-135, 139, 141; in novels, 181-182; in short stories, 205-206
*Peter Pan*, 253
Petrarch, 44-45, 51
*Pharsalia*, 89
*Philaster*, 233
Philips, Ambrose, 240
*Philosophy of Composition, The*, 61
picaresque novels, 154-155, 159-160, 162, 164, 185, 227
*Pickwick Papers*, 173-174
*Piers Plowman*, 19 n.
*Pilgrim's Progress, The*, 151, 155
*Pillars of Society*, 251
*Pills to Purge Melancholy*, 25
Pindaric ode, 52-53, 59, 63
Pinero, A. W., 250-251
*Pippa Passes*, 64
*Plain Dealer, The*, 241
*Plain Tales from the Hills*, 203
Plautus, 212-215, 220, 230-231
plot: of epic poetry, 111-112
Plutarch, 118, 120, 224
Poe, Edgar Allan, 60-61, 178, 193-199
*Poetics*, Aristotle's, 110, 211, 213
poetry a fine art, 2-4
*Pomander Walk*, 253
Pope, Alexander, 103-104, 125, 133
popular epic, 84-85
popular fiction, 149-150
Porter, Jane, 169
Porter, W. S., 204, 208
Praed, Winthrop M., 69
Pre-Raphaelites, 61, 65-68

*Pride and Prejudice*, 171
*Prince Arthur*, 98
*Princess, The*, 63
Prior, Matthew, 69
*Prioress's Tale*, 29
probability, 114, 187-188, 207, 259-260
problem plays, 251-252
*Prometheus Unbound*, 56-57
prose style, 136-137, 154, 177, 201, 208
"Prospice," 64
"Psalm of Life, The," 65
Purcell, Henry, 246
Puritanism, 95, 104, 137, 160
*Purple Island, The*, 48 n.

Q

*Quality Street*, 253
Quevedo, Francisco Gomez de, 129
Quiller-Couch, A. T., 204

R

*Rab and His Friends*, 201
Racine, Jean Baptiste, 244
Radcliffe, Mrs. Ann, 161, 168-169, 192
*Ralph Roister Doister*, 219-220, 226
*Rambler, The*, 131-132, 133 n.
*Rape of the Lock, The*, 103-104
Raphael, 65
"Raven, The," 61
Reade, Charles, 175, 177
realism, 71, 90-91, 126, 149-150, 153-155, 158-163, 173-175, 178-180, 182, 187, 195-201, 220, 227-230, 254, 260-261
refrains, 17-18, 27, 41, 66-67
*Rehearsal, The*, 103, 238-239
relations of the novel, 181-182
relations of the short story, 205
*Reliques of Ancient English Poetry*, 25-26
*Remorse*, 250
Renaissance, The, 7, 93, 117, 212

repetition in ballads, 16-17
Restoration drama, 236-243
*Return of the Native, The,* 207
revenge tragedy, 213, 221-222, 224-226, 231-232
reviews, the, 137-138
*Richard II.,* 223
*Richard III.,* 223
Richardson, Samuel, 148, 154, 157, 159-163, 173
"Rip Van Winkle," 192-193
Ritson, Joseph, 26
*Rivals, The,* 247-248
*Robbers, The,* 248
Robertson, Thomas W., 249
Roberts, William, 132
Robin Hood, 18-21, 33-34, 84
*Robin Hood, Little Gest of,* 7, 19, 21, 34, 84
*Robinson Crusoe,* 159
*Roderick Random,* 160
roman à clef, 126, 156-157, 161
*Romance of the Forest, The,* 169
romances, 7, 59, 89, 105, 126, 128, 148-157, 161, 169-170, 177, 179, 228, 233, 237
*Roman Father, The,* 245
romantic epics, 92-95, 106-107, 111-112
Romantic Movement, 25-26, 40, 54, 65, 105, 133, 137, 166
*Romola,* 176
rondeau, the, 69
*Rosalynde,* 151 n.
*Rosamund,* 246
Rosicrucians, The, 103
*Rosmersholm,* 251
Rossetti, D. G., 27, 65-67
Rostand, Edmond, 253
roundel, the, 43
Round Table, The, 106, 152
Rousseau, Jean Jacques, 159, 164, 187
*Rovers, The,* 249
Rowe, Nicholas, 239
*Roxana,* 160
Ruskin, John, 138
Russian short stories, 199-200

S

Sackville, Thomas, 219
*Sandford and Merton,* 164
Sappho, 38-39
satire, 104, 126-128, 130, 132, 133, 141, 143, 153, 160, 171-172, 174-175, 214-215, 220, 228-230, 237
*Saturday Visitor, The,* 194
*Scarecrow, The,* 253
Schiller, Friedrich, 248
"Scholar Gypsy, The," 64
*School for Scandal, The,* 247-248
*Scottish Chiefs,* 169
Scottish songs, 54
Scott, Walter, 26-27, 55, 134, 148, 170, 172, 201
*Secchia Rapita, La,* 103
*Second Jungle Book, The,* 203
*Second Mrs. Tanqueray, The,* 251
"Second Shepherds' Play, The," 217
secret histories, 156-157
*Sejanus, his Fall,* 231
*Semaines, Les,* 96
Seneca, Lucius Annæus, 117, 120, 130, 212-214, 220-222, 231-232, 258
*Sense and Sensibility,* 171
*sententiæ,* 214
sentimentalism, 62, 134, 158-159, 162-164, 169, 171, 173-174, 237, 239-240, 242-244, 247-249
*Sentimental Journey, The,* 163
*Servant in the House, The,* 253
setting: in primitive ballads, 30; in essays, 133; in novels, 187; in short stories, 206-208
Shakespeare, William, 24, 46, 49-50, 74, 150, 151 n., 153, 170, 176, 213, 218, 220, 222-228, 231-232, 234, 237, 239, 244, 248, 257, 259, 261
Shaw, George Bernard, 252
Shelley, Mrs. Mary W., 169
Shelley, Percy Bysshe, 40, 55-57, 59-61, 66, 69-70, 79, 169, 250

Shenstone, William, 54
Sheridan, Richard Brinsley, 244-248
*She Stoops to Conquer*, 247-248, 256
Shirley, James, 234-235
*Shoemaker's Holiday, The*, 228-229
Short Story, The, 178, 191-210
*Short View of the Immorality of the English Stage, A*, 242
Sidney, Philip, 46-49, 74, 151-155
"Signal Man, The," 201
*Sigurd the Volsung*, 107-108
*Silas Marner*, 176
similes, 87, 93, 110, 114
*Simple Story, A*, 165
simultaneous staging, 217
"Sire de Malétroit's Door, The," 201, 206
"Sir Hugh," 29
*Sir Launcelot Greaves*, 160
Sir Roger de Coverley, 130, 133, 142, 157
"Sister Helen," 66
situations in short stories, 191, 193-195, 206
*Sketch Book, The*, 192-193
Smollett, Tobias George, 159-160, 179
socialistic literature, 71, 165-166, 248
*Soldiers Three*, 203
"Solitary Reaper, The," 75-77, 79
"Song of England, A," 70
*Song of Roland*, 92
"Song of the Shirt, The," 61
songs, 49-51, 54, 61
*Songs of a Sourdough*, 71
sonnet conventions, 48
sonnet, the, 44-49, 58-59, 64, 66
*Sonnets from the Portuguese*, 64
sonnet themes, 47
Sophocles, 211
sound and sense, 79
*Spaniards in Peru, The*, 249
Spanish drama, 232

*Spanish Tragedy, The*, 225-226, 231
*Spectator, The*, 99, 111, 125, 127, 129, 130
Spenser, Edmund, 7, 46, 48 n., 69, 94-96, 109
Spenserian stanza, 59, 98
stage, the, 130, 183, 211-212, 217, 235-236, 245, 254, 258, 260-261
stanzas: in ballads, 17-18; in lyrics, 78-79
Statius, 89
Steele, Richard, 125, 127-129, 131, 133, 240, 243
Stephen, Leslie, 139
Sterne, Laurence, 158, 163-164
Stevenson, Robert Louis, 139-140, 177, 196, 200
stichomythia, 214, 221
*St. Leon*, 165
Stockton, Frank R., 203
Stowe, John, 222
strambotto, the, 44
*Stranger, The*, 249
*Strife*, 252
Strindberg, August, 251
Strunsky, Simeon, 140
subjectivity: in lyrics, 39, 58, 66-67, 74-75; in essays, 119-120, 133-135, 139, 141; in novels, 181-182; in short stories, 191-195, 197-199, 205-206; in the drama, 261
subjects for study: the ballad, 34-35; the lyric, 79-80; the epic, 115; the essay, 144-145; the novel, 188; the short story, 208-209; the drama, 262
sublimity in poetry, 100, 102
Sudermann, Hermann, 251
"Sumer is icumen in," 42
supernatural machinery, 87, 91, 93-94, 98, 100-101, 106, 109, 113, 168, 193
Surrey, Earl of, 45, 154
"Sweet and low," 63
Swift, Jonathan, 160

Swinburne, Algernon Charles, 40, 67-70, 77, 79
Sylvester, Joshua, 96
symbolism, 66, 253-254, 260-261

**T**

"Take, O take those lips away," 50
tales, 126, 192-193
*Tales of a Traveller*, 192
*Tales of Terror and Wonder*, 26
*Tamburlaine*, 223
"Tam Lin," 30
Tassoni, 103
Tasso, Torquato, 94-97
Tatius, 89
*Tatler, The*, 125, 129-130
*Tea-Table Miscellany*, 25
technique: the ballad, 29-34; the lyric, 73-79; the epic, 110-114; the essay, 141-145; the novel, 181-188; the short story, 205-208; the drama, 255-262
*Tempest, The*, 234, 237
Temple, Sir William, 125
Tennyson, Alfred, 61-64, 71, 74, 105-107
Terence, 212-215, 230-231
testament in ballads, 30-31
Texts, of *Faerie Queene* and *Paradise Lost*, 115
Thackeray, William Makepeace, 69, 137, 172-175
*Thaddeus of Warsaw*, 169
*Theagenes and Chariclea*, 89
*Thebaid, The*, 89
themes: of simple ballads, 29; of adventure ballads, 33; of sonnets, 47; of epic poetry, 88, 90, 93, 99-100, 111; of essays, 122
thesis plays, 251-252
"They," 202
Thompson, Francis, 70
Thompson, James, 54, 245
Thornton, Bonnel, 131
"Three Blind Mice," 50

*Thyestes*, 213
"Thyrsis," 64
Tieck, Ludwig, 58
Tilley, Prof. Arthur, 121-122
*Timber*, 125
*Tom Jones*, 155, 162
*Tom Thumb*, 245
*Tottel's Miscellany*, 45, 49
Tourneur, Cyril, 226, 232
tragi-comedy, 229-230, 237
tragic structure, 176, 186
*Travels with a Donkey*, 139
*Treatise of Christian Doctrine*, 137-138
*Tristram Shandy*, 163
*Troilus and Cressida*, 44
Trollope, Anthony, 175
troubadours, 44
Twain, Mark, 180
*Twelfth Night*, 231, 256
type-characters, 126-128, 152, 156, 169, 171, 174-176, 183, 214-215, 220, 228-231, 233-234, 240, 248, 259
types of literature, 4
type-studies in series, 11-12
*Tyrannic Love*, 238

**U**

Udall, Nicholas, 219
*Underwoods*, 139
*Unfortunate Traveller, The*, 151, 154, 159, 179
unity of action, 91, 99-100, 106-107, 111-112, 161-162, 170, 174, 176, 185-187, 213, 221, 233, 238, 250, 256-257
*Universal Chronicle, The*, 132
*Utopia*, 151

**V**

*Valentinian*, 234
Vanbrugh, John, 127, 241
*Vathek*, 167-168
*Venice Preserved*, 239
verbal melody, 40
*vers de société*, 69
verse form: in ballads, 17-18;

## INDEX

in sonnets, 49; in Romantic lyric, 59
*vers libre*, 72
*Vicar of Wakefield, The*, 163
Vice, The, 219-220
Victorian period, 61, 137-138, 177
Vida, 93, 110
Virgil, 7, 86-94, 97, 99, 109
*Virginibus Puerisque*, 139
*Visions, The*, 129
*Vittoria Corombona*, 232
*Volpone, the Fox*, 230
Voltaire, F. M. Arouet de, 245
Vorse, Mary H., 204

### W

Waller, Edmund, 52
Walpole, Horace, 167-168, 247
Walpole, Hugh, 180
Walton, Izaak, 24
"Wandering Willie's Tale," 201
Ward, Mrs. Humphry, 175-176
Warner, Charles Dudley, 140
*Waverley*, 172
Waverley Novels, 170
*Way of the World, The*, 241
Webster, John, 226, 232
Wells, C. J., 250
Wells, H. G., 179
*West Indian, The*, 244
"West Wind, The," 70
Wharton, Mrs. Edith, 180
*What-d'ye-call-it?*, 245
"What Was It?" 196
whimsicality, 135-137, 158, 163
Whistler, J. A. M., 71

Whitehead, William, 245
"White Ship, The," 27, 66
Whitman, Walt, 72
Whittier, John Greenleaf, 60
*Wieland*, 169
Wilkins-Freeman, Mary E., 204
"Willie and Lady Maisry," 20
"Will of the Mill," 206
Wilson, John, 138
*Winter's Tale*, 24, 227, 234
"Without Benefit of Clergy," 203
*Woman Killed with Kindness, A*, 228
women in literature, 46, 165, 168-169, 171-172, 242 n.
women on the stage, 236-237
Woodberry, George E., 139
Wordsworth, William, 54-60, 74-77, 249
"World is too much with us, The," 74
*World, The*, 131
*Wuthering Heights*, 172
Wyatt, Thomas, 45, 50
Wycherley, William, 127, 241

### Y

Yeats, William Butler, 40, 71, 253
Young, Edward, 245
"Young Waters," 29

### Z

*Zanoni*, 173
*Zapolya*, 250

# BIBLIOLIFE

Old Books Deserve a New Life
www.bibliolife.com

Did you know that you can get most of our titles in our trademark **EasyScript**™ print format? **EasyScript**™ provides readers with a larger than average typeface, for a reading experience that's easier on the eyes.

Did you know that we have an ever-growing collection of books in many languages?

Order online:
www.bibliolife.com/store

Or to exclusively browse our **EasyScript**™ collection:
www.bibliogrande.com

At BiblioLife, we aim to make knowledge more accessible by making thousands of titles available to you – quickly and affordably.

Contact us:
BiblioLife
PO Box 21206
Charleston, SC 29413

Printed in Great Britain
by Amazon